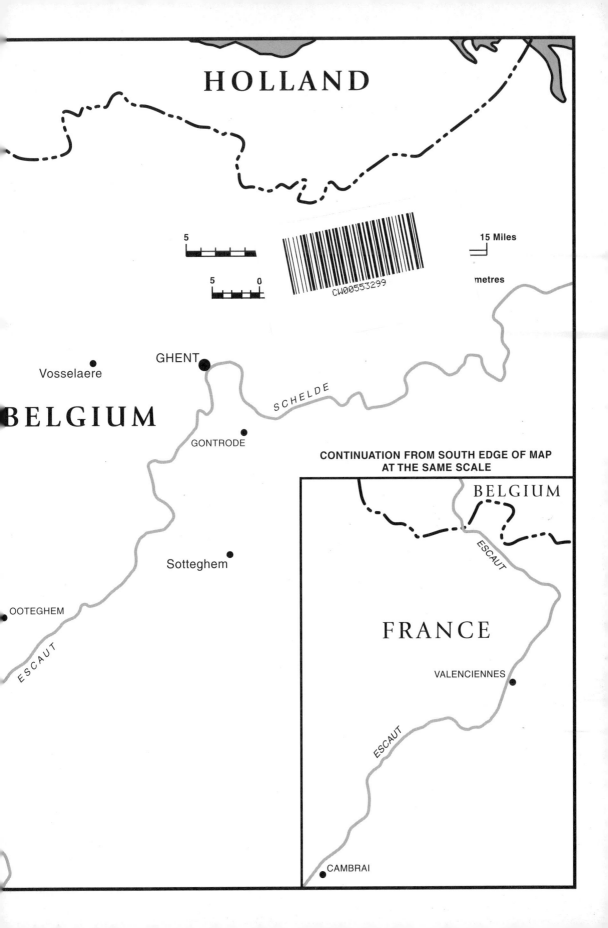

HOLLAND

BELGIUM

Vosselaere

GHENT

SCHELDE

GONTRODE

Sotteghem

OOTEGHEM

ESCAUT

5

5   0

15 Miles

metres

CW00553299

**CONTINUATION FROM SOUTH EDGE OF MAP
AT THE SAME SCALE**

BELGIUM

ESCAUT

FRANCE

VALENCIENNES

ESCAUT

CAMBRAI

BLACK FOKKER LEADER

This book is dedicated to my support team:
Judy, Cara, Karl, Clayton, Christine, Elaine and Tessa Kilduff – and Pearl

Other books by Peter Kilduff

The Red Baron

That's My Bloody Plane

Germany's Last Knight of the Air

U.S. Carriers at War

A-4 Skyhawk

Germany's First Air Force 1914-1918

Richthofen – Beyond the Legend of the Red Baron

Over the Battlefronts

The Red Baron Combat Wing

The Illustrated Red Baron

Talking With the Red Baron

Red Baron – The Life and Death of an Ace

Black Fokker Leader

Carl Degelow –
The First World War's
Last Airfighter Knight

Peter Kilduff

Grub Street • London

Published by
Grub Street Publishing
4 Rainham Close
London
SW11 6SS

British Library Cataloguing in Publication Data
Kilduff, Peter
    Black Fokker leader : the First World War's last airfighter
    knight
    1. Degelow, Carl 2. Fighter pilots - Germany - Biography
    3. World War, 1914-1918 - Aerial operations, German
    4. World War, 1914-1918 - Campaigns - Western Front
    I. Title
    940.4'4943'092

ISBN-13: 9781906502287

Cover design by Lizzie B Design

Book design and artwork by:
Roy Platten, Eclipse – roy.eclipse@btopenworld.com

Printed and bound by MPG Books Group, Bodmin, Cornwall

Grub Street Publishing uses only FSC (Forest Stewardship Council) paper for its books

CONTENTS

FOREWORD

In the summer of 1956, the novel *The Falcons of France* excited my fifteen-year-old mind in a way no book ever had. It recounted stories of idealistic and courageous young men who flew off to battle in the skies over France in biplanes made of wood and canvas. A thinly fictionalised account of the exploits of Charles Nordhoff and James Norman Hall as American volunteer pilots in the Lafayette Flying Corps, that 1929 book catalysed what has become a lifelong interest in World War I aviation history.

As my interest in the subject and book collection grew, one of the earliest titles I acquired was *War Birds – The Diary of an Unknown Aviator* written by Elliott White Springs, with artwork by Clayton Knight; both men were Americans who flew with the Royal Air Force in World War I. In 1961, I had the good fortune to meet and become friends with Clayton Knight, OBE, and he was the first of nearly thirty surviving World War I flyers I came to know in person or by mail.

Each veteran flyer referred me to one or more of his living former comrades and in this way, in 1967, I was put in touch with Carl Degelow. I knew him by reputation as a thirty-victory ace and a recipient of the military order Pour le Mérite, Prussia's (and, *de facto*, Germany's) highest award for bravery. It was a wonderful experience to correspond with him during the last three years of his life, during which he patiently – indeed, enthusiastically – answered my endless stream of questions. Carl Degelow was a living repository of history and I was determined to learn as much as I could about his air combat and other wartime experiences.

The initial result of our correspondence was the sixteen-page article 'Reminiscences of Jagdstaffel 40' in the Autumn 1971 issue of *Cross & Cockade Journal*, the quarterly publication of The Society of World War I Aero Historians. Unfortunately, Carl Degelow did not live to see the article, as he died on 9 November 1970 – fifty-two years to the day after he was authorised to receive the last Pour le Mérite awarded during World War I. Eight years and more research later, a much expanded account of Degelow's career appeared as my third book, *Germany's Last Knight of the Air*. Eventually the book went out of print, but my interest in Carl Degelow did not end. That enduring pursuit was best expressed in that 1979 book about him:

> 'During the three years following our initial contact, [Degelow's] letters to me were full of delightful anecdotes –… as well as unique photographs relating to his own or his comrades' exploits. He wanted no barriers to stand in the way of a complete telling of his experiences during World War I. While I adhered to a rigid code of linguistic

politeness so necessary for 'proper' relationships in German correspondence, [Degelow] tossed it all off in one line of an early letter, done in English, as he liked to do from time to time: "My friends all call me 'Charly', why not you, too?"'

In the following years, additional archival research revealed new information about Carl Degelow and his comrades, and brought me to a new review of the German-language texts used in the earlier book. It occurred to me that the new material, along with a fresh, edited translation of his letters and other texts, would enable me to tell a more complete story than before. By editing these texts, I believe I have made their tone as conversational as Degelow's letters had been.

Moreover, the new material and a review of other documents clarified certain points in Degelow's life story. For example, in recounting his unfortunate accident with another pilot in August 1917, Degelow identified the other man as 'Leutnant Kreuger', a name that does not appear on any rosters of the fighter squadron Jagdstaffel 36, to which both men belonged at the time. The summary of Jasta 36's war diary, which I obtained after my original Degelow article and book had been published, recorded the incident and identified the other man as Leutnant der Reserve Edwin Kreuzer, a native of the former Grand Duchy of Baden, which has since gained a special place in this author's heart. Thanks to material found in Baden's central archive, an amended and expanded account of the accident appears in Chapter Four of this book.

In a war of vast destruction and savagery, Carl Degelow was notably different. While so many fighter pilots aimed specifically at their opposing pilots and aerial observers, Degelow took to heart the lesson offered by one of his instructors at the Fighter Pilot Training School: 'Aim for the aeroplane, not the man. When you put the aeroplane out of action, you will take care of the man.' As difficult as it was to follow that admonition in the heat of combat, Carl Degelow did his best to achieve an unusual, humanistic approach to man-to-man air fighting and, consequently, he enjoyed the rare experience of greeting some of his aerial opponents in his Staffel's dining room.

Far more meaningful than my words are those of Degelow's long-time friend, the late Paul Nami. Paul's comments were published thirty years ago, but deserve to be read again, as they provide insight into a combatant who did not allow the exigencies of war to diminish his humanity:

'Carl Degelow's … [exploits] as a German fighter pilot on the Western Front provides a clear picture of what goes on in a pilot's mind when he is engaged in a life-or-death struggle in the air. Without such an account, it would be hard for people today to imagine what aerial combat was like during World War I. Performing the most disaster-laden manoeuvres in fabric-covered aircraft and flying without parachutes, the pilots of that era ran the daily risk of being set afire in the air or being hit in some vulnerable spot that would literally cause the airplane to break apart in the air, thousands of feet above the ground; add to these the dangers of shooting off one's own propeller if the machine gun synchronisation device malfunctioned, or having one's vision blurred by driving hail or rain – in addition to the normal hazards of flying. One of the greatest risks was that of mid-air collision; for, even the slightest brushing of one speeding aeroplane against another would cause one or both aeroplanes to crash to the earth. It was a slight collision of this nature that caused the death of the celebrated German fighter pilot Oswald Boelcke.

'Despite these and other dangers, Carl Degelow persevered. In so doing, he built up an enviable record, both as an individual pilot and as a squadron commander. A four-victory pilot when he joined Jagdstaffel 40 in May 1918, he went on to bring down another twenty-six enemy aircraft during the next six months, thereby accounting for almost half of the squadron's total "bag" of fifty-four enemy aircraft. His achievements were recognised during the closing days of World War I, when, on 9 November 1918, he became the last wartime recipient of the Pour le Mérite, popularly known as "The Blue Max."

'After the war, Charly could have remained in the German Army, as did many of his comrades. Instead, having done his duty for his Fatherland, he preferred to return to the paths of peace. Although a national hero and a knight of the Order Pour le Mérite, he resumed his prosaic work of cement manufacture. He became general director of nine plants in Pomerania. Charly had no sympathy for the Nazi movement and, typically conscientious and true to his beliefs, he was once arrested for failing to give the stiff-arm Nazi salute. He served in the German Luftwaffe during World War II, but he was not enough of an "organisation man" to attain the high rank that many of his more politically astute former subordinates did. That was one area where lack of success did not bother him. To his credit, it can be said that not once was the name Major Carl Degelow mentioned in connection with any war crimes activities. He was a soldier, pure and simply – a concept not easily understood amid the complexities of modern day global politics.'[1]

The reader will note many instances in which I postulate which air units and even individual airmen fought against each other. Such speculation is possible due to the wide use of aircraft heraldry – raising again the 'knights of the air' image of these early air combatants – and the availability of many archival sources that provide evidence of such encounters. In recent years, this research endeavour has become more (but not entirely) conclusive thanks to such books as *The French Air Service War Chronology 1914-1918*, *The Jasta Pilots*, *The Sky Their Battlefield*, and other valued standard reference texts published by Grub Street, which are included in this book's bibliography. I am grateful to the authors of those books and for the hard work and thought they applied to their works.

I also remain grateful for Paul Nami's encouragement in the initial stages of research into Carl Degelow's career in the 1970s. Paul desired only to have his friend Charly's exploits properly chronicled. Without his help, the work would have been infinitely more difficult to complete.

Again, I thank the fine people who were early helpers in this research: F.W. (Bill) Bailey, Norman Franks, and Alex Revell. Also remembered with heartfelt thanks are the following people who in various ways helped to shape this book and have since gone to their final reward: Dipl.-Ing Adolf Auer, Maria Degelow, Peter M. Grosz, Generaloberst a.D. Alfred Keller, my writing mentor Major Clayton Knight, OBE; Russell Manning, Generalfeldmarschall a.D. Erhard Milch, Neal W. O'Connor, William R. Puglisi, Anton

Raab, and my German military history mentor Oberstleutnant der Reserve a.D. Hanns-Gerd Rabe.

In more recent times, I have been helped by other valued colleagues and friends and extend sincere gratitude to them: Trudy Baumann; Roger Dhoore; Falk Hallensleben, Wissentschaftlicher Beirat des Fördervereins Luftwaffenmuseum der Bundeswehr in Berlin-Gatow and OSF a.D. des Jagdgeschwaders 71"Richthofen" (Richthofenmuseum); Elisabeth Karinski; Burkhard Klietz, Kaiser-Karl-Schule in Itzehoe; Achim Koch, Bundesarchiv Militärarchiv; Dr. Eberhardt Kettlitz, praeHistoria Büro für Archäologie und Geschichte; James Streckfuss; Julian Putkowski; Stewart K. Taylor; and Dr. Wolfgang Mährle, Judith Bolsinger and Manfred Hennhöfer of the Landesarchiv Baden-Württemberg, as well as Katherina Krickow, M.A. and Carolin Freund of the Technische Universität Darmstadt, and A. Julia Loeschke of the Universität Mainz. Kimberly Farrington and Francis J. Gagliardi of the Elihu Burritt Library of Central Connecticut State University exemplify the valued help received from my alma mater.

My thanks also go to a cadre of friends (in alphabetical order, as they all rank top positions for their contributions to this book): Ronny Bar for his excellent colour artwork portraying Jasta 40 aircraft, Jan Christian Bodenbender for helping locate important research resources, Russell Folsom for sharing his insightful knowledge of German military history, Judy and Karl Kilduff and my mentor David E. Smith for their helpful review of and comments on the manuscript, my cultural mentor Klaus Littwin for helping me understand German linguistic nuances and providing valuable assistance in locating important research sources, Dr. M. Geoffrey Miller for strengthening my research with his medical expertise, and my Belgian friend Lothair Vanoverbeke for helping me to better understand his homeland's role in World War I. Profound gratitude goes to my long-time colleague and friend Greg Van Wyngarden for his helpful suggestions and for sharing his artistic and historical resources.

No history-based book such as this one can ever be the work of one person and I am very glad for the friendship and assistance that all of the above-named members of this band of 'word warriors' have brought to this book.

Peter Kilduff
New Britain, Connecticut, USA
January 2009

1   Kilduff, *Germany's Last Knight of the Air*, pp. 18-20.

CHAPTER ONE
LIFE AND DEATH IN THE AIR

Life in the Air

Mist shrouded the troubled skies of Flanders on the morning of Friday, 20 September 1918. But the weather[1] also aided fighting forces on both sides of the lines in The Great War. It provided cover for air and ground contact patrols as they sought out their adversaries and marked them for destruction by hundreds of heavy artillery rounds that churned earth, trees and buildings into a ghastly thick wasteland stew.

Some 3,000 metres above the ground and away from the fractured landscape, a lone black Fokker D.VII fighter aeroplane flew in broad circles over Reckem airfield in German-occupied Belgium. Its pilot, Leutnant der Reserve [Reserve Second-Lieutenant] Carl Degelow, was test flying the 'plane, which mechanics had been working on for the past two days since the radiator and engine had been hit by ground fire. Degelow, the commanding officer of Jagdstaffel 40, knew that he could fly alone with confidence, as his men were watching him from the ground. If he were approached by unfriendly aeroplanes over his own airfield, his comrades would quickly take to the air to help him.

The Fokker leader's peaceful test flight was interrupted when his eye caught movement off to the south. He turned and the veil of mist parted enough for him to recognise the outlines of three Bristol two-seat fighter aeroplanes. They were heading east from their aerodrome at Boisdinghem[2] toward Roubaix, an industrial city in northern France that was an attractive target. While the Bristol Fighters could not match the Fokker's speed or agility, they could be formidable opponents, appearing from a distance to be cumbersome, less-manoeuvrable two-seat reconnaissance aeroplanes. The Bristol Fighter's 'pilot had the widest possible field of vision … [and his back-seat] observer was given a wide field of fire'[3] that provided the aeroplane with excellent defensive capabilities.

Degelow knew:

'These British two-seat fighters were frequently assigned to attack our frontline positions. The trio that came before my muzzle this day were a "line patrol", in which inexperienced aircrews were familiarised with the make-up and peculiarities of the Front. When breaking in a new crew over enemy lines, two or more experienced pilots would take a third in their midst and with this novice, known as a *Häschen* [young hare] in our flying circles, make their way carefully over the Front. In attacking the three British "tourists", I needed to catch the Häschen by surprise.'

At twenty-seven, Carl Degelow was five or more years older than many of his contemporaries and more mature in his judgement. Hence, as he was now totally on his own, he knew he had to proceed very carefully. It was too late to fire a flare to invite his comrades on the ground to join him in the fight he knew was coming. He wrote later:

'So I used the intervening time to climb to a more advantageous altitude, away from the approaching British aircraft. Three single-seat fighters would have been a good day's work, but three two-seaters – each equipped with an able gunner in the rear cockpit – required special effort.

'I waited for the trio to turn and then, from my higher position and with the rising sun at my back, I pounced on one machine that came out of the turn slightly out of formation and a bit behind the others. It seemed to be the most favourable target.'

Having culled the weak calf from the herd, and watched the other two British aeroplanes fly away, the German pilot had only to slip below the Bristol Fighter, as he knew from experience that the two-seater had a narrow blind spot just below and behind the observer's battle station. If he wanted to, Degelow could have aligned his aeroplane with the British observer's Achilles heel. Then, with a few well-placed bursts, he could have killed the observer and, as he chose, raked the two-seater's underside with machine-gun fire until it began to smoke and burst into flames.

But, in a few seconds of hesitation, the two-seater dipped and when Degelow fired, his rounds streamed over the head of the British observer. He was about to fire again when he sensed that his opponent's ring-mounted twin machine guns appeared to have jammed. The observer clearly had Degelow in his sights several times but did not open fire. His actions could have been a ruse, but as long as he held his fire, Degelow decided not to shoot at him.

Leutnant der Reserve Carl Degelow and a Fokker D.VII bearing his personal marking, a leaping white stag, which he used while commanding Royal Saxon Jagdstaffel 40 on the Flanders Sector. A good marksman, Degelow may have improved his accuracy as an air fighter in this Fokker by using the aeroplane's optical gun sight, visible above the pilot's head. This photo was taken shortly after he was awarded the Knight's Cross of the Royal House Order of Hohenzollern with Swords (pinned above his left breast pocket) on 9 August 1918. Below that award are his Iron Cross First Class and Military Pilot's Badge.

Then Degelow made a bold move, making use of his aeroplane as a gun platform. He pulled back and sent a burst of incendiary bullets alongside – but not into – his opponent. The prospect of capturing this pair of newcomers suddenly appealed to Degelow and the menacing grey smoke trails from his guns made it clear what the German *could* do, if he were so inclined. Had the observer returned fire at the black Fokker – which must have looked like the apparition of death, with tracer ammunition spitting out of two guns of the big, squared off front of its fuselage – Degelow would have moved his rudder bar to turn the aeroplane toward the observer and fire a lethal burst. For an instant, it was a matter of who would fire first – if at all.

Responding to Degelow's daring move with one of his own, the British observer took his hands off his twin Lewis machine guns and placed them on the ring mounting in plain sight – a sign of surrender. By now it was obvious that neither of the other two Bristol Fighters would come back to join the fight; as it turned out, they returned to Boisdinghem and reported optimistically that their missing squadron-mates were 'last seen [at] 11 a.m. over Roubaix diving on E.A [enemy aircraft].'[4]

As the lone Bristol Fighter headed lower and lower, with the Fokker right behind it, Degelow extended his right arm and vigorously moved his hand in broad motions to signal the crew to head south. The observer confirmed his understanding of the situation by nodding his head vigorously in the affirmative while keeping his hands visible during the transaction. The German fired one more burst, at which the pilot also raised his hands to indicate surrender. Degelow was now in the awkward position of having aerial 'prisoners' and not knowing quite what to do with them. It was a new experience on both sides.

Degelow recalled:

'The suddenly tame Tommies made an excellent landing in a nice flat meadow outside Roubaix. I could only hope that the fellow would set the 'plane down in one piece and not try to crash it. Meanwhile, as my engine RPMs had dropped to a very low level, I decided to land in the same field, rather than take a chance and fly some twenty kilometres back to Reckem.

'By the time I landed, German troops in the area were already converging on the British aeroplane. I got out of my Fokker and walked over to my prize and in my best English accent said: "Good morning, my fine fellows, how do you do?"'

The British flyers seemed quite nervous about their fate within enemy territory and their captor tried to assure them that they were safe. Degelow had worked in America for some eighteen months before the war and continued to talk to his opponents, glad for the opportunity to practice his English.

The stillness of the meadow was disturbed by the roar of automobile engines, as several cars arrived on the scene bearing even more curious soldiers who had never seen a captured British aeroplane. Degelow quickly asserted his authority as an officer and directed a corporal to find the nearest field telephone.

'Call Jasta 40 at Reckem airfield and tell them that their commanding officer needs two lorries to haul away some aeroplanes,' he ordered.

Jasta 40 men celebrated Carl Degelow's fifteenth aerial victory, on 20 September 1918, by posing with the aeroplane he forced to land. According to Staffel member Adolf Auer, Bristol F.2B serial numbered D.2260 of 48 Squadron, RAF, landed in an open field north of Annappes, France and was soon appreciated by (from left): unidentified enlisted ground crewman, Ltn.d.Res Hermann Gilly, unidentified, Degelow, Ltn Hans Jeschonnek (in pilot's seat), Ltn.d.Res Willy Rosenstein (in observer's position), *Feldgendarm* [military police enlisted man], unidentified pilot, and Ltn Frodien.

Reckem was close enough that the Jasta 40 vehicles arrived in short order. The Staffel members hauled away their leader's aircraft and his trophy while Degelow rode back to his airfield in a car with the two British airmen.

Degelow later recalled:

'My prospective guests, who had no idea what their fate would be at the hands of the "dreaded Huns", as we were called in the popular British press, sought to end their perplexity by asking: "What will happen to us?"

'I was amused by the question and all that it implied and answered, again in English. "I never discuss business on an empty stomach. Let's talk about it after lunch."

'My British colleagues were somewhat bewildered and, from looking at them, I could see that our short exchange in the air must have made them feel quite warm under their thick fur-lined flying suits. They were steaming like a pair of overworked race horses and did not show the usual calmness of spirit that one was accustomed to seeing displayed by British flyers who had been brought down. I could understand their anxiety, since these harmless air-fighters had proven themselves to be inexperienced in the business of aerial combat. This was further confirmed by the brand new sport clothes they wore beneath their flying suits – all bearing the label of the exclusive Robinson & Co. of Regent Street in London.

'From the formal introductions, I learned their names: Lieutenant Mahony[5] and Second Lieutenant Kier[6] of No. 48 Squadron, one of the better two-seat fighter units that opposed us. Indeed, once we learned that they were from such an illustrious unit, I was surprised that the event had ended so peacefully. But I am sure they were surprised, too. What happened, quite simply, is that their luck ran out and their first aerial battle did not end the way they had imagined it would. In any event, we spent a pleasant day together.'

Degelow chatted further with Mahony and Kier and, after a comforting lunch, Mahony presented his new fleece-lined leather coat to the victor. No doubt, the twenty-three-year-old Briton was glad to be alive and grateful for Degelow's charitable nature. In return, Degelow gave his new friend a German army overcoat to help him ward off the cold weather yet to come. (Almost fifty years later, Carl Degelow made a gift of the British coat to the German Luftwaffen-Museum, which today numbers it among its World War I artefacts.)

Degelow also learned that the crew were not as inexperienced as he thought. It turned out that surviving their encounter with a Fokker over German territory was Mahony's and Kier's second piece of good fortune in less than a month. The moonlit night of 24/25 August 1918 enabled five German ground attack two-seaters from Schlachtstaffel 16 [Attack Section 16] to attack the RAF aerodrome at Bertangles and inflict such extensive damage on 48 Squadron's facilities, aircraft and personnel that the unit 'had to be withdrawn from the line to Boisdinghem to be re-equipped'[7]; among the thirteen squadron members wounded in the raid were Lieutenants Mahony and Kier.[8]

Later in the day, the British flyers were turned over to rear-area authorities for transport to a German prisoner-of-war camp, where they would spend the next seven weeks or so until the German war effort collapsed and the armistice went into effect.

Earlier in the war, the captured Bristol Fighter would have been shipped back to the Inspektion der Fliegertruppen [Inspectorate of Military Aviation] in Germany for flight testing and a complete examination of its construction. The aircraft's serial number, D.2260, indicated it was from the first production batch of Bristol F.2Bs to be fitted with the 200-horsepower Hispano-Suiza engine,[9] which may have had some special interest for the inspectorate engineers. But at this late stage in the war, Germany's most optimistic

A current view of the fully restored pilot's flying coat that Lt Martin Mahony presented to Carl Degelow following their 20 September 1918 aerial combat. The coat is now displayed in the Luftwaffe museum in Berlin-Gatow, Germany.

military planners could only hope to keep the army intact for an orderly withdrawal back to Germany, from whence a better position might be negotiated during the clearly inevitable armistice.

For the moment, the nicely intact trophy was counted as the fifteenth enemy aircraft brought down by Carl Degelow, whose successes as a fighter ace were increasing steadily. Indeed, his aerial combat victories were occurring with such regularity that the staff of the Kommandierende General der Luftstreitkräfte [Commanding General of the Air Force] singled him out as an example for other fighter pilots to emulate. Degelow's achievement was noted in the 20 September combat summary in the Commanding General's weekly intelligence digest.[10] Thirteen German air combat triumphs were confirmed for that day, and the five pilots to receive special notice were Leutnant der Reserve Paul Bäumer for his twenty-seventh victory, Vizefeldwebel [Sergeant-Major] Otto Fruhner for his twenty-fifth, Ltn.d.Res Hermann Frommherz for his twenty-third, Ltn.d.Res Georg Meyer for his twentieth, and Carl Degelow for his fifteenth. There were higher rewards for successful airmen but, of that quintet of German air heroes, only Bäumer and Degelow went on to become among the eighty-one aviation recipients of the Orden Pour le Mérite, officially the Kingdom of Prussia's highest bravery award for officers, but generally accepted as Germany's ultimate award for bravery in combat in World War I.[11]

Death in the Air

Exactly a week later, Degelow was leading a patrol in partly cloudy skies near Armentières when once again he spotted a trio of Bristol Fighters. The encounter that followed seemed to be a replay of the previous Friday's adventure and Degelow knew it would be quite an accomplishment for him to 'capture' another Bristol Fighter and its crew. Before initiating the fight he signalled his comrades to hold back and assure no enemy attacked him. After that, they could go after their own targets.

Degelow recalled:

'As soon as I launched my attack by diving on the enemy formation, two noble defenders deserted the novice, while he, who did not appear to be burdened with an abundance of orientation points, stubbornly flew southeast, under the impression he could get back to his own aerodrome by proceeding in that direction. Through a fast manoeuvre I got into an attack position behind and slightly below the two-seater so that I could fire undisturbed at the enemy airplane while I myself was protected from the unpleasant action of the observer's machine gun.

'To be sure, the Bristol Fighter pilot bolted left and right, trying to shake me off. The efforts of the lost one were in vain, as, in the meantime, other aeroplanes of my Staffel quickly gathered around and joined in this chase. Despite our numerical superiority, the Bristol pilot did not think of capitulating, even though he was offered a very favourable opportunity to land at one of our airfields, as, in the course of the chase, we had already reached German aviation facilities in the vicinity of Lille.

'Finally, I gave up my vantage point when the "Tommy" fired off three red flares, one after the other during a lull in the battle. I took the red star-shells to be the well-known emergency call of sailors, S O S, although it did not seem to me that this distress signal would save these tormented souls.

'I ceased firing and came almost alongside the Englishmen. The observer stood at his battle station with his hands raised. I directed hand signals to his pilot to make him understand that he must land immediately. Perhaps this "hands up" was a trick by the observer, who may have seen something hostile in my hand motions. In any event, suddenly he clattered away furiously with his twin machine guns, even though the cease fire had been understood by both sides. Righteous indignation over this unfair manner of fighting incited my battle fury, and rightfully so, for the conduct of the British airman certainly deeply offended the universally applicable concept of chivalrous manners of fighting in aviation.

'Now I was angry and pursued him southward, over the city of Douai, through the whole German 6th Army sector, down into the region of the 17th Army and then east into the 2nd Army sector. As Valenciennes came into view, my opponent finally prepared to land, presumably because his engine had run out of steam.

'The landing should have been successful, as both crewmen were resigned to it. Their machine glided in at about fifty metres above the ground, when suddenly it dropped to the ground without my firing at it. Perhaps during the long rearguard action, the Bristol Fighter had taken so many hits that the aeroplane's framework could no longer take the stress of a long descent.

'The wreckage of the machine fell almost at the feet of a farmer who was ploughing his field with a team of oxen. The startled man left the team in the lurch and by leaps and bounds ran into the nearby house. He was not at all accustomed to such dramatic incidents during his contemplative occupation and I could sympathise with him, who, in the face of this scene of destruction, first of all wanted to safeguard his valuable self and then the oxen.

'Somewhat relieved after this adventure, I steered towards my airfield, where the successful encounter with these hard fighting opponents was credited as another aerial victory. As I learned during my landing at Reckem, the Bristol Fighter's observer had taken some small measure of revenge. His shots had hit my landing gear tyres and I had a very bumpy ride along the airfield.'

A review of British air operations reports of 27 September helps to explain the long, erratic course taken by the Bristol Fighter's pilot, Lieutenant Cuthbert Foster, and his observer/gunner, Sergeant Thomas Proctor, of 88 Squadron, RAF. Both men perished on a day when Britain's air arm deployed 'forty reconnaissance and eighty-three contact and counter attack patrols'[12] to support initial ground efforts to storm the German defensive bulwark known as the Hindenburg Line; in the course of the day's operations, thirty-six aeroplanes were lost.[13] On this crucial day, RAF units were sent out in unusual patterns. Hence, Foster and Proctor took off from Allonville aerodrome[14] on the Somme Sector, over ninety kilometres south of their objective, Armentières, and flew over unfamiliar territory during most of their mission. In trying to save himself and his observer/gunner, Foster could only hope that, by heading south, he might reach advancing British forces. He must have fired the red flares to attract friendly aircraft to come to his aid and did not realize he was so deep into German-held territory.

At the end, the bullet-riddled Bristol Fighter plunged to the ground, killing both men and leaving their bodies in such a friendless place that they were not accorded a proper burial – not even by the farmer whose country they were trying to help liberate. To this day, Foster and Proctor are listed as having 'no known grave'.[15]

While Carl Degelow received credit for bringing down the Bristol Fighter – it was recorded as his eighteenth aerial victory – this grim achievement was not mentioned in the Air Force Commanding General's weekly intelligence digest. Apparently, there was more morale-building to be achieved by recognising other, higher-scoring aces and, significantly, the 300th aerial victory of Jagdstaffel 2, the unit formed and once led by one of Germany's greatest fighter aces, Oswald Boelcke.[16]

The Beginnings of German Military Aviation

Nearly half a century after the end of World War I, Carl Degelow, by then a veteran of both world wars, was well qualified to look back and offer some perspective on the early development of aerial combat. He shared the following thoughts with this author:

'Prior to World War I an army depended on the daring exploits of its cavalrymen to dash ahead of the main force and to scout the route it should follow. Their trusty horses provided the cavalrymen with the element of speed and manoeuvrability to perform this vital mission. They were aptly named "the eyes of the army".

'But it soon became apparent that World War I was to be fought differently. Unlike the running battles of previous wars, World War I was marked by a long line of trench fortifications running from southern France all the way to the North Sea. Men on horseback simply could not cross the lines without stumbling into shell holes or being cut down by withering machine-gun fire from well-placed fixed locations.

'Consequently, the newly constituted airmen became the new cavalry. Impassable roads and heavily defended ground fortifications did not hamper the "soldiers of the sky" from performing their missions. Indeed, the new breed of forward scout proved to be even more valuable than his equestrian predecessor, for aircraft could carry high precision cameras with which, from great altitudes, many of the enemy's secrets could be photographed with relative impunity. This form of intelligence gathering was much more helpful to the high command than the random notes sketched by a cavalryman from his saddle. Finally, aircraft could be fitted with wireless telegraphic equipment with which an aerial observer could tap out artillery ranging corrections to help the big guns on the ground zero in on their targets. Even the stuffiest, most hidebound infantry generals eventually had to concede that the new air weapon would revolutionise the arts of warfare. Indeed, the military planners became inventive to the point of ordering the construction of bigger aircraft with greater range and the ability to carry heavy loads of bombs beyond the reach of even the best artillery pieces. Thus was born the "terror bombing" that attained such a zenith of horrible perfection during World War II.

"There is a popular misconception, aided no doubt by the air of romanticism still surrounding the events of World War I, that great numbers of fighter aeroplanes were sent aloft specifically to do battle with similar numbers of opposing aircraft. From most accounts of aerial combat, including my own experiences, this was not the case. In fact, measures against aircraft were taken only after it was discovered what a great threat they were to ground forces.

'At the outbreak of war in August 1914, aeroplanes were regarded by many as the playthings of the rich or, at best, as items of curiosity. But, when they were employed as a more efficient replacement for the cavalry, planners on both sides of the lines began thinking about ways to oppose the enemy's aeroplanes. The first military aircraft were so underpowered, however, that the added weight of a weapon would have made the difference between taking off and failing to get into the air.

'Once again, technology came to the rescue. More powerful engines were developed and installed in sturdier aircraft. Then, when an enemy reconnaissance aeroplane flew overhead, an army official could order its removal by sending up another aircraft with the intention of discouraging the enemy or shooting him down. Light rifles were used first and then air-cooled machine guns. The next mark of progress is obvious. If one army's reconnaissance aircraft were going to be attacked by the opponent's aircraft, then the reconnaissance aeroplane would be escorted by an aircraft specifically intended to protect it. Thus, fighter aircraft tactics were developed for use by whole squadrons whose only purpose was to attack other enemy aircraft or keep their own planes from being attacked.

'From the outset of World War I, the German Army expected to be fighting against a numerically superior enemy. The so–called Triple Alliance of Germany, Austria-Hungary and Italy formed before the war could not hope to match the resources of manpower possessed by the so-called Triple Entente of England, France and Russia. When, in 1915, Italy joined the war on the side of the Entente, Germany and Austria-Hungary were left alone to face the major nations of Europe. It was only the great German spirit – which our detractors labelled as "militarism" even though they tried to emulate it – that kept us going in the face of such adversity. That German spirit, which includes a fierce love of the Fatherland, enabled our flyers to resist the far more numerous flyers opposing them, even though the opposition brought to bear the combined technology of the several countries involved.

'The disproportion of power in the air was often five to one against us, and the enemy swarmed over our lines in increasingly greater numbers. With every offensive of our enemies, each of which used a different cockade tri-colour design to identify the nationality of their aeroplanes, our ground troops must have gained the idea that German flyers were being crowded out of the air. Such was not the case, however, for the enemy's swarm-like advances were repulsed time and time again. What we could not win, however, was the war of attrition and, finally, the British and the French – reinforced by virtually limitless American resources – simply outlasted us.

'Aerial combat during World War I is often compared to the tournaments of the Middle Ages, in which one knightly contestant was pitted against another and thereby locked in individual conflict. There is some truth to this. We were certainly different from our comrades on the wrinkled face of Mother Earth, who utilized protective ground formations and conducted an often distant battle in which companies of soldiers exchanged fire with opponents who were often never seen and thus fought a battle utterly impersonal in character.

'In our aerial encounters, however, the opposite was the case. Here one clearly saw his opponent, protected only by a pair of goggles amid the vast expanse of air space over the front. This circumstance, seldom found in other forms of combat, lends itself to a form of chivalric behaviour in which the battle is a contest of wits and the opponent is more of an adversary at one's own level of talent – in this case, the art of flying – rather than an enemy whose presence is part of the larger international political struggle going on. We aviators are special people and that fact was as well recognized among squadrons during World War I as it was across the battle lines.

'The advent of aerial operations during World War I created a new type of German military man. The eternal class distinction – the officers above, the enlisted men below, and ne'er the twain shall meet – was an idea that had to perish in order to give rise to the special camaraderie found in German air squadrons, in which enlisted and officer pilots served together. Each man's life depended too much on the other's and so in the air we all had to be equals, joined in a common cause.

'Since there are no trees, boulders or other natural barriers to offer protection from an enemy in the sky, there were moments when a fighter pilot's life depended entirely on the assistance of his comrades. Hence, on more than one occasion, after luckily returning from an aerial combat, I had cause gratefully to shake the hand of one or more of my fellow fighter pilots for their timely aid.

'This mutual assistance in the air – a determination to meet danger together – soon created not only a very close relationship among pilots, but also a feeling of belonging to the next best thing to one's own family. This feeling was particularly evident in the evening, after a hard fight, when all of the pilots gathered in the *Kasino* [pilots' mess] to share a good meal and some good cheer. Such a genuine friendship inspired these men to gain new successes, with the watchword being: camaraderie in the air, camaraderie on the ground.

'It was only after more than a year of combat during World War I that fighter pilots began to gain the recognition they deserved. Initially, German Army pilots were simply those men foolhardy enough to seek out aggressively enemy aircraft. But that situation changed when Hauptmann [Captain] Oswald Boelcke and Oberleutnant [First-Lieutenant] Max Immelmann and several other pilots of single-seat aircraft began to shoot down enemy airplanes on a regular basis, thereby proving that such activity could be more than a random occurrence.

'Consequently, it did not take long for the German Supreme High Command to recognise the propaganda value of these air heroes. Accordingly, a pilot who shot down five enemy airplanes and qualified as a *Fliegeras* [flying ace] soon became a prominent figure in the popular press and his every deed was covered in great detail. And so it was that, on 12 January 1916, Boelcke and Immelmann became the first flyers to receive the Pour le Mérite, Prussia's highest bravery honour. It is said that when Immelmann's decoration was fastened around his neck, the blue enamel of the Pour le Mérite medal cast a reflection on his otherwise pale countenance and, from that time forward, the decoration became known as "the Blue Max".

'Although the number of enemy 'planes shot down was not supposed to be the determining factor in awarding the Pour le Mérite, such numbers no doubt entered the minds of those "higher ups" who made recommendations for the honour. For example, Boelcke and Immelmann had each shot down eight enemy aeroplanes when they received the high award. But, a year later, the famous Red Baron, Rittmeister [Cavalry Captain] Manfred Freiherr von Richthofen, received it after he shot down sixteen enemy aeroplanes, and his protégé Erich Loewenhardt after he had downed twenty-five. By late 1918, the criterion seems to have risen to thirty, the number I attained within two weeks of the war's end and which no doubt contributed to my receiving the last Pour le Mérite authorised during World War I.[17] Several other noteworthy pilots were recommended for the time-honoured award, which was established during the reign of Prussian King Friedrich II (best known as Frederick the Great) in June 1740,[18] but it was not authorised for them before the government of Kaiser Wilhelm II went out of existence on 9 November 1918 and could not be awarded thereafter.'

1 Kofl 6. Armee, *Flieger-Wochenbericht*, 20 September 1918, p. 1.

2 At the time the most recent aerodrome of 48 Squadron, RAF, ref: RAF, *War Diary* entry, 26 August 1918, p. 2.

3 Bruce, *British Aeroplanes* 1914-1918, p. 127.

4 RAF, *Combat Casualty List*, 20 September 1918, which also noted: 'report received 1.11.18 states both are prisoners.'

5 Lt Martin Francis Ronayne Mahony, born 28 February 1895 Dublin, Ireland, commissioned T/2Lt Royal Irish Fusiliers 11 November 1914, promoted T/Lt 23 May 1915, designated Flying Officer, RFC 29 June 1917, Lt 1 April 1918, BEF 7 August 1918, wounded while with 48 Squadron 24 August 1918, returned to duty 2 September 1918, captured 20 September 1918, repatriated 23 December 1918 [Ref: National Archives file 9870-9878].

6 2/Lt James Neil Kier, born 19 July 1899, joined 48 Squadron, RAF as observer 19 July 1918, wounded while with 48 Squadron 24 August 1918, captured 20 September 1918, repatriated 23 December 1918 [Ref: National Archives file 9759-9769].

7 Jones, *The War in the Air*, Vol. VI, pp. 479-480.

8 RAF, *War Diary*, 24 August 1918

9 Bruce, op.cit., p. 142.

10 Kogenluft, *Nachrichtenblatt der Luftstreitkräfte*, Vol. II, No. 31, 26 September 1918, p. 472.

11 O'Connor, *Aviation Awards of Imperial Germany and the Men Who Earned Them*, Vol. II, p. 62.

12 RAF, *War Diary*, 27 September 1918.

13 RAF, *Combat Casualty List*, 27 September 1918.

14 RAF, *War Diary*, 31 August 1918 listed 88 Squadron as being based at this location.

15 Hobson, *Airmen Died in the Great War 1914-1918*, pp. 141, 180.

16 Kogenluft, *Nachrichtenblatt der Luftstreitkräfte*, Vol. II, No. 32, 3 October 1918, p. 492.

17 Confirmed in O'Connor, op.cit., p. 65.

18 Zuerl, *Pour le Mérite-Flieger*, p. 547.

CHAPTER TWO
PEACE AND WAR

Münsterdorf is a village on the Jutland peninsula between the Baltic and North Seas in Schleswig-Holstein, Germany's northernmost state. The village, on an open plain of pastoral beauty, is bounded on the south by forests and on the north by the Stör, a winding river that flows into the Elbe above Hamburg. Münsterdorf's website notes proudly that it is the hometown of a nationally renowned nineteenth century painter and an internationally known twentieth century fighter pilot who was awarded Germany's highest bravery honour.[1]

The Early Years

The second famous local son is Carl Degelow, who was born in Münsterdorf on 5 January 1891[2] and whose early years were formed by life in the hardy northern German countryside. He received his primary education at the Kaiser-Karl-Schule, which was founded in 1866 in the town of Itzehoe, a community central to Münsterdorf and other villages in the immediate area. At the time young Degelow was a student, he was one of some twenty youngsters from Münsterdorf to be taught at the school from Kindergarten through preparation for the *Abitur* examination for university admission after twelve years of study.[3]

A review of some of Carl Degelow's early grades at this school showed that he was better than average in personal orderliness, behaviour, diligence and attentiveness, but he began to slip in the areas of religion, German and French. He perked up in geography and the natural sciences. He also did well in singing and physical education. Young Carl developed an inquiring mind and a sense of patience that would serve him well in the military – although, as a constant questioner, probably not as a career.

The area's main industry at the time was the Alen'schen Cement Factories in Itzehoe and neighbouring Lägerdorf, so it was a natural development that, when the nineteen-year-old Degelow attended the University of Darmstadt, he prepared himself for a career related to the cement industry. He audited courses in mechanical engineering and, with a view toward an eventual management position, he also studied psychology.[4] Degelow related to this author that, at the end of his studies, one of his early life's great joys was the year-and-a-half he spent in the United States, working for cement companies in Chicago, Illinois and El Paso, Texas. The US was then the technological leader in the industry and Degelow was determined to return to Germany with knowledge and practical experience to give him advantages over his peers.

Back in Germany, Degelow rejoined his family, then living in Hamburg. There he became friends with Paul Nami, a young American who had gone to Germany to learn more about automobile engines. Nami, who also wanted to advance his career back home by studies and experiences gained overseas, recalled:

'I met Carl (or, as we called him, "Charly") Degelow and his brother John in a wrestling academy in Hamburg, some months before the outbreak of World War I. We exercised together and learned to wrestle under the tutelage of one of Germany's champion wrestlers. We also practiced boxing, a sport in which Charly became interested while visiting the United States. Although I was a few years younger than Charly and Johnny – and a foreigner, to boot! – they invited me to their home in Altona, near Hamburg, to meet their family. Carl Degelow, Senior was a prominent businessman and well-known poet. His elder son and namesake possessed many of his father's fine qualities and sensitivities, including a sparkling sense of humour. He also played the piano and sang with a good voice. I enjoyed many pleasant hours of music and good fellowship in the Degelow home during my stay in Germany.

'Johnny and I became deeply interested in the fledgling art of flying. But Charly was absorbed in industrial chemistry, his speciality being the manufacture of concrete. With the outbreak of war on 1 August, 1914, Charly became one of the millions of young Germans who eagerly entered the army, full of patriotism and idealism – and confident that it would all be over by Christmas.'[5]

Called to Duty

When Carl Degelow began his studies in Darmstadt in 1909, he came under the authority of the Grand Duchy of Hesse and, as every German male was subject to military service from age seventeen to forty-five, the Münsterdorf native was enrolled in the local Landsturm [Home Guards] First Battalion.[6] Hence, during his time in Darmstadt he received enough basic training and military indoctrination to understand his military responsibility if Germany were to prepare for war. Degelow was in the Hessian city of Mainz when mobilisation was announced and volunteered for service with a local unit, the 2. Nassauischen Infanterie-Regiment Nr. 88 [Second Nassau Infantry Regiment No. 88].[7] He was one of thousands of volunteers who clogged the streets of Mainz at the outbreak of war[8] and stood in long lines during the next several days among the new Landsers [Privates of the lowest rank] being processed and placed within companies to complete the regiment's roster.

While the troops were already well motivated, General der Infanterie Hugo von Kathen, Military Governor of the Mainz District, addressed the regiment with a forceful reminder that concluded with:

'In unshakeable trust in God and our good and justified cause, all of Germany takes up arms and will carry out the fight, no matter what the cost. All of us who call ourselves Germans and feel German are imbued with the singular feeling of securing the most precious gift for Kaiser and *Reich* [realm], hearth and home, of protecting German prestige, German reputation, and German customs and traditions. Firm and loyal as ever before, the citizenry and military men of our dear Mainz will stand closely together

Carl Degelow (seated) and his comrade Felix Debertshauser wore their new uniforms while proudly posing for this photo just before the 2. Nassauisches Infanterie-Regiment Nr. 88 went off to war in August 1914.

in this grave hour of danger. And all of that we now reaffirm in the call: His Majesty, the Kaiser, our most gracious supreme war lord, and His Royal Highness, the Grand Duke of Hesse, our beloved sovereign of this land. Hurrah!'[9]

Early on the morning of Friday, 7 August 1914, the men of Inf.-Reg Nr. 88 with previous training were fully organised by company and sent out on foot to engage their new enemies in World War I. Untrained or not fully trained men – and Degelow was in the latter category – remained in Mainz for three weeks of basic infantry instruction. Degelow's good state of physical fitness served him well, as he (an 'older' man at age twenty-three) easily outpaced many of the less fit teenagers who flocked to the regiment during the early war patriotic frenzy.

On Sunday, 23 August, Degelow and the second wave of recruits went by train to catch up with and reinforce their regimental comrades, who were already fighting in France. When they arrived, the regiment was advanced south, into hilly terrain southwest of Les Deux Villes. Well placed French forces inflicted casualties of two officers and sixty-eight enlisted men of Inf.-Reg Nr. 88 that day.[10] Those incidents set the tone for what Degelow's unit encountered in weeks to come: as their troops advanced, they came under attack and responded with greater firepower, reinforced by artillery. The Germans pushed their opponents as far south as the Marne Canal, but those advances were hard won, often fought at close quarter with bayonets.[11]

Trench Warfare

During the epic Battle of the Marne, where British and French forces held the line and reversed their fortunes, Inf.-Reg Nr. 88 and other elements of the German 2nd Army were forced back to Reims. As that city is just over 140 kilometres east-northeast of Paris, it was imperative for French forces to stop the German advance at the time-honoured cathedral city in the Champagne Sector. Subsequently, Degelow's regiment moved east to Roye and dug in for protracted warfare. In the autumn of 1914, a trench system of irregular ditches, each as deep as a man's height, began to take shape. 'The area between the opposing positions was known as no man's land … [varying] in width from 30 to 800 yards,' as one historian noted. 'With typical thoroughness, the Germans constructed … large dugouts where platoons and companies could find shelter from the heaviest bombardment …'[12]

Before Degelow and a large number of his regimental comrades could settle into their trenches in France, in December they were culled out for transfer to the newly-forming Hessian Reserve-Infanterie-Regiment Nr. 253. As the German Army shifted emphasis in various sectors, it typically created new 'reserve' units to respond to changing circumstances and opportunities. In this case, Res-Inf-Reg Nr. 253 was part of a large force created for the new German 10th Army organised for Generaloberst [Colonel-General] Paul Ludwig Hans Anton von Hindenburg und Beneckendorf, the Eastern Front commander who became better known as von Hindenburg. Following his success at Tannenberg in August, Hindenburg hoped for a second major victory that might knock Russia out of the war.

The resulting conflict, known as the Second Battle of the Masurian Lakes [now in Poland], began during a snowstorm on 7 February 1915. Less than two weeks later, the

Russian XX Army Corps surrendered and Hindenburg tried to keep the momentum going. Despite tremendous losses, the Russians managed to fend off a major German incursion into the Russian homeland. At this time, Degelow's leadership potential came to the attention of his superiors, as on 1 February 1915, he was promoted to the rank of Gefreiter [Lance Corporal] and granted more responsibility within his infantry company.

The German 10th Army suffered relatively light casualties in the winter fighting, but among those who had to be removed from the battle zone was Gefreiter Degelow. While leading a small party of men against the enemy, he took a bullet in the right arm. Before he was sent back to Germany for further treatment and convalescence, Degelow was awarded the Iron Cross Second Class.

He was treated for his wound at the *'Weisser Hirsch'* [White Stag], a famous spa hotel on the edge of Dresden, capital of the Kingdom of Saxony. Then run by the German Army Medical Corps, the spa had excellent facilities to help its patients recover and return to duty. Degelow was so impressed by the White Stag that, two years later, he had its emblem of a silver stag with golden antlers painted on the side of his fighter aeroplane as his personal battle symbol.

After being discharged from medical treatment, Degelow was assigned to another newly-created Hessian unit, Reserve-Infanterie-Regiment Nr. 358. He was happy that the new unit was located on the warmer and more hospitable Champagne Sector in France – rather than in Russia.

By the time of his arrival, Res-Inf-Reg Nr. 358 was in secure trenches that signified the stagnation that was a hallmark of World War I. The trenches provided immediate protection, but, as the months wore on into the spring of 1915, the soldiers' discomfort grew. Degelow remembered:

'Infantrymen of World War I were not at all pleased to have to live in the trenches that were a vital part of the frontlines. Indeed, there were times when the unpleasantness of that kind of lodging sank to a new low of discomfort and became practically unbearable. Anyone familiar with our corrugated zinc-covered bunkers admitted that the nickname "Villa Bend Down" was most appropriate in distinguishing these low-ceilinged lodgings from those in the "real" world back home.

'Eventually, the "comfort" of our frontline dwelling was undermined even further by an industriously propagating family of rats that had become fellow tenants. What this rodent invasion did to the soldiers' composure may perhaps only be understood by someone who was forced to be a mute witness to the nightlong love orgies of the rat denizens in our underground quarters. Living in a hole like this eventually got on my nerves, particularly when the rat nuisance was reinforced by torrents of water pouring down onto us. Resistance to the latter was accomplished to some extent by nailing down everything that was liable to float away, right down to the chairs and tables.

'Apparently we were not alone in our discomfort and its after–effects. The Frenchmen across the lines from us seemed unenthusiastic about attacking us and, thus, did nothing to arouse the warlike virtues dormant in us. Each of us young soldiers felt that such inactivity was not for him and was, therefore, depressed and ashamed that other comrades were attacking and winning daily, while he fought the mud and the rats.'

The latter comment is typical of the modesty that remained with Carl Degelow for life. Far from being involved only in fighting 'the mud and the rats', he had been so active in combat that he had been decorated and identified as a man with leadership potential. By the end of April 1915, at a time when French artillery fire was increasing in intensity in the Champagne Sector,[13] Gefreiter Degelow gained further recognition from his superiors: he was posted back to Germany for officer training.

First, he travelled to a rear area cleaning station for a decent bath, haircut and shave, as well as fresh uniforms. Degelow did not yet have an officer's shoulder boards on his uniforms, but certainly looked and felt much more presentable. A long train ride took him out of France and into the German heartland. As he approached his destination, the broad, flat greenery of the Lüneburg Heath reminded him of his hometown in Schleswig-Holstein. Even the name of the training centre was similar: Munster-Lager.

Officer Training

The first army unit to train at Munster-Lager, in 1893, was commanded by then Oberst [Colonel] Paul von Beneckendorf und von Hindenburg.[14] By the time Carl Degelow arrived there, that officer had risen to the rank of Generalfeldmarschall [Field Marshal] and led the German Army for most of World War I. In Hindenburg's day, most officers 'came through the regimental ranks in a special grooming program lasting about eighteen months,'[15] while many others were products of the Royal Prussian Cadet Corps, 'a system of state military secondary schools … that fed students at about age fifteen into the central cadet school in Berlin'[16] for about three years. But the high rate of attrition among junior officers in World War I required an infusion of fresh young military leaders who could be prepared for lower level command positions in about four weeks. Trained by seasoned non-commissioned officers and *aktiv* [career-oriented] officers, enlisted men such as Carl Degelow who completed the course were awarded Leutnant der Reserve commissions.

Briefly stated, the majority of regimentally-trained officers was intended 'to ensure that the brotherhood of officers of a regiment was a socially, philosophically, and professionally homogeneous unit.'[17] Cadet Corps officers came from a broader spectrum of society, as the result of a competitive entrance examination and were better educated. Wartime Reserve commissions were awarded most often to combat-experienced men who displayed natural leadership ability. In all cases, 'the sober Prussian military leaders, whatever their regional loyalties or class biases, recognized that their purpose was to produce military leaders with the attributes – intellectual, spiritual and physical – required for vigorous field service.'[18]

On Sunday, 1 August 1915, the first anniversary of Germany's mobilisation for war, Ltn.d.Res Carl Degelow departed Munster-Lager to assume his new duties with Res-Inf-Reg Nr. 358. While he was away, his regiment was in the German-occupied Lorraine Sector of France, allowing the men time to recuperate from a steady pace of combat.

A month later, Degelow's regiment went back to living in trenches in the Champagne Sector, where the latest danger came from the air. Degelow remembered that:

'French flying activity increased daily. French aeroplanes crossed over our position, came down low and strafed our trenches with machine-gun fire. Our own aeroplanes showed themselves from quite a distance or not at all. It turned out that of only six aeroplanes on hand, two combat aeroplanes were available and of course they could have no success against the numerically superior French flyers.'

The air attacks decreased during worsening weather in December, but then the poor hygiene of trench life caught up with Degelow's regiment. Instances of 'a typhus-type malady' were reported. Most likely, the ill soldiers suffered from trench fever, which was widespread on the Western Front. According to a medical expert: 'The Germans constructed deep, shellproof dugouts … which were usually better drained [than British trenches] … however, louse infestation and trench fever affected the Germans just as badly as it affected the British.[19] The disease was generally not fatal, but restricted the soldiers' ability to fight. It was addressed by 'de-lousing' the men and their living quarters with disinfectant. The down side of the procedure was that having the men leave the safety of the dugouts made the remedy more dangerous than the illness.

Good weather in the spring of 1916 encouraged French air units to resume their bombing missions and strafing runs over the German trenches. Carl Degelow recalled:

'From time to time the monotony along our sector was broken by the steady hum of an aeroplane engine. Peering over the battlements we could see the aeroplanes of both sides freely moving through the air. The immediate thought was: "How pure and clean it must be up there!" The combined circumstances of life in the "Villa Bend Down" quickly led my thoughts to the aviation branch of the army, which in those days was called the Fliegertruppe [Flying Force].

'During World War I the Fliegertruppe was but a small part of the German Army. In order to get into aviation, one had first to be in the army. Some lucky fellows, such as Hauptmann Oswald Boelcke, got into flying right away. Others either did not know how to go about transferring, or became discouraged by the mass of bureaucratic manoeuvring it took to win such a transfer. Furthermore, the longer a man was with a ground unit, the more valuable he became to that unit by virtue of his experience and, hence, the less likely it would be that his superior would willingly let him go. Determination and perseverance were the keys to success.

'Of course, not every German soldier was eager to leave the solid security of Mother Earth for the thousands of feet of air above his head. But there were some things about the life of a ground soldier that made the air look more attractive – particularly when one is looking up at the clean air from out of a muddy, cold trench. To realise this ambition, it was now up to me to discuss my plan with my battalion commander and to override all ninety-nine of his objections to my request for a transfer.'

From the Mud to the Clouds
The spring rains were good for the trees and plants that survived the artillery barrages, but only added to the misery of human existence in the frontline trenches, where rivulets of water were abundant. But then, as Degelow joyfully recorded: 'The blooming flowers of May 1916 brought with them my orders to leave the trenches and report to the Deutsche Flugzeug-Werke [German Aircraft Works] at Lindenthal, outside of Leipzig.

'In short order I was across the Rhine and back into Germany and what an incredible difference it was from what I had left behind. The natural beauty of the Rhine provinces was peaceful and undisturbed, unlike the endlessly deserted and shattered countryside of France, where grenades and landmines had transformed quiet villages and cities into heaps of rubble. In its May dress of green, Germany was learning the results of how, in the west, the wall of our field-grey soldiers had advanced far into enemy territory. Their sacrifices served only to strengthen our sense of duty and our determination to triumph. It was a marvellous feeling to belong to such a brotherhood.'

At the time, Germany's need for pilots was greater than its military establishment's capability to train hundreds of men to fill and replace billets in the 108 two-seat reconnaissance and artillery cooperation squadrons, thirty bombing units, six single-seat fighter units and other smaller, specialised aviation units that were in the field by May 1916.[20] Hence, private contractors helped to fill the gap and one such firm was the Deutsche Flugzeug-Werke (DFW), whose primary business was constructing aircraft for the war effort. Established in 1912 in the Kingdom of Saxony, DFW ran a lucrative secondary business of training pilots. When the war began, 'the DFW Flying School employed eight flight instructors and fourteen … aircraft to train some thirty to forty students.'[21] Not surprisingly, DFW two-seat aeroplanes were the exclusive training machines at the school. The favourable instructor to student ratio assured competent and complete training for the would-be aviators.

The atmosphere and the training regime at the DFW Flying School were described by another pilot who had much in common with Carl Degelow. Julius Buckler, who also became a fighter pilot and recipient of the Pour le Mérite, later described his impressions of Leipzig-Lindenthal:

'The airfield lay close to a wood. Upon my arrival, the first thing I saw was a burned and charred something-or-other … between the trees. Bewildered and with the feeling that aviation was a damned dicey business, I reported to the flying school office. In no time at all the formalities were completed, I was assigned to living quarters and a short time later I stood among the student pilots, many of whom had already flown solo and believed themselves to be demi-gods. The hair-raising stories these fellows served up to the novices could be really creepy. But I had already learned thoroughly about horror on the nocturnal field of death at the Front, and so I listened indifferently to their grotesque babbling. Inwardly, however, I was so agitated by all of the great detail of the frightful experiences of the babbling demi-gods that I could not sleep at night. Moreover, I was afraid that I would over-sleep.

'At 0430 hours the following day, my flying duty began. Punctually, I set out for the airfield … [where] the big doors on the hangars were closed. On one hangar roof, attached to a pole, was an inflated tube-shaped thing that looked like an air-filled trouser leg. As I later learned, it was a "windsock". And due to this inflated, wildly tugging and flapping "sock" on the pole, all was not right here. Because of this, the student pilots had gone home, the hangar doors were closed and not a single aeroplane stood outside. For those in the know, the agitated windsock signified "flyers' weather", that is to say: no flying weather.

'The old hands … did not even come to the airfield and the others just turned back. They let me, the novice, calmly walk on. Everyone has his own experiences and so this was as it should be.'[22]

Learning from the Best

Despite such minor annoyances, Julius Buckler – and later Carl Degelow – learned to fly from highly qualified instructors. Buckler noted that the school's commanding officer was Hauptmann Willi Meyer,[23] who had earned *Deutsche Luftfahrer-Verband* [German Aviators Association] License No. 136 on 18 November 1911 under the tutelage of aviation pioneer Hans Grade.[24] The school's chief pilot was Heinrich Oelerich, who had earned DLV License No. 37 on 21 October 1910,[25] and at least five other instructors were licensed before World War I began.[26]

In Degelow's case, certain preconceived notions needed to be dispelled before he began this phase of his instruction:

'I knew that an instructor would teach me how to fly; however, my passion and zeal for flying were soon dampened. I had imagined that the procedure would simply be to appear at the airfield, put on a helmet, jump into an aeroplane already prepared for the occasion, and fly off into space. I was soon freed from this illusion. It turned out that, instead of what I had imagined, we students had to have the patience of an angel and wait until those in charge – the instructor pilots – granted permission to make the first flight. They had their own system and one had to admit that it was not the worst. The words we heard were: "Always observe, gentlemen. You will learn how to fly sooner from sharp observation than by taking over the airplane's controls prematurely."

'I must admit that this waiting time was not entirely uninteresting; for, watching fledgling pilots getting themselves and their *Kisten* [crates], as we called the old training 'planes, into comical situations from lack of experience kept one from becoming too serious about this business. For eight long days after my arrival I had to remain inactive, while all the time being stuffed with flight theory to such an extent that I came to think of myself as an experienced aviator.

'At last, one morning in the middle of May, after the proper authorities had ascertained that not even the smallest leaf on a tree had fluttered, that no air current had moved the windsock and the air was calm, I was permitted to take off accompanied by my instructor. Poetically minded persons might tell of the musical song of the engine, but actually the first-time flyer is more prosaically inclined. In any event, the roaring of my training aeroplane's engine was not melodious to me. Despite that, during my first flight I immediately felt that here was a devilishly delightful thing to do.

'Flying produces a pleasing sense of freedom that is not only due to being separated spatially from the bounds of earth, and this purely external circumstance has a soothing effect on one's innermost feelings. In flight, a pilot has also to observe the technical requirements demanded of him. To become lost in a philosophical reverie of inner concerns can bring disastrous results, as I was soon to discover.

'After numerous flights with my instructor in a dual-control training aircraft, I was sent up alone in this machine, which was nicknamed "The Buffalo". I had proved on our training flights that this "crate" possessed the nature of the animal for which it was named and I learned to my cost that it also had a will of its own. During its long service, my "Buffalo" had tamely flown its rounds, but now that I was alone in the air for the first time, it seemed to become stubborn and wilful. Contrary to my intention, the aeroplane suddenly turned to the left and, instead of pursuing its regular circular course, it headed with increasing speed toward the neighbouring woods.

'Despite my giving the 'plane all the right rudder that I could, due to the engine's tendency for extreme torque to the left, the machine maliciously took me ever closer to the menacing forest. In my mind I could see the grinning faces and hear the scornful laughter of the people at the airfield, and I could imagine the anxiety on my instructor's face. The thought occurred to me that perhaps the mechanics had committed sabotage by attaching the steering cables backwards. With one last desperate effort I pulled the machine up just above the treetops. Still turning to the left, I suddenly saw the airfield beneath me and, easing back on the throttle, I glided down and made a three-point landing.

'From all sides came the silent witnesses of my narrow escape. Leading them was my instructor, his arms waving. "How could you do such a thing?" he yelled. "By a whisker you avoided crashing and smashing up my beautiful machine."

'The second censure came from Chief Pilot Oelerich: "Get that man out of the machine. He has no feeling for flying. I can see that he will never learn. Give him twenty more training flights."

'My comrades later confided that they had already agreed on the sum of money they would spend to buy me a burial wreath.'

The weather improved during the summer months and Degelow flew more often, from early in the morning until as late in the afternoon as good sunlight allowed. On those days of 'flyers' weather', with little to do at the airfield, he slept for awhile. But, being innately curious, he also spent time with the mechanics, watching them disassemble and repair engines, and asking many questions about the 'heart' of the aeroplane.

A Look at the Man
Life at the flying school was not all work and there were opportunities to enjoy the sights and cuisine of nearby Leipzig. Carl Degelow's American friend Paul Nami recalled their last wartime get-together:

'I had originally come to Germany to learn how to drive and repair automobiles. When the war broke out, I became an aeroplane mechanic. The United States had declared its neutrality, so working in a German defence industry presented no problems then to an American national. While Charly was receiving pilot training at Lindenthal, I worked at the Halberstadter Flugzeugwerke [Aeroplane Works] in Halberstadt, a city not far from Leipzig. I was installing engines and synchronisation gear to allow machine-gun fire to pass through the propeller arc of the Halberstadt D.II biplane fighter.

A sign in the student pilot's cockpit of a two-seat training aeroplane reminds the 'Emil' [pilot] to pay attention to the spark advance while advancing the throttle during the ignition cycle.

'Accepting Charly's invitation to visit him in Leipzig, I went there by train one Sunday in July 1916. Charly met me at the main railroad station, traditionally the one place in almost every German city where one of the best restaurants is to be found. The dining establishment in Leipzig was no exception. Charly ordered river salmon for both of us – and what a marvellous treat that was!

'As a civilian in wartime Germany, I joined the general population in subsisting on *ersatz* [substitute] foods; civilians could get no flour, meat, fat, sugar, nor certain other foods normally considered necessities of life. Instead, we had to live on substitutes, and hard work, besides. We soon learned that survival is not dependent on the luxury foods that we were denied. The sumptuous meal that Charly and I enjoyed was no doubt "arranged" because he was a German officer.

'The day was sunny and warm, and our youthful spirits were high. Leipzig's location in eastern Germany kept it secure from the aerial bombardment that so badly damaged it during World War II. From the railroad station, Charly took me to the museum on the Augustusplatz, where, among the priceless art exhibits, we could contemplate Max Klinger's famous statue of Beethoven, and be deeply touched by Arnold Böcklin's painting *"Die Toteninsel"* [Isle of the Dead]. Next we went to the elite Café Felscher for coffee and cake. While enjoying these virtually forbidden luxuries, Charly described to me the opera he had seen the night before, Wagner's "Tristan und Isolde". I marvelled at the many sides to the character of this dedicated soldier.

'Leaving the café, we walked past some of Leipzig's famous buildings and my host provided a complete rundown on their histories. Then came one of the greatest thrills of my life: dinner in Auerbach's Keller, the scene of a noted episode in the Goethe drama "Faust".

"The memorable day ended with Charly seeing me off on the train that took me back to Halberstadt, where I had to be at work the following morning. I mention this wartime visit because I think it provides insight into the character of the man who, although he went on to become an accomplished fighter pilot, actually killed few of his opponents. Indeed, his nature was such that it was an even greater challenge, despite the furious pace of the killing going on around him, to bring down his opponent alive.

'Carl Degelow was a man of refined taste, with the soul of a poet. Despite the horror of war and the destructive passions unleashed during aerial combat, he could still admire the beautiful face of nature. During our long association, I never once saw him in an angry mood. At the height of his air combat success, he maintained an even balance regarding the events around him; indeed, had he been the one shot down, he would have accepted his fate calmly as the fortune of war and he would have held no rancour toward his opponent.'[27]

The Winds of Change

In August, Degelow was transferred to Flieger-Ersatz-Abteilung 6 [aviation replacement section 6] in Grossenhain, northwest of Dresden, the capital of Saxony. Despite its location, FEA 6's twenty-one establishing officers came from other parts of the German Empire,[28] making it an all-German – and not just a regional – facility. As Degelow observed, FEA 6 demonstrated that cooperative regionalism could work within the German national military framework that was created after the Franco-Prussian War of 1870-1891:

'The Fliegertruppe became a melting pot of Germans from all points of the empire. There were, to be sure, some Bavarian, Saxon and Württemberg squadrons, but, while most air units bore the "'Royal Prussian" designation, they were made up of men from around the country. As time went on, even the regional air units had to accept replacements from places outside of their own sections of Germany.'

Degelow himself was a good example of the military integration that evolved in Wilhelmine Germany. He was born in Schleswig-Holstein, which had been annexed by Prussia in 1866,[29] fulfilled his military obligation by enlisting in a Hessian infantry regiment, later served in a Royal Württemberg reconnaissance squadron, two Royal Prussian fighter squadrons and went on to command a Royal Saxon fighter unit. As he noted:

'In a local regional unit, a soldier could freely converse in his own dialect and be readily understood by all present. But in the Imperial German Navy, which had no localized ships or units, Hochdeutsch [High German] had to be used as a common medium of oral communication. The situation quickly became the same in the Fliegertruppe, where clear communication was essential.'

Degelow saw a bit of humour in the growing melding of elements in aviation units:

> 'At the time, there was no official Fliegertruppe uniform – aside from flight clothing, which also came in a variety of forms – so it was perfectly all right for a new member of an aviation unit to wear the same uniform he had worn while serving with his previous local or Prussian Army unit. This development led to some interesting displays of uniforms and military heraldry at a facility such as FEA 6. During a troop review or similar occasion, many a visiting dignitary was surprised to see several fellows in the field-grey of the infantry, while, in the same line-up, there might be a fancily-dressed hussar or a colourful musketeer in his regimental uniform. The one piece of uniform apparel they all had in common was the small pilot's or observer's badge, which was worn on the lower left portion of a uniform jacket. Other than that, it was each man for himself and according to his tailor.'

Degelow's lessons and seemingly endless practice flights at FEA 6 enabled him to refine the basic skills he learned at the flying school, but, meanwhile, German military aviation itself was changing. Following the disastrous Verdun campaign, on 29 August 1916, General Staff Chief Erich von Falkenhayn stepped down and was succeeded by the highly acclaimed commander of the Eastern Front, Generalfeldmarschall Paul von Hindenburg,[30] who brought with him a number of air-minded staff officers to help him make sweeping changes, including reorganising the Fliegertruppe. Consequently, on 8 October 1916, the flying service was upgraded as a command by having a general officer placed in charge and renamed the Luftstreitkräfte [Air Force]. The commanding general, fifty-six-year-old Generalleutnant Ernst von Hoeppner, was not a flyer; he was a seasoned cavalryman accustomed to leading widely deployed forces over a broad area, roughly analogous to aviation units. The Fliegertruppe's loose command structure[31] was succeeded by a more cohesive organisation.

Carl Degelow's role in the new Luftstreitkräfte would begin after he successfully completed a series of ever more difficult requirements to become a two-seater pilot. These examinations included solo flights and figure eights in the air, as well as gliding descents from varying heights and within fixed perimeters, cross-country flights with an instructor present, mock aerial combats, night-time take-offs and landings without an observer or instructor, and sustained higher altitude flights. In order to qualify for his pilot's badge, Degelow also had to demonstrate knowledge of flight theory, aircraft construction and engine operation (which were aided by his previous engineering studies at Darmstadt University and time spent with the mechanics at FEA 6), as well as navigation and map reading.[32] He would not receive the badge, however, until he had made the number of combat flights required by the officer in charge of aviation in his battle sector. At the end of the course, Degelow proudly noted:

> 'Although my further training at Grossenhain did not proceed without difficulties and minor accidents, I soon became familiar with all of the aircraft controls and learned how to master their technical difficulties and peculiarities. The rough landings that gave me black eyes and a bloody nose on several occasions were all behind me. Now I was a

fully qualified pilot and could earn my flyer's badge.

'At the end of December 1916, I received orders to report to Flieger-Abteilung (A) 216, a Royal Württemberg reconnaissance squadron on the Somme Sector in France. And there, on New Year's Day 1917, my flying adventures would begin.'

1   www.muensterdorf.de

2   Zuerl, *Pour le Mérite-Flieger*, p. 177.

3   Kollegium, *Kaiser-Karl-Schule Itzehoe 1866-1991*, pp. 96-107.

4   Ref: Alumni Association, Technische Universität Darmstadt.

5   Quoted in Kilduff, *Germany's Last Knight of the Air*, p. 15.

6   Imperial War Museum, *Handbook of the German Army in War*, p. 9.

7   Zuerl, op.cit.

8   Schmidt, *2. Nassauisches Infanterie-Regiment Nr. 88*, p. 9.

9   Ibid.

10 Ibid., p. 17.

11 Ibid., p. 23.

12 Esposito, *A Concise History of World War I*, pp. 79-80.

13 Ibid., p. 45.

14 Hindenburg, *Out of My Life*, p. 63.

15 Moncure, *Forging the King's Sword*, p. 15.

16 Ibid., p. 5.

17 Ibid., p. 16.

18 Ibid., p. 223.

19 Miller, "Of Lice and Men: Trench Fever and Trench Life in the AIF," p. 2.

20 Neumann, *Die deutschen Luftstreitkräfte im Weltkriege*, p, 64

21 Grosz, *DFW C.V Windsock Datafile 53*, p. 1

22 Buckler, *Malaula! Kampfruf meiner Staffel*, pp. 56-58.

23 Ibid., p. 60.

24 Supf, *Das Buch der deutschen Fluggeschichte*, Vol. I, p. 565.

25 Ibid., p. 563.

26 Hans Grade students Hans Steinbeck, holder of DLV License No. 68 on 27 February 1911, and Hermann Gasser, DLV License No. 202 on 14 May 1912, as well as Reinhold Boehm, DLV License No. 382 on 18 April 1913; Walter Höfig, DLV License No. 585 on 8 November 1913; and Kurt Rehse, DLV License No. 735 on 25 April 1914 [Ref: Supf, Vol. I, pp. 564, 567 and Vol. II, pp. 663, 665, 667].

27 Kilduff, op.cit., pp. 16-18.

28 Aviation stations in Döberitz (Prussia), Metz (German-occupied Lorraine), Strassburg (German-occupied Alsace), Darmstadt (Hesse) and Cologne (Rhineland) [Ref: Täger, Heerde, Franke & Ruscher, *Flugplatz Grossenhain – Historischer Abriss*, p. 7].

29 Clark, *Iron Kingdom*, p. 542.

30 Ibid., p. 610.

31 Hoeppner, *Deutschlands Krieg in der Luft*, (1921), p. 82.

32 Neumann, op.cit., pp. 268-269.

CHAPTER THREE
OVER THE FRONT AT LAST

Carl Degelow concluded 1916 on the happiest of notes. It was a blustery Sunday morning on 31 December, when he boarded the officers' car of a troop train departing westward from Dresden's main railroad station. Some officers brought various bottles with them to ease the boredom of more than half a day's journey to Belgium and France, but Degelow, ever mindful of his Christian upbringing and earlier athletic training, did not join them. With his pilot qualification papers and new orders in hand, the prospects of what lay ahead in his first squadron assignment filled him with more euphoria than any liquid ever could. He had endured twenty months in the trenches, followed by eight strenuous months of pilot training, and now he was eager to go to war in the air – and to begin with a clear head.

He and a group of other new pilots got off the main train in Brussels and changed to a slower local train that plodded along to Valenciennes, France. There, they climbed into the back of a lorry that took them to a big aviation depot, where some men left the group. Degelow rode on for an additional several hours to his new airfield farther south, in the Somme Sector. Even that long, bumpy and chilly ride did not dampen his spirits. Very early in the morning of New Year's Day 1917, he arrived at a nameless flat expanse alongside the road; in the dim light of a few lanterns, he could make out the hangar sheds that housed his new squadron's airplanes. A drowsy duty officer pointed him in the direction of a small house that served as the officers' quarters, where Degelow was left on his own to find an empty bed.

Flieger-Abteilung (A) 216

For all of his enthusiasm, Degelow could not imagine that Royal Württemberg Flieger-Abteilung (A) 216 (abbreviated Fl.-Abt (A) 216), had quite a sad history.[1] Later, he learned that some six weeks earlier the squadron had suffered its initial fatalities: its first commanding officer, twenty-three-year-old Leutnant Max Arand von Ackerfeld,[2] and his pilot, Ltn.d.Res Günther Friedrichs.[3] On 17 November 1916, about twenty-five minutes after taking off, suddenly and for no apparent reason their aeroplane plunged to the ground; both crewmen were found dead in the wreckage.[4] Ten days later, the unit's previous officers' quarters burned to the ground from a swift fire of unknown origin; all of the officers' clothing and equipment was lost in the blaze.[5] Perhaps due to their precarious existence high in the air with little external protection and no parachutes, many airmen became superstitious and they worried about omens.[6]

Degelow later wrote to this author:

'When I first arrived at the Abteilung, the winter weather had put a chill in military operations. There were exchanges of artillery fire, but heavy winds and occasional driving rains curtailed extensive flight operations. In the absence of formal missions to perform and not content to sit in the officers' mess most of the day, I requested and was allowed to make a series of orientation flights in our immediate vicinity.'

When he suited up for his first flight over the Somme battlefield, Degelow saw that none of his new brothers-in-arms wanted to leave their warm quarters and join him. An experienced observer in the backseat would have acquainted the new pilot with the area and helped him fend off enemy single-seat fighters whose pilots considered a bigger, slower two-seat reconnaissance airplane to be a good target. But Degelow was less interested in personal comfort than in beginning his combat flying career. As a junior officer, with no command authority, he could not give orders to his peers; he could only direct the ground crew to secure a 100-kilogram sand bag in the observer's seat. The ballast would make up for the weight lost by the lack of a more aggressive flying companion.

The German Military Pilot's Badge, authorised by Kaiser Wilhelm II on his birthday, 27 January 1913, was awarded to enlisted and commissioned officer pilots alike after they completed all qualifications. The symbol within the badge, a Rumpler Taube [Dove], was an aeroplane familiar to many pre-war airmen.

The German Aviation Observer's Badge, authorised by the Kaiser on 27 January 1914, was awarded only to commissioned officers, as enlisted men could become only pilots or aerial gunners. Within the badge was a black and white checkerboard surrounded by a red border to symbolise an Army Group, which would benefit from an observer's visual and photographic reconnaissance duties.

That first flight was uneventful, despite the danger of flying alone and becoming lost in the air. German flyers even coined a word for it: *verfranzt*. For reasons never made clear, a two-seater pilot was referred to as the 'Emil' and the observer as the 'Franz'. Degelow deduced that the nicknames evolved: 'In much the same way as that which causes people to substitute words for names they cannot immediately remember, such as the use of "Friedrich" by hotel guests for male members of the hotel staff.

'Such a lapse of memory is said to have given rise to the name "Franz" for the observer in reconnaissance aircraft and, despite the complexity of his duties, he became known as the "Franz". Later, to get even with the pilots who had given them a nickname, the observers christened their pilots with the nickname "Emil". I trust that this digression on the subject of fliers' jargon, done in the spirit of fun, will permit the reader to understand what I mean by saying that a "Franz" has "franzt" or guided himself. If one became "verfranzt", then, of course, he was lost.

'Being verfranzt was not so bad when it happened during the daylight; for, even if all attempts to find the right direction fail, the pilot might have made an emergency landing on favourable terrain to ascertain his whereabouts. This navigational hazard was much more dangerous when it happened to a pilot flying alone at night; for, if he had no observer on board to answer his pregnant questions of "whereto?" and "how far?" with a simple nod or shake of his head, even his experienced eye could not pick out a landing place in the darkness.'

First Night Flight

As he later wrote, during his first month at the Front, Carl Degelow experienced the perils of flying alone at night:

'It was a bitterly cold day in January 1917 that began with a snowstorm. I paid a visit to some friends in a squadron at a neighbouring airfield and was preparing to return to my own 'field when it began to get dark. The twilight was fading as I started my engine and prepared to take off. Casting to the wind all warnings that the storm blowing in the wrong direction would hamper my journey, I gunned the engine and took off. The houses and railroad tracks passed like shadows beneath me. Now and then I saw lights from farmhouses and pairs of glaring automobile headlights on the country road below me that gave me the impression I was being followed by two glow worms of equal speed. Thus, my attention was dreamily distracted from my aeroplane to the darkened earth below. It was not uncommon for such a circumstance to occur during wartime, for that sense which registers danger to be lulled and for drowsiness to creep over one's awareness.

'At this point, one might tell the story of the soldier who slept one night on an unexploded shell that had been fired into his mattress by enemy artillery and which he did not discover until the following morning. Similarly, on this flight I did not realise the unpleasantness of my situation until I glanced at my fuel gauge and found that I only had enough gasoline to last me a quarter of an hour.

'Soon after taking off, I was forced by the unfavourable wind to fly at almost treetop altitude. The wind at higher altitude was almost twice as strong as that closer to the ground and would give me an even slimmer chance of making it back to my own airfield. But because of low-altitude flying, soon I lost my bearings. In short, I had gotten myself verfranzt. I had laughed when I heard other airmen telling of a similar misfortune, and now I was in the same dilemma. Moreover, it was night-time and any search for a landing place would be in vain. Such moments produce thoughts of the worst possibilities and you can see yourself hanging from a high-tension wire, with the prospect of an immediate flaming death assured.

'Strange feelings, arising from the desire to survive, came into my mind and caused me to think: "Just because of a casual visit, my flying career is coming to an end!" Suddenly, I had a foreboding vision that hundreds of high, menacing church steeples were in my path and at any moment I would crash into the roof of one of the sacred edifices. Thoughts of disaster clouded my mind and I had the overwhelming feeling: "You have not got a chance. Everything is over for you. Prepare yourself for the worst, for you will soon run into something and be dashed to pieces."

'It is well known that at such times, when the end of his destiny seems near, the story of a person's life passes in quick review before his eyes. Such were the thoughts that filled my mind as I held onto the control column of my reconnaissance biplane as it plunged through the darkness. I did not know whether I was on a course to London or to Brussels or whether, like a lost bird of passage, I would in the next instant smash into some unyielding object protruding from the earth. My compass had long since ceased to function and a glance at my fuel gauge showed that I now had only enough gasoline to last about five minutes. "Therefore," I thought, "may fate speed this lost soul to his doom by a swift crash!"

'Then, calm thinking took over and pointed a way for me to escape my almost certain doom. I let the 'plane climb and, spiralling upwards, I soon gained a better view of the earth beneath me. There to my left I saw the brightly shining pools of water that filled the shell holes on the Somme's battle-scarred face. Hurrah! I was once again on a true course and very close to my Abteilung's airfield.

'Due to the darkness, which is deeper close to the ground than it is hundreds of feet higher, I had been unable to recognise the topography and so I lost my way – I was verfranzt in the truest sense of the word. Someone at my airfield heard the roar of my 'plane and hastily ordered beacons to be lighted and the landing area marked out with magnesium flares. Again, hurrah! Throttling down the engine, I cautiously descended and, in due course, stood once again on good solid ground. I solemnly swore that I would never again permit myself to lose my way – at least not at night.'

That misadventure and a steady run of bad weather put a damper on Degelow's plans for making regular flights over the frontlines:

'Once again the word was patience and still more patience. We knew the British and the French would wait until springtime to launch an offensive aimed at driving us back. We also knew that our generals were plotting some counter-move either to entrap the Entente forces or find some weak link in their lines and have our armies drive right through it. Meanwhile, we could do nothing but wait.'

Preparing for the Spring Offensive

During the winter of 1916-1917, Generalfeldmarschall Paul von Hindenburg's chief of staff, General Erich Ludendorff, ordered the construction of a vast defensive system that would eventually run from Lens in north-eastern France through Cambrai and St. Quentin south and east to Reims. The new strategy's effect was felt immediately by German aerial reconnaissance crews, whose high perch gave them a broad view of changing events on the ground, as Carl Degelow recalled:

'The first hint of the impending battle came when we spotted troop movements along a section of the front north of us and known as the Siegfried Line, named in honour of the legendary Germanic hero. Acting on the supposition that the enemy's strongest pressure during the anticipated spring offensive would be on the southern angle of our defence line, which our adversaries called the "Hindenburg Line", the German Supreme High Command ordered most of our aviation units to the southern area, near the Aisne Sector.

'When we arrived at our new base of operations in the 7th Army Sector,[7] we were greeted by some of the most difficult landing areas we had ever seen and which could not always be overcome by skilful flying. Consequently and to the regret of our Abteilungsführer [squadron leader], Oberleutnant Bodo Creydt, our aircraft graveyard of broken and bent machines began to reach monstrous proportions. There was nothing we could do except attempt to cope with the situation.

'The High Command was most anxious to obtain precise information about the movement of enemy troops facing us across the frontlines. Hence, Flieger-Abteilung (A) 216 was one of the units ordered to take aerial photographs that would reveal the marching routes, resting areas, degree of artillery advance, and other preparations that precede a massive attack. Our squadron leader set up a schedule under which a group of three of our two-seat aircraft would make repeated flights behind enemy lines.

'My observer, Ltn.d.Res Kürten, and I were assigned the lowest position in the trio. Once in flight, however, we discovered that the speed of our good Albatros C.V, which we nicknamed "the furniture wagon", left us far behind the other two aircraft, to our misfortune. Our colleagues were already crossing the frontlines when we, slowed down by the strong west wind, seemed to hang in the air above Laon. Our vulnerable position made the local anti-aircraft batteries and the French single-seat fighters quite rambunctious. We had scarcely flown ten kilometres over the French lines when their accurately-aimed anti-aircraft bursts enveloped us.

'Turning steeply, first on one wing and then on the other, I tried to evade this uncomfortable greeting from the ground. Just as we began to feel safe from ground fire, we suddenly had five Nieuport single-seaters on our necks. My "Franz" bobbed about in his observer's seat like a sparrow under attack, fidgeting with his ring-mounted Parabellum machine gun that could so easily fail us in a critical moment.

'He opened fire. Tak-tak-tak-tak-tak …Just a few rounds fired off and the gun jammed. Probably due to an oversized cartridge stuck in the breech and there was not a thing we could do about it. That was the end of our defence.

Ltn.d.Res Degelow (seated) and his observer, Ltn.d.Res Kürten, standing by an Albatros C.V they flew in over the Champagne Sector while serving with Royal Württemberg Flieger-Abteilung (A) 216.

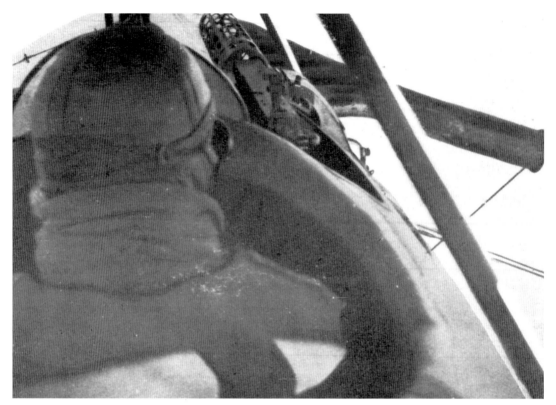

This backseat view of a two-seater pilot in the air is what Kürten saw when Degelow fired his Spandau LMG 08 machine gun at an enemy aeroplane directly in front of him.

"The speedy fighter 'planes recognised our plight and came so close to us that we could almost tell the colour of the pilots' eyes. They fired away in a lively fashion. One series of bullets made holes in our fuel tank and oil reservoir, and another cut our steering cables to pieces. Also, the defenceless Franz, who was bustling about behind me, had received a slight scratch. I worked on the steering apparatus with all of my physical strength – or what was left of it – to keep our poor Albatros out of the enemy's stream of bullets.

'We dropped almost straight down in a column of smoke, both of us thinking that we would soon come down, like a flying crematorium, into some ravine along the Aisne River. The black smoke column that we left fooled the Frenchmen and they flew off, certain that we had been shot down and destroyed. Not until we reached tree-top level was I able to restart the engine after switching over to the reserve fuel tank. Barely a few metres above the ground, we practically "crawled" home and safely reached our airfield. There, we examined closely the damage done to our crate. That was my first flight under combat conditions and our comrades were quick to assure us: "You put up a very good show. Half as much would have been enough."'

While the German two-seater squadrons did their best to keep track of enemy ground forces and their fighter squadron comrades strived to fend off enemy air reconnaissance units, army engineer troops strengthened Siegfried Line positions with ruthless efficiency.

While Ltn Degelow flew the aeroplane, one of Ltn Kürten's duties was to take aerial reconnaissance photographs, such as this view he made of a portion of the Champagne Sector showing French troop movement (dotted line) on 6 March 1917.

According to one description: 'Houses were demolished, trees cut down, and even wells contaminated, while the wreckage was littered with a multitude of explosive booby-traps. And on the night [of 12 March] the German forces began a methodical retirement, by stages, to the new … "Siegfried" … line. A consummate manoeuvre, if unnecessarily brutal in application, it showed that Ludendorff had the moral courage to give up territory if circumstances advised it.'[8]

Making use of artillery advancement tactics that were successful at Verdun, French Général Robert Georges Nivelle ordered his forces to move into the seemingly abandoned German territories. 'Everything that could possibly go wrong [for advancing French forces] did so. The retreat of the Germans to the strong defensive position of the [Siegfried] Line, which was completed by April, was disregarded by Nivelle … [and] carelessness that involved the German capture of two vital documents in trench raids revealed the exact boundaries of the [French] attack between Reims and Soissons …'[9]

From the perspective of the air units, Degelow noted:

'The German plan was to have our army fall back at certain points and then have it confront the British and French armies at points within our own region that were well fortified. The plan was successful, but it depended heavily on our ability to provide the High Command with accurate reports on a quick and regular basis. Hence, my observer, Kürten, and I flew many far-ranging reconnaissance missions that gave me, as the pilot, much to do.

'We also flew missions in support of our artillery units. The Luftstreitkräfte employed one-way wireless telegraphy in combat and, from its inception in January 1917, that means of communication proved to be an effective instrument of warfare. Hence, during our artillery-ranging missions, Kürten would be very busy in the backseat of our Albatros, tapping out messages in Morse code to the ground crews, telling them whether their shells were falling short of the target or needed to be brought closer on one side or the other. Once the artillery battery was right on the mark, Kürten would signal them to commence regular firing and we would go on to the next battery and perform the same service. Kürten was very busy during these flights, but there was little for me to do except fly regular patterns over the front to give him a constant view of the intended targets.'

First Successful Aerial Combat

With warmer weather came the beginning of spring rains, which made flying difficult on both sides along the German 7th Army sector. What became known as the Second Battle of the Aisne, from 16 April to 7 May 1917, grew ever worse for Général Nivelle's armies. It has been noted that the offensive 'was poorly organised and fell into confusion … Nevertheless, Nivelle persisted in ordering successive futile and costly attacks. By early May, widespread mutiny had broken out in the French armies.'[10]

Despite his observer's successful efforts and the positive course the battle was taking from the German standpoint, Degelow fell into a certain malaise. However, in his usual take-charge manner, he shook himself out of it and achieved a combat hallmark for Fl.-Abt (A) 216:

'The artillery-ranging flights were so mechanical in nature that I felt like nothing more than an aerial chauffeur. I preferred to leave such contemplative work to other people. I craved something more exciting and one fine day in May, I took more than usual interest in a two-engined French Caudron observation 'plane that was over Laon, performing a mission similar to ours, but on our side of the lines. We seemed to be the only two aeroplanes in the entire sky, so, when Kürten finished photographing various emplacements along the frontlines, I got his attention and pointed to the Caudron. Kürten pointed towards home. Again I pointed to the French 'plane and, throttling back on the engine, I shouted to my comrade: "Let's go after him!" Kürten did not seem interested and again, but rather vaguely, pointed toward our airfield. Generally, two-seater pilots were enlisted men and the observers were officers, thereby establishing a relationship in which the pilot was a "driver", while the observer was in charge of the aeroplane and made all major decisions on the mission. But Kürten and I were both reserve officers of equal rank, so there was little he could say if I wanted to delay going home long enough to have a look at the Caudron.[11]

'As we approached the two-seat French 'plane, its pilot spotted us and his observer took up his gunnery position, but we were much too far apart for the fire to be at all effective. When I noticed the French observer stopping to change the ammunition drum on his machine gun, I moved in close enough to give Kürten a good shot at him. My trusty Franz opened up and got many hits on the Caudron. But the Frenchman soon returned fire and I pulled away. This round of activity went on for some minutes, as, all the while, the clever French pilot made greater headway south-east toward his own lines, where his comrades in single-seat fighters would soon come up to rid him of us. Therefore, this situation called for direct action, which could best be provided by my forward-firing Spandau machine gun, fixed to the cowl in front of me.

'Because of its design, we gave the nickname "Gitterschwanz" [lattice tail] to the two-engine Caudron; the fuselage, engines and wings were attached to the tail control surfaces by two long sets of tail-booms and bracing wires. Viewed from the side, the

A Caudron G.IV 'lattice tail' reconnaissance aeroplane of the type encountered in combat by Ltns Degelow and Kürten on several occasions.

crew appeared to be sitting inside a large bird cage, and that's what gave the idea to have Kürten attack from the side. The Frenchmen would continue to expect me to fly alongside them, to give Kürten a chance to fire, but they would be surprised if I were to pull away and dive at them from their side and slightly below – all intended to keep us out of their range of fire.

'Kürten must have thought I had gone mad when I performed this unexpected manoeuvre, but soon I had the Caudron lined up in my gun sight and opened fire. The French 'plane shook from front to back as my bullets poured into it. The pilot attempted to dive away, as it became apparent that his 'plane had been very badly hit. That is when Kürten had yet another opportunity to fire a few rounds, which added to the Frenchmen's demise. We followed them down and observed their crash near Braye, not far from the Aisne River, near our forward lines.

'It was no joy to watch the stricken French 'plane fall helplessly to the earth; for, by a different turn of events, that could just as easily have been us. But there was a certain pride in the accomplishment of denying the enemy the valuable intelligence information that his Gitterschwanz had gathered, as well as causing him the loss of an aeroplane.'

According to German Army records, this first air combat success occurred on 22 May 1917 and was credited to Degelow and Kürten.[12] The Caudron G.IV came down at the town of Berrieux, south-west of Braye. Fl.-Abt (A) 216's records list the crash site as being 'just behind French lines',[13] which may indicate the aircraft was salvaged and, for whatever reason, not entered into the French casualty registry.[14]

Second Aerial Combat

Buoyed by that success, Degelow became even more interested in pursuing other air combat opportunities, as he wrote:

'Three days later, on 25 May, Kürten and I were over the southern perimeter of our sector when we spotted another Caudron heading for Laon. Again, Kürten had finished his work and we were going home. And again, I throttled down and attracted his attention so I could point out the French warbird near our nest. Having once enjoyed the thrill of the hunt, Kürten was now enthusiastic about going after the cheeky fellow. So, on with it!

'What worked once may well work again, so we tried the same manoeuvre. I approached the enemy from such a position that he thought only my observer was armed. Then, at the last moment, when he had been deceived about my lack of a forward-firing machine gun, I charged headlong at him and brought his mission to a swift end. But this fellow was in no mood for a fight. Apparently, he had completed his work over our lines and was now most anxious to go home. Therefore, he preferred to run. First he headed south, toward Braye, but, when I cut him off and too quickly revealed my forward-firing machine gun, he headed west toward Compiègne. Kürten remained ready at his post, but now it was I who had to stop the Caudron from getting home. This was no time for fancy manoeuvres to allow Franz to use his gun.

'My best position was always almost directly behind, but to one side of the opponent. If I could remain there, the enemy observer risked shooting at his own control surfaces to fire at me. Meanwhile, at various moments I managed to get off a good series of shots at him. Then I hit one engine, which began to smoke profusely. More rounds were fired into the fuselage and the enemy gunner was silenced. The stricken engine soon caught fire, which spread to the fuselage. When the Caudron finally dipped and went into its death dive, we knew this was no ruse. Down, down it went, crashing into some trees outside the town of Bailly. We watched from a safe altitude and then headed for home.

'I was still shaking so much from the excitement of the chase that I had to grip the control column tightly to keep from becoming a quivering mass all over. My stomach was performing aerobatic manoeuvres of its own and seemed to want to do somersaults right out of my abdomen. For a few minutes I felt as though I was going to become sick, but I leaned my head alongside the fuselage, away from the protection of the windscreen, and the fresh air revived me and made me feel better.

'That evening in the flyers' mess, Kürten and I were interrogated by our comrades, eager for every detail of the fight. All were in agreement that our French adversaries met with a horrible end that none of us hoped would happen to him.'

This aerial victory was also recorded in the weekly summary of news and intelligence issued by the Commanding General of the Air Force.[15] The Caudron was seen to crash south-west of Bailly, near Braye, but the official French casualty registry did not mention that type of aircraft in its listing for that day.[16] According to Degelow, his Abteilungsführer, Oblt Creydt, told him that he and Kürten would each be credited with achieving two aerial victories. Later, Degelow questioned the mathematical logic of such a record-keeping system, which implied that he and Kürten had shot down a total of four aircraft. He was proved to be right some months later, after he shot down his first opponent as a single-seat fighter pilot. That triumph was recorded as Degelow's second, acknowledging that, under the strict German rules pertaining to credit for aerial victories, he and Kürten had received a half-score for each of the two Caudron G.IVs they shot down as a team; hence, one full victory apiece.

Transferred to Fighter Pilot School

No matter how the scoring was kept, Degelow had proven to be an aggressive combat pilot and became intent on luring other French aeroplanes within range of his guns. However, his commanding officer, who held a Regular Army Royal Prussian commission[17] and was a career officer, had other ideas about how a two-seater pilot should carry out his primary mission, essentially being the observer's driver, as Degelow related:

'Less than two weeks later, Kürten and I engaged another Caudron in a long fight. Many bullets were exchanged by both sides and the fight seemed to end in our favour, when the Caudron headed for the ground, leaving a smoke trail behind it. We followed it briefly, but were driven off by ground fire before we could learn our opponent's fate.

'A sort time later, Oblt Creydt called us in for a discussion of our air combat tactics.

After congratulating us on the recognition we received in the Air Force Commanding General's weekly publication, his smile changed to a frown. As much as he appreciated our efforts in depriving the enemy of information and aircraft, he said, our primary mission was that of a normal two-seater unit; aggressive aerial combat was to be undertaken by fighter pilots. He went on to itemize the amount of damage that our aircraft had suffered during our three air fights and pointedly noted that such encounters might well have resulted in the loss of the photographs and information that we had been sent out to obtain. In short, there was to be no more of this "adventuring". That is the price we paid for telling the truth. We should have claimed the Frenchmen attacked us. Then we would have been hailed as valiant defenders.

'In the days following I made no secret of being unhappy with the order to use our guns only for defensive and not offensive purposes. Again I was summoned to the Abteilungsführer's office. This time he told me quite bluntly that I would be of more use to the Fatherland and be more personally satisfied if I were transferred to a Jagdstaffel [fighter squadron]. From the tone of his voice it sounded as though his decision to send me away was meant to punish me, whereas, from my point of view, he had just given me the grandest gift.

'"Jawohl, Herr Oberleutnant!" I said and saluted snappily.

'I returned to my quarters and informed my comrades of the decision. I would remain with Fl.-Abt (A) 216 until all of the paperwork had been processed and then I would be transferred to a forward area training airfield to learn the rudiments of aerial combat in a single-seat fighter airplane. Meanwhile, I was expected to be a "good boy" and not get into any mischief over the lines. To ensure the latter, I was paired with another observer, a Regular Army Oberleutnant who was quick to inform me that he was my superior officer and, as such, definitely in charge of the airplane at all times. Meanwhile, my erstwhile colleague, Ltn.d.Res Kürten, was assigned an enlisted pilot, who clearly understood who was the "boss" of the aeroplane.'

The first phase of Carl Degelow's air combat career was over, but he had not been singled out for correction of a behavioural or disciplinary problem. Rather, his transfer was in keeping with an identified need at the top echelon of the Luftstreitkräfte. Indeed, Degelow's departure from the Flieger-Abteilung at the end of July was preceded three weeks earlier by the unit's transfer of another overly eager two-seater pilot, Regular Army Leutnant Hans Joachim Wolff,[18] who later gained fame as a protégé of Germany's famed 'red baron', Rittmeister Manfred Freiherr von Richthofen.

Luftstreitkräfte Commanding General Ernst von Hoeppner described the need that would shape Carl Degelow's service for the remainder of the war:

"The organizational concentration of the existing single-seat fighters into Jagdstaffeln [fighter squadrons] was begun on the Western Front in August 1916 … The first four Jagdstaffeln were deployed to the Somme Sector … Their further increase stood in the forefront of the program drawn up … to strengthen the Luftstreitkräfte and, accordingly, the number of Jagdstaffeln was raised to thirty-six by spring 1917. But their number alone could not guarantee success. The lifeless aircraft needed their pilots to breathe into them the spirit of fearless gallantry and unshakeable desire to attack. Selection of pilots intended for the Jagdstaffeln required special care. Only those pilots whose flying skill had already been proven while they were with Flieger-Abteilungen were recommended for training as fighter pilots. Following a short course of instruction at newly formed *Kampfeinsitzerschulen* [single-seat fighter schools] in Grossenhain and Paderborn, they received special training at Jagdstaffelschule I [fighter squadron school No. 1] in Valenciennes, after which they were sent to Staffeln to face the enemy.'[19]

On the last day of July, a rainy Monday,[20] Ltn.d.Res Carl Degelow's last official act in Fl.-Abt (A) 216 was to ride in the back of an open lorry – wrapped in a heavy canvas cloth to keep him dry – on the long journey to Valenciennes.

1 Established on 8 January 1916 at Flieger-Ersatz-Abteilung 10 at Böblingen in the Kingdom of Württemberg, Artillerie-Flieger-Abteilung 216 was sent to the Front on 24 January [Ref: *Württ.Art. Flieger-Abteilung 216 Bericht Nr. 2944*, 15 November 1916, p. 1].

2 Arand Edler von Ackerfeld, born in Stuttgart on 23 September 1893, previously served with Feldartillerie-Regiment Nr. 29 [Ref: *Ehrentafel der Flieger … der Königl. Württ. Armee … ,* p. 1].

3 Friedrichs previously served with Reserve Hussar-Regiment Nr. 2 [Ref: Uebe, *Ehrenmal des preussischen Offizier-Korps*, p. 192].

4 *Württ.Art. Flieger-Abteilung 216 Bericht Nr. 3225*, 2 December 1916, p. 1.

5 Ibid.

6 Richthofen, *Ein Heldenleben*, pp. 220-222.

7 Fl.-Abt. (A) 216 moved from the 2nd Army to the 7th Army Sector on 27 February 1917 [Ref: *Württ. Flieger-Abt. A 216 Bericht Nr. 5345*, 6 June 1917, p. 1].

8 Liddell Hart, *The Real War 1914-1918*, p. 300.

9 Falls, op.cit., p. 94.

10 Ibid., p. 93.

11 In fact, the observer was in charge of the airplane, but Kürten did not exercise his authority as forcefully as he could have.

12 Kogenluft, *Nachrichtenblatt der Luftstreitkräfte*, Vol. II, No. 16, 14 June 1917, p. 26.

13 *Württ. Flieger-Abt. A 216 Bericht*, op.cit.

14 Bailey and Cony, *The French Air Service War Chronology*, p. 123.

15 *Nachrichtenblatt*, op.cit., p, 27.

16 Bailey and Cony, op.cit.

17 In Moser, *Die Württemberger im Weltkrieg*, p. 125.

18 Franks, Bailey and Guest, *Above the Lines*, p. 232.

19 Hoeppner, *Deutschlands Krieg in der Luft*, pp. 85-86.

20 Western Front weather report in RFC, *War Diary* entry for 31 July 1917.

Chapter Four
Becoming an Eagle

Carl Degelow arrived at Jagdstaffelschule I in Valenciennes as a pilot with aerial combat experience, but it was based only on reactions to situations in which he found himself as a two-seater pilot. At the fighter pilot school, he was trained in proven methods of going on the offensive against a variety of aerial adversaries based on collective – albeit quickly learned – knowledge about the art and science of flying a single-seat fighter aeroplane. Due to the relative newness of aerial combat, the first Jagdstaffelschule was established on 29 November 1916,[1] the school's curriculum was in a continuing state of development, but it was grounded in a series of tactics put into written form by one of Germany's most successful early fighter aces, Hauptmann Oswald Boelcke.

Boelcke's Dicta

From August 1915 until the following June, Boelcke and his squadron-mate, Oberleutnant Max Immelmann, competed to become Germany's premier fighter ace. In that time, their combined score was thirty-three enemy aircraft shot down[2] and, on 12 January 1916, they were the first flyers to be awarded the Pour le Mérite.[3] Boelcke's emerging skill as a tactician was recognised by the Chief of Field Aviation, Oberstleutnant [Lieutenant-Colonel] Hermann von der Lieth-Thomsen, who asked the young pilot to summarise the tenets of aerial combat. The eight key points, now known as Boelcke's dicta and still used by fighter pilots, are:

'Seek the advantage before the attack. Whenever possible, have the sun at your back.
'Always follow through once the attack has been launched.
'Open fire only at close range and then only when your opponent is right in your sights.
'Keep your eye fixed on your opponent and do not let yourself be misled by ruses.
'In every attack it is important to go at your enemy from behind.
'If your opponent attacks you from above, do not try to elude him; rather, fly right at him.
'When over enemy territory, never forget your own line of retreat.
'In Staffel operations: Attack principally with four or six at a time. When the battle devolves into individual fights, several pilots should not pursue one opponent.'[4]

Carl Degelow and other students at the school practiced Boelcke's dicta in the skies above Valenciennes and over the Escaut River – far enough away from the frontlines to allow them relative safety from experienced Allied fighters. Degelow appreciated the importance of the lessons, noting:

> 'As a novice single-seat fighter pilot, I soon learned that it takes a lot of work for a "little man" to become what we called *eine grosse Kanone* [a big gun]. The will to achieve is not sufficient by itself. Rather, it is essential to apply oneself diligently to the study of air combat tactics.'

Such tactics did not exist during the early days of World War I. During his training, Degelow was told:

> 'There were times when, lacking any other means of attack, a pilot or aerial observer would desperately resort to using his service pistol or even his flare pistol as a means of vanquishing his foe. Such air skirmishing was seen less often in those early days when friend and enemy, on meeting in the air, would usually dip their wings in salute to each other. On many other occasions each flier would act as though he had not even seen his counterpart from the other side.'

The latter point was challenged by British accounts, which maintained that air-to-air combat occurred early and evolved with the aeroplanes' ability to carry offensive and defensive weapons, due to stronger aircraft construction and more powerful engines – as well as a good measure of pluck. A noteworthy example, in August 1914, was mentioned in the official RAF history:

> 'Aeroplanes at this time had no special armament; [flying] officers carried revolvers and sometimes a carbine; but the confidence and determination with which they attacked did the work of a machine gun, and brought the enemy down. In one instance … a British pilot and observer, who were destitute of ammunition, succeeded by manoeuvring boldly above a German machine in bringing it down and taking it captive.'[5]

Air combat made a giant leap forward some nine months later when engineers and craftsmen at the Fokker Aeroplanbau [aircraft construction factory] in Schwerin, Germany perfected an interrupter gear, a device that would enable the pilot's forward-firing machine gun to fire through the propeller arc without hitting the blades. The gear would 'interrupt' the firing sequence when the propeller would be hit, thereby leaving the propeller fully functional. '[A]nd when two-seaters were armed with a forward-firing gun, the Fokker gear was modified to operate from a cam fitted to the front of the engine.'[6] The interrupter gear made it possible for reconnaissance aircraft pilots to use their guns offensively.

Learning Air Combat Tactics

Now, however, Degelow was more fully occupied with air warfare waged by single-seat fighter aeroplanes:

'Encounters with enemy aircraft led to air battles of extraordinarily tenacious manoeuvring, as each opponent sought to gain the advantage over the other. These aerial combats soon took on a regular and recurrent form, which, depending on the tactics used by a particular squadron leader, evolved into certain methods of attack or defence. Since so much depended on prevailing circumstances at the front – the wind conditions and the sunlight, as well as the personality of the individual fighter pilot – it was difficult to lay down definite rules for each new fighter pilot to follow. But it was possible to prescribe certain procedures, which, based on long experience, could deal with most circumstances.

'One such method of attack was one I later advocated to the members of the Jagdstaffel I commanded. It was: *"Immer ran auf Meter, Meter!"* [Ever closer, metre by metre!]. Born of the instructions I received at Valenciennes, I impressed on the novices the need to wait until the target was within range. I am convinced that it was the chief reason for the successes of my squadron over British flyers in Flanders.

'But more than just the strict observance of this air fighting rule was necessary for success. Many other details affected the course of an aerial combat. Sharp observance of such matters often gave the experienced flyer the advantage over his less attentive opponent, thus enabling him to outwit and eventually shoot down his foe.

'One of the first lessons for a neophyte fighter pilot was carefully to scan the weather reports. Issued twice daily from our Armee-Oberkommando [Army Group Command], they were definitely not just rain or shine predictions for an automobile trip. To us flyers, the main importance of the weather reports was their reporting of the different wind velocities in kilometres per hour at the various altitudes at which the air fights occured, namely, from chimney height to levels above 6,000 metres. Further, it was extremely important to know the direction of the wind at these various levels, for the wind that blows in one direction at ground level, often blows in the opposite direction at 1,000 metres or more above the ground. This was a lesson I should have learned at Valenciennes, as a pilot would find himself at a great disadvantage if not correctly informed about wind direction.

'About a year after I left the Jagdstaffelschule, prior to an afternoon flight I read the wind velocity measurement hastily and surmised that at 3,500 metres – the average altitude for air fights at that time – a much stronger west wind was blowing. Leading my Staffel at that altitude, I came upon a far superior number of British single-seat fighters, heading toward us between Bailleul and Armentières. I wanted to start fighting after first using the wind to bait the enemy to a position behind our lines, so I spiralled down into the hostile pack and scattered them in confusion, which would increase our chances of success. By this manoeuvre, I soon had three Englishmen behind me; in falling for my ruse, they had become separated from the rest of their squadron. Dropping to about 1,000 metres, I was ready to attack and I cast a quick glance over the terrain, a custom of mine before every attack in order to orientate myself. I thought myself to be far behind our own lines, but one downward glance showed me that the opposite was true; I realised immediately that I was over British-held territory. The wind had switched direction in the lower air level and an easterly wind had driven me westward. As a result, I was vigorously pursued by three British fighters and only after an anxious, retreating battle at treetop altitude could I shake them off.

'Had I studied the wind velocity information more carefully before taking off, I would have learned that at 2,500 metres an east wind was blowing. Thus, my tactic of luring the more numerous opponents to a lower altitude was useless in this instance.

'At the Jagdstaffelschule one of Boelcke's Dicta in attacking aerial opponents was emphasized: Always seeking to surprise the opponent by coming at him from out of the sun. Because it was taxing and tiring, an inexperienced pilot did not turn to look behind him when the sun was at his back and such neglect was always dangerous. Even experienced pilots fell into this mistake because they did not keep the air space behind them clear by turning around often enough. Our instructor pointed out: "Always look around you. Always! Then you will stay alive long enough to look at the pretty girls when you get back home!"

'From my own experience I knew that one could gain an enormous advantage over an enemy flyer by skilful use of existing light conditions. That is another way to surprise an unsuspecting quarry. Here is how lighting played an important role in air operations over the Flanders Front: during the morning, German fighter aircraft, with the sun rising from the east at their backs, were always more eager to attack than were their rivals, who were flying right into the sun's harsh rays. During the evening, however, the enemy airmen sought to take advantage of moving toward us with the sun at their backs. Hence, they became even more aggressive. Every pilot preferred to fight with the sun behind him.

'Another lesson concerned the fundamental difference in attacking single-seaters as opposed to two-seaters. The latter could resist attack from the front or the rear, as both pilot and observer were well armed. Indeed, the observer's ring-mounted machine gun – which we nicknamed "the paintbrush" because it could be applied in such broad sweeps – was very effective in keeping attackers at a respectful distance. But by adroit manoeuvring, a fighter pilot could get himself into such a position that he could avoid being sprayed by the observer, while being effective with his own fixed, forward-firing machine guns. The desirable position was about ten to twenty metres behind and somewhat below the enemy two-seater. The attacker could fire at will, with little fear that the observer, now blocked by his own fuselage, would return the fire.

'From my own experience, the prime objective in aerial combat was to get as close to my opponent as the length of my own aeroplane, even as close as three or four metres. This tactic reduces the possibility of missing the target and the bullets are so well placed that vital parts of the target will be instantly shattered and put out of business. As mentioned earlier, our instructor at Valenciennes told us: "Aim for the aeroplane, not the man. When you put the aeroplane out of action, you will take care of the man."

'The problem with getting close to an adversary was that a pilot had an almost insurmountable fear that, by coming so close, he could easily ram into the other machine. That is where he had to prove that he had what it took to be a fighter pilot. He had to estimate with lightning speed the hazards involved, for the speed of both planes and the absence at that time of parachutes increased the possibility of a collision in the air with no chance of a safe return to earth. I believe that in such a situation certain psychological factors came into play, arising from the basic human instinct for self-preservation. These factors warned against pressing closely after the enemy – hence, the general rule of not coming closer to the opposing aircraft than "three aeroplane lengths". The words of Nietzsche – "Man is something that must be overcome" – could be applied to a man who became a flyer and be paraphrased as: "Conquer the negative feelings that weaken your spirit of attack." Usually, inner voices cautioned the pilot, but often they were only disguised feelings of anxiety and had to be avoided. Therefore, the fighter pilot had to close in on the enemy, getting ever closer to him.

'I found the proof of the soundness of this policy in the statement of one of our most successful flyers,[7] who often preached to his pilots: "When you are nearing the enemy and you are about fifty metres away, take your right hand from the control column, stretch your arm out slowly and thoughtfully and bring your thumb back to your mouth – and then, and not until then, press the firing button on your machine gun." With that advice the squadron leader wanted to impress upon his pilots that they were to open fire only when they were very close to the enemy. It was a very severe test of patience for one to see the tri-colour cockades of an Englishman or a Frenchman in front of him and yet refrain from shooting. As I made it my rule to shoot only when very close, I often left a Tommy unmolested because I could not get closer to him than 300 metres.

'The great Manfred von Richthofen made a clear distinction between "hunters" and "shooters".[8] On all sides, the former were very deliberate and did not open fire until they knew they could hit their prey; the latter always fired too soon and thereby wasted much valuable ammunition that might be needed to save their lives. A frequent occurrence was that from a great distance behind me, perhaps 4,500 metres or more, an enemy single-seat fighter's guns were popping away. Immediately, I knew that the pilot of the attacking plane was a beginner – a "shooter" – and that fact made me anticipate the fight with a great deal more confidence.

'Many fighter pilots claimed that their main successes were gained by the use of a telescopic gun-sight positioned between their two forward-firing machine guns. This method was supposed to have enabled them to hit their target from a greater distance with fewer misses and less personal danger to themselves. Well, telescope here, telescope there, I stuck to our policy, which brought us many successes. Therefore: *"Immer ran auf Meter, Meter!"* Ever closer, metre by metre!"'

Briefly a Member of Jagdstaffel 36

The Jagdstaffelschule course for pilots with previous combat experience lasted only two weeks. After that, the graduates were assigned to frontline Jagdstaffeln to begin their duties as fighter pilots. Carl Degelow recounted:

'Of course, we all wanted to be assigned to the illustrious units about which we had heard so much. The better known Staffeln invariably received better and newer aircraft, and a neophyte, such as I was at the time, could learn a great deal from a Staffel-Führer [squadron leader] of proven ability – that is, with an impressive number of aerial victories to his credit.

'Consequently, I was overjoyed when I was assigned to Royal Prussian Jagdstaffel 36,[9] commanded by Ltn Walter von Bülow, who had been a fighter pilot since 1915 and who

A line-up of Albatros D.V fighters of the kind used by Jagdstaffel 36 when Carl Degelow reported for duty with the unit.

up to that point had received credit for shooting down seventeen enemy aeroplanes. Now I would be part of a fine fighting unit and make a meaningful contribution to Germany's war effort.

'On the morning of 17 August 1917, several other prospective fighter pilots and I piled into the back of a big open Mercedes touring car and set out from Valenciennes for the Front. At various airfields along the way, the car stopped and delivered its cargo of individual replacement pilots to the sorely pressed Jagdstaffeln. One man to this Staffel, another to that one, and so on. Finally, the big car bumped and rattled down a winding road leading to a long, flat field outside the Flemish town of Kuerne, about three kilometres north of Courtrai. This place was the site of Jasta 36's airfield. Even before the car stopped I could see the Albatros and Fokker Triplane fighters bearing the distinctive blue-painted noses that identified this Staffel to friend and foe alike as a tough bunch of boys!

'My hopes of meeting Ltn von Bülow himself were dashed when I learned that he was away on leave, no doubt to celebrate his seventeenth victory. I knew that he was also a son of my native province of Holstein[10] and would therefore be a fellow with whom I could talk candidly when the occasion demanded, even though he was my superior officer. Events later proved that he was every bit as good a man as I expected. He went on to command the famed Jasta Boelcke, the fighter squadron named after its legendary founder. Like his noted predecessor, Walter von Bülow went on to earn the Pour le Mérite and continue fighting in the sky until fate intervened. After having shot down twenty-five aeroplanes and three captive balloons, he simply failed to return from a mission one day. Neither his body nor his aeroplane was ever found.[11] One can only wonder whether he met his end swiftly and cleanly in the air, or was forced down in no-man's-land only to be obliterated by one of the countless artillery barrages unleashed with equal fury by both sides.

'In any event, when I arrived from Valenciennes, the officer whom von Bülow had deputised to take over in his absence assured me that the Staffel-Führer would spend much time with me when he returned from leave. The acting leader [Ltn.d.Res Hans Hoyer[12]], I might add, was a stiff-necked Prussian, all spit and polish and true to the type. The German word *hochnäsig* [for haughty, but literally "high-nosed"] must have been coined with such fellows in mind. I was just as happy that he was not the regular officer in charge, for his cool, methodical ways of dealing with people were not at all to my liking.

'Now that I belonged to a regular Staffel, I had to become accustomed to a new routine. First there were orientation flights in the different aircraft, the Albatros D.III, Albatros D.V (faster than its predecessor) and the remarkable Fokker Dr.I triplane. Even though I had combat experience and had done very well at the Jagdstaffelschule, I was still not allowed to approach the frontlines. The feeling was that I should be exposed to that danger only under Ltn von Bülow's direction and in company with the rest of the Staffel. Meanwhile, I was to study maps and photo-mosaics of the area.

A Fateful Gunnery Exercise

'The day after my arrival, I was ordered to report to the gun pits for target practice. I was strapped into the cockpit of an Albatros which had been rolled into a special pit to keep it from taking off while the procedure took place. With the tail propped up to put the aeroplane on an even keel, I started the engine and began firing the machine guns down the long pit. To get the feel of the guns at different attitudes, the aeroplane's tail was raised and lowered, the point of the exercise being to watch how the lines of bullets converged and thereby get the feel of how much actual range there was to the guns.

'Following that, I went aloft in an Albatros to fire at various targets placed on the ground. This is where I ran into trouble. I did not quite understand the instructions prior to take-off – amid the rumble of the engine warming up – that I was first to make a low pass to line up on the targets and then, on the second pass, to open fire. That was to give everyone time to leave the shooting range. My first pass had me so perfectly lined up with the target that, in hopes of impressing my new comrades, I immediately commenced firing, pouring a series of shots into the best portions of the target.

'As I curved up and around at the end of the range, I could see a great commotion on the ground, with some men running out onto the range, while others fired flare pistols, apparently to signal me to hold my fire. I swooped down in a low, slow pass and

A gun pit used to align machine guns. In this case for two-seaters, but not much different from the exercise Carl Degelow underwent in Jasta 36.

saw, to my great horror, my comrades carrying from the 'field a man who had been behind one of the targets!

'Oh my God, I thought to myself. Oh my God! I have killed one of our own men! In my impetuous desire to develop and display my skills quickly, I have done something horrible.

'I landed the aeroplane quickly and, before the propeller stopped spinning, I ran across the airfield to the spot under a tree where the injured man was taken. Oh dear God, I said over and over to myself, please let him be alive!'

The unintended victim was twenty-four-year-old Ltn.d.Res Edwin Kreuzer,[13] with whom Degelow had made friends at their first meeting and exchanged air combat stories over dinner the night before. Kreuzer had also shot down a Caudron,[14] and Degelow greatly admired that his new friend's first aerial victory had been achieved in a single-seat fighter. This pair of flyers was as opposite in temperament as any two people could be; Degelow came from Germany's far northern province of Holstein, where so many people are reputed to be cool and distant; Kreuzer came from Germany's southeastern area, in the

Grand Duchy of Baden, near the Swiss border, where warm *badische Gastfreundlichkeit* [Badenese hospitality] is legendary. Now, the northerner's carelessness had brought the two men together in an odd binding of brotherhood, as Degelow noted in his tale of remorse:

"Kreuzer lay on the late summer grass, pale and still. A medical orderly wrapped a bandage around one of his feet, for that is where one of my bullets had hit him. But, thank heaven, he was still alive and, indeed, was probably not seriously injured. I was shaking like a leaf in a strong wind. One or two of my new comrades came over and tried to comfort me. Only one said, "You should have waited before you fired." But I knew that only too well.

'At length, Kreuzer was carried to a first aid station near the pilots' mess, where an ambulance took him to a nearby field hospital. Of course I rode with him, telling him over and over how sorry I was for my stupid mistake.

'Kreuzer was a very understanding fellow, however, and told me that he knew I meant him no harm. Indeed, my emotional state seemed to affect his own, for I was now weeping and he began to weep with me. But his tears of consolation and my tears of bitter regret could not wash away what happened.

'Back at the airfield, I was met by the ice cold stare of the acting Staffel-Führer. His eyes were like two blue jewels of frigid rage and his words to me were brief: "Pack your bags, Herr Leutnant, you are finished here."

'It was pointless to object. He was my superior and he gave me an order. *Befehl ist Befehl.* [Orders are orders.] Those are the Prussian's holy words.'

As touching as it may be, Carl Degelow's account of the incident is at odds with the official account, which appeared in Jasta 36's war diary. It infers that, at the very least, Degelow committed procedural errors:

'Ltn Degelow test flew his machine. During the test flight he carried out aerial combat practice and [then] fired his guns at a target set up on the 'field without regard for that action being prohibited. As firing at this target was to be done only under special instruction, no one knew what his intention was. But at that very moment Ltn Kreuzer was pasting [paper covers] over bullet holes in the target and – fortunately – was only injured in the foot by Degelow's shots. Ltn Kreuzer had to be transported immediately to a field hospital.'[15]

Despite the serious consequences of his disregard for orders and injuring a fellow combatant, Carl Degelow was neither court-martialled nor punished for his offences. But, as he told this author, his conscience imposed a penalty of its own:

'It would have been merciful indeed if I had simply been kicked out of Jasta 36 that evening. But, as it turned out, I had to languish there while communications travelled back and forth between the Staffel and German 4th Army Headquarters. I was not formally placed under arrest, but my presence seemed so awkward that I probably would have felt more comfortable in the guard house.

'I felt that I was finished as a pilot and probably in the army. After this, who would want such an impetuous fool in his unit? That was the question I asked myself for the next two days, when, at last, an orderly came to put my bags into the back of the same Mercedes that had brought me to Jasta 36. What must the driver have been thinking? Probably something like: "In on Friday, out the following Monday; here's a fine fellow for you!" Yes, a fine fellow going back to Valenciennes for some senior officer to be confronted with the problem of what to do with me![16]

'My leaving was quiet. Just after sunrise, I simply got into the back of the car and was driven back to the Jagdstaffelschule. No one was there to say good-bye or wish me well, or even tell me again (as if I needed to hear it) how stupidly I had acted. *Schluss! Kaput! Das ist alles!* That was all there was to it.'

A fond farewell to someone going off in a Mercedes touring car in front of an expropriated estate building. That is the way Carl Degelow would like to have departed Jasta 36, rather than the ignominious way he was sent packing after his brief and ill-starred experience at his first fighter unit assignment.

1   Cron, 'Organization of the German Luftstreitkräfte' in *Cross & Cockade Journal*, Vol. VII, p. 53.

2   According to Franks, Bailey and Guest, *Above the Lines*, pp. 76, 135, Boelcke attained sixteen aerial victories and Immelmann seventeen by this time.

3   O'Connor, *Aviation Awards of Imperial Germany and the Men Who Earned Them*, Vol. II, p. 62.

4   Quoted in Werner, *Boelcke der Mensch, der Flieger, der Führer der deutschen Jagdfliegerei*, p. 168.

5   Raleigh, *The War in the Air, Vol. I*, p. 329.

6   Woodman, *Early Aircraft Armament*, p.183.

7   Unfortunately not identified by Carl Degelow.

8   Degelow would have known this Richthofen comment by reading the famous ace's popular World War I-era memoir *Der Rote Kampfflieger*, published in 1917.

9   Reichsarchiv, *Kriegstagebuch der königlichen preussischen Jagdstaffel 36* (summary), p. 4.

10 Born on 24 April 1894 at Birby near Eckenförde, Holstein into an aristocratic family, Walter von Bülow-Bothkamp was a *Fideikommissherr* [hereditary estate holder] of Bothkamp, Holstein [Ref: Perthes, J. *Ehrentafel der Kriegsopfer des reichsdeutschen Adels 1914-1918*, p. 37].

11 Walter von Bülow-Bothkamp was shot down and killed on 6 January 1918 and, even though the wreckage of his aeroplane, Albatros D.V 2080/17, was not salvaged, it was listed as RAF captured enemy aircraft G.123 [Ref: Franks, Bailey & Guest, *Above the Lines*, p. 90; Robertson, *British Military Aircraft Serials 1911-1917*, p. 87].

12 Hans Hoyer was born on 20 September 1890 in Rostock in the Duchy of Mecklenburg-Schwerin. He joined the army in October 1911, served with two artillery regiments and was commissioned in Reserve Feld-Artillerie-Regiment Nr. 23. He became an eight-victory ace and may have attained another victory in his last fight, on 15 November 1917, when he was shot down and killed while flying with Jasta 36 [Ref: Franks, Bailey & Guest, op.cit., p. 132; Zickerick, *Verlustliste der deutschen Luftstreitkräfte im Weltkriege*, p. 36].

13 Ltn.d.Res Edwin Kreuzer was born 3 June 1893 in Messkirch in the Grand Duchy of Baden. He enlisted in Fuss-Artillerie Regiment Nr. 14 in 1913 and rose to the rank of Vizefeldwebel before the war began. He was transferred to Fuss-Artillerie Regiment Nr. 13 and, upon completion of officer training, Kreuzer was commissioned Leutnant der Reserve on 30 September 1915. On 11 March 1916, he was transferred to FEA 11 in Breslau for pilot training. After serving with Fl.-Abt 30 in Macedonia, he returned to Germany, where, after fighter pilot training, he was posted to Jasta 36 [Ref: *Personal-Bogen*, p. 2].

14 While flying with Jasta 36 on 6 April 1917, Kreuzer shot down a Caudron over Berry au Bac, thereby achieving his first aerial victory [Ref: Kogenluft, *Nachrichtenblatt der Luftstreitkräfte*, Vol. I, No. 11, 10 May 1917, p. 126].

15 Reichsarchiv, *Jasta 36*, op.cit.

16 In fact, Degelow's journey to Valenciennes was a brief interim measure; a decision had already been made to transfer him to Jagdstaffel 7 [Ref: Kofl 4. Armee, *Tagesbefehl Nr. 59*, 31 August 1917].

CHAPTER FIVE
EARLY AIR FIGHTING SUCCESS

The French city of Valenciennes was once known as 'the Athens of the North' and its 1,300-year cultural heritage remains alive in its intricately delicate lace. The 19th century exploitation of coal deposits in the area, however, transformed the once mainly artistic community into an industrial centre and an important segment of the French steel industry. That new role made Valenciennes a rich prize when it was captured by rapidly advancing German forces in 1914 – and subsequently it became a target for British airmen.[1]

The development of improved German fighter aircraft opened a new role for Valenciennes. A flat expanse on the outskirts of the city became an important training centre. A humbled and still fretful Carl Degelow reported to this location for undefined duties. As he recalled, his fears were soon allayed:

'It soon became apparent that I was just another pilot, awaiting reassignment. To occupy my brief time at the Jagdstaffelschule, I attended several lectures that I had enjoyed previously and that I felt would be worth listening to again. These included such practical instruction as how to clear a jammed machine gun in the air. The answer was simple: if an oversized round became lodged in the breech (the most common cause of a jam), the pilot used a wrench placed in the cockpit for just such an occurrence. He reached over the low windscreen in front of him and banged away like blazes on the exposed portion of the guns and hoped that action would dislodge the stuck round of ammunition. If the "wrench trick" did not work, the pilot was advised to try some of the divine entreaties recommended by the chaplain's office.

'The following morning, 21 August 1917, I received orders and was underway to my new assignment, and I could scarcely believe my good fortune. I had been assigned to Jagdstaffel 7, commanded by Leutnant der Reserve Josef Jacobs. At the time I joined the Staffel, he had been in many aerial combats, but had only six confirmed aerial victories to his credit. Jacobs went on to become one of the highest scoring German aces of The Great War, with a final tally of almost fifty confirmed victories.

'Again, I piled my bags and personal effects into the back of the big old Mercedes touring car. I was the only passenger that day, so we had an uninterrupted ride for the sixty kilometres or so from Valenciennes north to Thourout in West Flanders. My new Staffel was billeted in a château at the nearby Wynendaelsveld estate.'

Jagdstaffel 7 Background

Even before the Fliegertruppe was reorganised into the Luftstreitkräfte on 8 October 1916, Chief of Field Aviation Hermann von der Lieth-Thomsen developed plans for the first Jagdstaffeln, which would provide coordinated tactical air support for each army corps. Oberstleutnant von der Lieth-Thomsen authorised the first Jagdstaffel on 10 August[2] that year and selected Germany's top scoring fighter ace, Hauptmann Oswald Boelcke, to hand-pick aggressive pilots to fly the new Albatros biplane fighters needed to help German ground forces in the Battle of the Somme. Boelcke's most inspired choice was Manfred von Richthofen, whose marksmanship and singular bravery led him to become the war's most successful fighter ace. By the end of August 1916, six more fighter units had been formed, the last one being Jagdstaffel 7. Its first Staffel-Führer, the Hannoverian aristocrat[3] and seasoned pre-war flyer[4] Oberleutnant Fritz Erhard Bronsart von Schellendorf, had previous command experience with an early fighter unit, the Fokkerstaffel attached to Infanterie-Division Nr. 34.[5]

Bronsart von Schellendorf's best choice was an enlisted pilot, Vizefeldwebel Friedrich Manschott, who from 5 January to 16 March 1917 achieved eleven of his twelve confirmed aerial victories with Jasta 7; following his last triumph, a French captive observation balloon south of Fort Vaux near Verdun,[6] the twenty-four-year-old native of the Grand Duchy of Baden was himself killed in combat with four French Caudrons defending the balloon.[7] Nearby on the same day, Bronsart von Schellendorf shot down a balloon at Belleville, thereby achieving his first (and only) aerial triumph.[8]

Manschott was succeeded by twenty-two-year-old Oberflugmeister [Chief Petty Officer] Kurt Schönfelder, a pre-war flyer,[9] whose military service began as a pilot with the Imperial German Navy. He was transferred to Jasta 7 to gain experience to bring back to a naval fighter unit. Early in his time with the Staffel, Schönfelder claimed two enemy aircraft and a balloon as 'kills', but did not receive official confirmation of an aerial victory until 20 July 1917.[10] While over Passchendaele, Belgium at 8:25 p.m. that day, he shot down an S.E.5[11] from amongst a flight of one of the top Royal Flying Corps units, 56 Squadron. The pilot, thirty-year-old Canadian Lieutenant Robert G. Jardine,[12] crashed within German lines and was killed; due to heavy ground fighting in the area, his body was never recovered.[13] The following evening, the same British S.E.5 squadron was back in the area and may well have had their revenge on Jasta 7, as Staffel-Führer Bronsart von Schellendorf was shot down in flames and killed[14] in an area where several air combat victories were credited to 56 Squadron.[15] He was buried in the nearby German military cemetery in Thourout.[16]

The Jacobs Era Begins

The skilled pilot and seasoned air fighter selected to succeed Bronsart von Schellendorf was Ltn.d.Res Josef Carl Jacobs, an air combat veteran who had been posted as an instructor at Valenciennes.[17] Jacobs was also a pre-war flyer and, when he enlisted in the army in August 1914, he was sent to Flieger-Ersatz-Abteilung 3 in Darmstadt[18] to complete his aviation training. He was subsequently posted to Feld-Fliegerabteilung 11 commanded by Hauptmann Helmuth Wilberg,[19] who later became Kommandeur der Flieger [Officer in Charge of Aviation] for the 4th Army. Following a series of early aerial victories, Jacobs

Three luminaries of the German Luftstreitkräfte who had an effect on Carl Degelow's aviation service in World War I (from left): Oberstleutnant [Lieutenant-Colonel] Hermann von der Lieth-Thomsen, Air Force Chief of Staff; Rittmeister Manfred Freiherr von Richthofen, the highest scoring fighter ace of all nations involved in the war; and Generalleutnant Ernst von Hoeppner, Commanding General of the Air Force.

was posted to the Jagdstaffelschule at Valenciennes, where, most recently, he was recovering from the flu[20] when he was assigned to command Jasta 7.

On Friday, 3 August 1917, Jacobs departed for his new post and, as he noted in his diary: 'I left with Ltn [Georg] Meyer and Ltn [Otto] Kunst, who were allowed to join me at Jagdstaffel 7 … Of the original officers who were with the Staffel when it was formed, only Ltn [Johannes] Kintzelmann and Oberflgmstr [Kurt] Schönfelder were on hand.'[21]

Upon Jacobs' arrival, the Staffel's aerial victory score stood at forty-eight. Still under his leadership at war's end fifteen months later, Jasta 7 recorded a total of 150 enemy aircraft and balloons brought down. Jacobs was known to be a tough but fair commanding officer, who led his unit by example rather than admonition. The Rhinelander's warm smile and friendly words for everyone led to his being nicknamed 'Köbes'. In his Rhenish culture, 'Köbes' was a centuries-old traditional way of addressing the friendly and ever-helpful waiters in the best beer halls in Cologne, Düsseldorf and other cities in the area of central western Germany called the Rhineland. According to Degelow, Jacobs bore the nickname with typical grace and charm.

An increase in the number of victories for the Staffel was slow to start. A three-aeroplane flight that Jacobs led on 21 August was marked by an aerial mauling that occurred when he and his men tried to use low cloud cover to attack British observation balloons near Ypres. They ran into a swarm of Sopwith Camels and S.E.5s that peppered them with machine-gun fire at every turn. Finally able to get back to his airfield, Jacobs and his shot-up Albatros had to make an emergency landing. Unbeknownst to him, one of his comrades was landing at the same time. The two Albatros fighters collided at low altitude just above the edge of the small landing field. Jacobs was uninjured and walked away from the crash, but the other pilot, Ltn Kunst, was unconscious and had to be extricated from the wreckage of his 'plane. Kunst was in hospital for a few days, but soon returned to action and scored further victories.

Unser erfolgreicher Ka... fliege.
Leutnant Jacobs

Sanke
...ich verfolgt.

Ltn.d.Res Josef Carl Jacobs, Jagdstaffel 7 commanding officer, was the subject of a popular postcard in a series eagerly collected during the war. Jacobs went on to receive the Pour le Mérite, but is seen here wearing the Knight's Cross of the Royal House Order of Hohenzollern with Swords (above his left breast pocket), Iron Cross First Class and Military Pilot's Badge.

Jacobs did not score again until 10 September. Meanwhile, on 21 August, he welcomed the pilot who would become his most successful protégé, Carl Degelow, who recalled:

'I approached my first meeting with Staffel-Führer Jacobs with some trepidation, but the Rhinelander's easy manner made me feel quite comfortable within the shortest space of time. We had a long discussion, during which I asked him about his experiences and he asked about mine, particularly about the two Caudrons that Ltn Kürten and I had shot down with our two-seater. Then we came to "the incident" at Jasta 36.

'"We will discuss the matter just once," Jacobs said, "and then neither of us will ever mention it again. Agreed?"

'After a few moments devoted to that unpleasant subject, we were soon able to dispense with the matter. The slate was clean and I could make a fresh start.'

With more aerial combat experience than the new arrival, Jacobs understood that the war existed on a daily basis for pilots and aircrews on both sides of the lines. They gave little thought to the long-range scope of operations because their activity was generally limited to a small area of a few hundred square kilometres. Moreover, while ground positions can be secured by infantry, the aerial arena remains the same despite the movement of troops below. The struggle for the sky was a daily exercise, as airmen from each side struggled to deny their opponents use of the air over the battlefields.

As Jasta 7 and its sister units ranged across the Flanders sky in autumn 1917, they were part of a direct reaction to plans formulated that spring, which was typically the season of military offensives. Both sides launched all-out land and air attacks early in 1917. At that point Germany enjoyed aerial superiority to the extent that high British aircraft losses in one month alone led to the name 'bloody April' that has identified that four-week span ever since. With the failure of the Allied spring offensive on the Aisne Front, the emphasis was shifted northward to Flanders. Sir Douglas Haig planned for British armies in Flanders to take on the bulk of German opposition in June.[22] Haig's move would buy time for the French to restore confidence to their own soldiers and for the arrival of fresh troops from the United States, which had entered the war on 6 April. Haig understood that the infusion of men and materiel from America would be needed to complete the defeat of the German Army.

Germany was then fighting a two-front war, with troops deployed in Belgium and France, as well as in Russia. Hence, it was fair to assume that intensive British pressure in Flanders would call for the diversion of German forces to that area. Also, Haig had been warned by high naval authorities that failure to clear German units from the Belgian coast would seriously affect the Fleet's ability to hold the Channel. Loss of the Channel would affect the capacity to continue the war into 1918.

The Allies' Flanders campaign began in June with an attack on the group of hills that form the Messines - Wytschaete ridge, a distance of some 2,000 metres. Taking this ridge from the Germans would deprive them of an excellent observation post over a large section of the countryside and would enable British forces to prepare for a much larger campaign.[23] Defences in that area were manned by the German 4th Army under the command of sixty-five-year-old General der Infanterie Friedrich Sixt von Armin. The battle at Messines and subsequent engagements at Ypres and Cambrai all involved elements of von Armin's 4th Army, including, of course, Jasta 7.

There was little time for orientation flights for a pilot who had frontline experience and Carl Degelow was quickly put into action. According to his flight logbook, his first flight with Jasta 7 occurred on the afternoon of 22 August, when he took part in an escort flight for reconnaissance aircraft for Flieger-Abteilung 40. It was uneventful – much to Degelow's dismay. Three days later, however, he took part in a major operation:

'There was great excitement in the air. The order had been given by headquarters: "Immediate readiness to take off. Big day of battle!" Ltn Jacobs had got us up at an ungodly early hour, and a brisk run to the flight line took the place of breakfast. The mechanics had our aircraft lined up like a company of Frederick the Great's guardsmen, with Albatros D.V and Pfalz D.III fighters perfectly aligned with each other. The pilots slipped into their flying suits more hastily than usual and swore that their Tommy opponents would get a bellyful for waking them so early.

The cockpit of an Albatros D.V was Carl Degelow's battle station when he began his service as a successful single-seat fighter pilot. At the lower centre of the photograph is the control column with the buttons that activated the aeroplane's two Spandau LMG 08 machine guns.

'After sitting in our planes waiting for the word to go, the starting bell finally rang and we took off for the Front. Our flight of eight single-seat fighters, with the Staffel-Führer at its head, circled the airfield, then closed formation and flew northeast to Ostende and proceeded from there along the Flanders coast to Nieuport. Then we turned south, along the Yser Canal, to the Ypres Sector, where we were on the lookout for British aircraft. As we climbed to about 3,000 metres, we saw bursts from our own anti-aircraft guns firing at something within our lines between Roulers and Courtrai, some thirty to forty kilometres away. Just as tracks lead a hunter to his prey, the black anti-aircraft fireballs told us that we would soon have targets in our gun-sights.

'From out of the clouds of anti-aircraft fire there emerged a squadron of about twenty-five British two-seaters, heading for Ghent to drop bombs on our main army arsenal. We manoeuvred into position to attack the enemy, each of us trying to pick out an opponent, but ready to break away if a comrade had a better shot at it.

'This was my first big air fight and I was all the more determined to shoot down the foe and thereby prove myself worthy of being a fighter pilot. I fired continuously at the opponent I had selected, but he held his course with no visible damage. His apparently unconcerned attitude made me very angry. He seemed hardly to notice me! Over Ghent, the enemy squadron curved and, on the flight leader's flare signal, dropped its bombs. In close formation, the aircraft then sought to reach their own lines.

'The enemy plane I was attacking seemed to have been assigned to protect his squadron's rear. The formation's turning manoeuvre worked to my advantage, for it enabled me to get closer to my quarry. Again and again I peppered him with lively machine-gun volleys. His only reaction was to wave his arm. That broke the thread of my patience. I dived steeply on the enemy and again pressed both buttons of my machine guns. But suddenly the reassuring "tak-tak–tak" ceased and, to my dismay, I saw the empty cartridge belt flutter down into my cockpit. My ammunition was used up!

'Just as I discovered my incapacity for further fighting, my opponent turned and our roles were reversed. I was the hare and he the hound. The fellow did not shoot badly and soon smashed my oil tank, resulting in my goggles being covered with a fine spray of oil. Egyptian darkness settled around me. Like a wild man, I jerked the control stick and tried with quick turns to evade the Englishman's fire.

'I was able to escape my enemy only after a bitter twisting and turning flight. Tearing the oil-covered goggles from my eyes, I looked around in time to see the proven *Kanone*, Ltn Jacobs, make quick work of destroying the two-seat fighter. I was lucky to be alive and, in not exactly high spirits, I returned to our airfield. This encounter with the British two-seater impressed upon me very firmly that I still had quite a way to go before I would become an ace.'

Despite Degelow's report of a fight with two-seaters and his confirmation of a victory for his Staffel-Führer, Jacobs did not receive credit for shooting down a Bristol F.2B in that fight. On 31 August, Degelow noted in his logbook that Jasta 7 participated in a flight with the *Richthofen-Geschwader* [a Group composed of four Staffeln commanded by the famous Red Baron], recognisable by the large patches of red on the Fokker triplanes. But it was also not fruitful. Three days later, however, Jasta 7 had much more success.

Anatomy of an Air Fight

Jacobs wrote in his diary that 3 September was:

'A great day for Jagdstaffel 7! We brought down five enemy aeroplanes. We took off in two flights: Leutnants Meyer, [Erich] Thun, Degelow and me; and [Paul] Billik, [Hans] Horst, [Adolf] Techow and Kunst. As we circled over the Front at 7:40 a.m., we noticed some anti-aircraft bursts in the vicinity of our airfield, and soon I spotted an enemy formation, so I signalled my flights to fly above them. I noticed a German Albatros fighter in great difficulty and gave my engine full throttle to go to his assistance, but I was too late, as the Albatros exploded and went down in flames. I had a Sopwith Camel beautifully lined up in my sights when I was jumped by a Spad. I started to side-slip but fell into a spin and lost altitude so that, when I finally regained control of my 'plane, I had to go home.

This undated Jasta 7 photo shows (from left): Ltn Carl Degelow, Ltn Willi Nebgen, Uffz Jupp Böhne, unidentified captured pilot, Ltn Josef Jacobs, unidentified pilot, Oberflgmstr Kurt Schönfelder and another unidentified pilot. As Jacobs was wearing only his Iron Cross Second Class ribbon on his tunic, the photo was most likely taken before he was awarded the Knight's Cross of the Royal House Order of Hohenzollern with Swords on 3 August 1917.

'The two flights landed … and reported as follows: Ltn Meyer, one Sopwith Camel, down in flames over Dixmuide; Ltn Billik, one Camel, forced to land within our lines; Ltn Degelow, one Camel, forced to land. And Ltn Thun, a Spad shot down within enemy lines.

'All successes were confirmed by witnesses on the ground … The attack on my machine by the Spad resulted in an amount of hits in the fuselage and I have come to the conclusion that I do not particularly care for the Albatros D.III fighter.'[24]

Carl Degelow had a less dispassionate view of the encounter:

'The whole scene was a mass of confusion. The British sent over a large formation of two-seat Bristol Fighters and single-seat Sopwith Camels and Spads to greet us after breakfast. But we rose to the occasion in two groups … Meyer, Billik and I each brought down a Camel, while Thun got a Spad. Meanwhile, Jacobs became involved with another Spad and lost a great deal of altitude. He managed to make it back to our airfield. That evening, the score was raised one more notch when Ltn Kunst shot down a Spad.'

Keeping track of successes in the highly competitive matter of scoring aerial victories was highly subjective on both sides of the lines. Medals and a certain measure of fame went to the high scorers and all fighter pilots aspired to be among that élite group. But there were many instances of two or more pilots firing at the same enemy aeroplane at different altitudes and later claiming the same 'kill'. Plus, pursued pilots often feigned being hit so they could dash for home once their pursuers had given them up for dead or crashed. Hence, victory claims were often matters of interpretation and, aside from examples of pursuers landing near their defeated adversaries, assigning credit for downed aircraft was very speculative. Performing the latter task more than ninety years after the fact – as this author and other researchers do, based on studying reports from both sides, and aligning times and locations – also does not guarantee complete accuracy.

A case in point is Degelow's claiming credit for forcing a Sopwith Camel to land near Dixmuide in Western Flanders on the morning of 3 September. The weekly report for the 4th Army Sector lists only a Sopwith sent down at 8:25 a.m. near Dixmuide 'on the other side' of the lines.[25] The German Air Force Commanding General's report for the period credits Billik with his sixth victory, a 'Sopwith single-seater' shot down near Eesen, Degelow with forcing a Sopwith single-seater to land near Dixmuide, and Thun with forcing a Spad single-seater to land near Pervyse.[26]

The best documented aspect of the air fight over Dixmuide on 3 September was the Albatros fighter loss witnessed by Ltn Jacobs. The German sector commander's weekly report identified the casualty as twenty-eight-year-old Hauptmann Otto Hartmann,[27] leader of Royal Württemberg Jagdstaffel 28 and a seven-victory ace. Very likely, he was shot down and killed by the Bristol Fighter crew of Lt R. Dodds and 2/Lt T.C.S. Tuffield, members of 48 Squadron; the pilot later reported:

'While escorting [two-seat] D.H.4s on bombing [mission], we were attacked by two Albatros scouts on our return. The first machine attacked us, but I manoeuvred and got my front gun on him and he passed under my right wing, and my observer emptied a drum [of ammunition] into him and drove him down appearing out of control. The second one appeared immediately on our tail and above us: my observer fired into him at 200 yards range, and I turned and got between him and the sun, and we went head-on, firing from a range of 100 yards and finally 25 yards, after which … [the Albatros] went down with flames issuing from his engine, which was completely out of control.'[28]

Jacobs' witnessing the demise of Hptm Hartmann in an Albatros D.III and the disparaging comments about that aircraft type in his diary, presaged his more formal report that added to negative feelings about that aeroplane. As aviation historian Peter Grosz wrote: 'Only a few weeks after the first [D.III's] exposure to combat, it became patently obvious that something was seriously amiss with the wings of the new Albatros D.III fighters; fortunately the aircraft came down safely – a situation that could soon change for the worse.'[29]

While Jacobs eagerly awaited the arrival of new Pfalz D.III fighters, he had to make do with the aeroplanes he had. In fact, a week after complaining about his Albatros, Jacobs flew it and scored his seventh victory when he and three comrades jumped five French Spads over Keyem, a small town just north of Dixmuide. The French pilot, who was killed when the aircraft exploded on impact with the ground, was subsequently identified as Capitaine Georges Matton, a nine-victory ace and member of France's Escadrille Spa 48. Like many other German fighter pilots, Jacobs liked to collect souvenirs from enemy aeroplanes that he shot down and, on this occasion, he noted with disappointment that 'very little could be saved from the wreck' of Matton's Spad.[30]

There was a celebration that night in Jasta 7's pilots' mess set up in a small expropriated castle in Thouroube [Torhut]. Despite the deprivations suffered by ordinary citizens on the home front, aerial victories scored in Albatros fighters could still be toasted with a supply of wine gladly furnished by the Albatros-Flugzeugwerke in Schneidemuhl – no doubt to 'buy' some good-will.

Across the lines, meanwhile, there would be a solemn salute to the empty chair in the dining room of Escadrille Spa 48, one of a small number of French fighter squadrons in Flanders. But the mood among so many aviators of that war was mercurial; one dinnertime solemnity could be quickly replaced by the following evening's joy over triumph in an aerial battle. Pilots on both sides accepted this condition with a form of emotional anaesthesia that allowed them to witness a comrade's – or even an adversary's – flaming death without dwelling on the unpleasant reality of the event, and certainly without giving a great deal of introspection on one's own frail mortality. The key to combat flyers' mental survival was to live a day at a time.

As Carl Degelow observed:

'During the war there appeared with great regularity treatises of varying lengths by medical doctors with a specialized interest in the new art of flying. A primary subject of such discourses was the physical effects of lengthy combat flying on pilots and observers. To be sure, we were aided by certain technological advances, as seen in such specially-developed equipment as electrically-heated flying suits and high altitude

The château at Ruddervoorde, less than ten kilometres north-northeast of Thorout, was one of several stately homes in Flanders expropriated for use by Jasta 7.

breathing apparatus. But the role of the bespectacled gentlemen of medicine – the forerunners of today's flight surgeons – was then rather limited. They were not yet able to prescribe preventive measures or remedies to counter-act the physiological damage that the delicate mechanism of the human body sustained during strenuous flying activity.

'An even more unexplored area of medical science was the psychological effects on combat airmen. Stethoscopes and other instruments of auscultation were incapable of sounding the flyers' mental state, the variations of which cannot be registered on a graph, as pulse beats can. Amongst ourselves, we fighter pilots were able to recognise some of the thoughts flashing through the minds of our comrades; they became evident in the hunting fever that sparkled in a man's eyes or in the determined set of his jaw.

'After the war, I was asked one question most often: "When fighting in the air, do you feel any fear?" That one was difficult to answer because the dangers that surround a flyer, particularly a combat pilot, differ from those to which other kinds of soldiers are exposed. In addition to the chance of being shot at, which the pilot shared with every soldier, there was always the possibility of crashing to the ground due to mechanical failure or atmospheric conditions. True, some of the danger was removed later in the war, with the development and use of parachutes and improvements in aircraft construction methods, but the chance was always there, hanging over the pilot's head like the sword of Damocles. Engrossed in handling his machine, however, a pilot gave little thought to these hazards. His insensibility to peril stemmed from his ingrained trust in modern technology, which made him less fearful than his ancestors were in the horse and buggy days. Flying had – and still has – more to do with control of the aeroplane than with personal daring. The pilot and the aeroplane are a team, but the hand at the controls had to recognise the limitations of the machine, or his mission would come to naught.

'During the early days of flying, people had an exaggerated admiration of flyers, due to the newness of flying and a natural reluctance to leave terra firma. Far be it from me to belittle the work of our brave comrades of the air, whose deeds live on as highlights of the war. But let us face the facts. Generally speaking, ninety per cent of all normal men could qualify for flight training; the remaining ten per cent would be unsuited; not just due to dizziness while flying, but usually because they did not have the perfect eyesight and depth perception required, or because they had some physical handicap that hindered efficient handling of the aeroplane. But my observations about fitness are for flying in general, and do not contend that ninety per cent of all normal men would be suited for combat flying. That is where we separate the men from the boys.

'One needs to understand why the flyer did not become dizzy at high altitude, as the general public supposed he might. If you were to climb way up in a church tower and look at the buildings below you, your being so high above everything else produces an uncomfortable feeling and dizziness. The impression from an aeroplane would be entirely different, for you would then be separated from the earth and high above everything connected to the earth. It is a matter of your relationship to and with the ground. Thus, our aerial observers were taken to very high altitudes to perform their photographic work and never had any cause to be frightened or suddenly think: "Now I am falling!" Their orientation was to the aeroplane and, as long as it remained on an even keel, their stability was never threatened.

'As for a fighter pilot, he had to use all of his willpower to fend off any feelings of doubt when he had to attack. Certain experiences tended to weaken one's willpower and the mental reaction to a frightful aerial adventure caused some fliers to give up flying completely. On the other hand, I once saw a pilot whose machine was set afire in the air and who was saved from "roasting" by his parachute. When he got to the ground, he could hardly wait until he could get into another aeroplane to go up and renew the fight, carrying it to a victorious end. Such fellows were cut from good wood. If, in addition to such iron nerves, they also possessed expert flying ability, they belonged to the corps of excellent men who were destined to become successful fighter pilots.'

New Pfalz D.III Fighters Arrive

Structural problems with the Albatros D.III and its successor, the D.V, left Jagdstaffel leaders hoping for a new aeroplane that would offer good performance and safety for their pilots. Initially, the Pfalz Flugzeugwerke in Speyer seemed to have a new fighter that filled the bill. It was a sleek streamlined aircraft and, as the late Peter Grosz noted: 'There is little doubt that the Pfalz D.III was of more rugged construction than its Albatros counterpart and, like most German aircraft, the workmanship where it counted was of high quality … [and] the Pfalz D.III was regarded as equal to the Sopwith Camel (probably the most over-rated and accident-prone fighter in the Allied inventory) and surprisingly only the [Airco] D.H.5 was superior [to the Pfalz D.III] in speed, climb rate and manoeuvrability.'[31]

Pfalz D.IIIs began arriving at Jasta 7 at the end of the month, but they were not without their surprises, as Jacobs' diary entry for 30 September indicates:

'Ltn Kunst, flying his new Pfalz for the first time, joined our patrol near Nieuport. Just as we decided to go after a flight of Sopwith fighters, Kunst's Pfalz suddenly flipped over and spun down. I followed immediately, as did a Camel that dived toward his [own lines] when I fired a burst at him. I continued on to within 500 metres of the ground but could not spot the Pfalz. While [we were] flying home, Kunst's Pfalz suddenly appeared alongside me. The sensitivity of his aeroplane's controls had almost been fatal to Kunst, but he had been able to straighten out when he was fifty metres above the ground.'[32]

Later, more Pfalz D.IIIs and allegedly improved Albatros D.V fighters arrived to replace the Albatros D.IIIs, but, with the approach of winter in Flanders, even the elements seemed to turn against the aerial combatants. In addition to the shorter period of daylight, the weather became colder and the wind more turbulent. These factors contributed to a decrease in flights and the subsequent reduction in aerial hostilities.

Nonetheless, Staffel-Führer Jacobs continued to add to his bag of aerial kills while his pupils – including Degelow – tagged along with little success. On Thursday, 6 December, Jacobs wrote in his diary:

'During the afternoon patrol …we came down on some British single-seaters, who immediately high-tailed it for home. I went after an R.E.8 and poured bullets into him, but he would not fall. As Ltn Degelow pulled up alongside me, I perceived another R.E.8 to the left and below me, and had to give him up for lost because I had overshot him in my dive.'[33]

Of course, no one dared to criticise the Staffel-Führer. His subordinates were with him to learn how to survive duels in the air and how to protect their leader's flanks. It was a method of operation that Degelow himself later used when he went on to command Jasta 40. To be sure, while the weather was a factor in restraining the newer pilots, the proper motivation was enough to make them disregard the elements and plunge into whatever action occurred.

A case in point is the afternoon patrol flown by Jasta 7 on 8 December, 1917. In his diary, Jacobs noted the morning patrol had been 'cut short because the air was quite bumpy and there were low clouds.'[34] Yet, during the day's second mission he passed up an opportunity to pounce on four Spad two-seaters – choosing instead the more difficult challenge of a flight of Sopwith two-seat observation aircraft and their Sopwith Camel fighter escorts.

Jacobs claimed a Camel west of Passchendaele and Degelow a Sopwith two-seater south-west of the same town.[35] It was recorded that both Camels went down within British lines, but, if so, they did not show evidence of damage or injury sufficient to be noted in Royal Flying Corps reports.[36] Likewise, the Royal Naval Air Service did not list any of its Sopwith Camels as casualties for that day.[37] The German 4th Army's weekly report noted that Jacobs and Degelow had forced (but not shot) down two Sopwiths. The official publication of the Air Force Commanding General rendered its opinion, which was final and, in terms of aerial combat on 8 December, made no mention of either man in that day's summary of German aerial victories.

In a similar incident four days later, Jacobs led a flight over Houthulst Forest, where they encountered a superior number of Sopwith Camels. Jacobs stated that Degelow shot down one of them. He also credited Vizefeldwebel Hans Horst with shooting down a 'Spad' [sic] and Ltn Billik with downing a Camel. In fact, according to Jacobs' diary: 'Lucky day for Jasta 7, since we shot down three enemy aeroplanes, one of which landed intact on our field … [and the] Camel pilot, Flight Sub-Lieutenant Clark, a Canadian, twenty years old, was our guest for the evening. This chap made an extremely fine impression on all of us.'[38]

The 4th Army report granted credit to Horst and Billik for each shooting down a Sopwith Camel. Degelow's claim, however, was disallowed. The British account of the fight states:

'While making a sweep round by Ghistelles and Dixmuide, nine Camels from No. 10 Squadron [RNAS] encountered six Albatros scouts. A general engagement took place in which one of our machines was attacked and shot down by an Albatros. Flight Commander Macgregor immediately attacked the E.A. [enemy aircraft] and drove him down out of control … Confirmation of the destruction of this E.A. has since been received from the Belgians, who state that a British and a hostile machine were seen to go down at this time, near Leke.'[39]

Ltn.d.Res Carl Degelow had a landing accident in this all-black Pfalz D.IIIa which he flew while assigned to Jasta 7. It was the first aeroplane to bear his 'white stag' personal insignia, which he took with him to Jasta 40.

The same report listed F/S/L John G. Clark of 10 Squadron, RNAS as missing in action on 12 December.[40] It also inferred that Flight Commander Norman M. Macgregor avenged Clark's loss by shooting down the Canadian's victor, Ltn Paul Billik – even though Billik made it home intact that day and flew with Jasta 7 through the end of 1917.[41]

Degelow was frustrated by his further lack of success, knowing that he could not rest on the old laurels of his Flieger-Abteilung (A) 216 achievements. He knew he had to produce results and would have to try harder to succeed as an air fighter. To cheer himself up, Degelow had his Pfalz D.III decorated in a special manner so his comrades could easily identify him in the air. Following the example of Ltn Jacobs, who had his new Albatros D.V fuselage painted all black with two silver rings around it,[42] Degelow had his aeroplane's fuselage painted all black. As one of Jasta 7's mechanics was a particularly talented artist – and, indeed, had painted an attractive gold six-pointed star on both sides of Oberflgmstr Schönfelder's black fuselage – Degelow presented a more challenging project. He wanted the artist to replicate the symbol of the *Weisser Hirsch* [white stag] sanatorium in Dresden, where Degelow had convalesced after being wounded in ground fighting in 1915.

A short time later, Degelow's Pfalz D.III bore a faithful rendering of the stag – exquisitely executed with a silver body and gold antlers. He neither knew nor cared that another fighter pilot, Dresden-born Rudolf Windisch, would use a similar battle emblem. Carl Degelow, whose father had read him many writings from German mythology – including Ludwig Uhland's poem, '*Der weisse Hirsch*', about a magical white stag that eluded all hunters – now had an appropriate battle symbol to wear with pride in air fights yet to come.

Uhland's poem[43] hinted at the agility such a symbol promised:

Es gingen drei Jäger wohl auf die Pirsch, sie wollten erjagen den weissen Hirsch.	Once three hunters went out a-stalking, wanting to hunt down the white stag.
Sie legten sich unter den Tannenbaum, da hatten die drei einen seltsamen Traum.	They laid themselves down under the fir tree, where the three had a peculiar dream.
Der erste. Mir hat geträumt, ich klopft auf den Busch, da rauschte der Hirsch heraus, husch husch!	The first, I dreamed that I beat upon the thicket, there the stag rushed out, quick, quick!
Der zweite. Und als er sprang mit der Hunde Geklaff, da brannt' ich ihn auf das Fell, piff, paff!	The second, And as he sprang out with the dogs a-barking, I shot and hit him, bang, bang!
Der dritte. Und als ich den Hirsch an der Erde sah, da stieß ich lustig ins Horn, trara!	The third, And as I saw the stag on the ground, then I blew happily into the horn, tra-ra!
So lagen sie da und sprachen, die drei, da rannte der weiße Hirsch vorbei.	While they lay there and talked, the three, just then the white stag went right past them.
Und eh' die drei Jäger ihn recht geseh'n, so war er davon über Tiefen und Höhn. Husch husch! Piff, paff! Trara!	And before the three hunters really saw him, he was off, over gorge and hill-tops. Quick, quick! Bang, bang! Tra-ra!

1 The first such attack took place on 26 September 1915, when Lt M.G. Christie of 7 Squadron, RFC and 2/Lt G.G.A. Williams of 5 Squadron 'bombed the locomotive sheds at Valenciennes' [Ref: Jones, *The War in the Air*, Vol. II, p. 132].

2 Kriegsministerium, *Teil 10 Abschnitt B, Flieger-Formationen*, p. 234.

3 Perthes, *Ehrentafel der Kriegsopfer des reichsdeutschen Adels 1914-1918*, p. 34.

4 Supf, *Das Buch der deutschen Fluggeschichte*, Vol. I, p. 116.

5 Franks, Bailey, & Duiven, *The Jasta Pilots*, pp. 20-21.

6 Kogenluft, *Nachrichtenblatt der Luftstreitkräfte*, Vol. I, No. 7, 12 April 1917, p. 16.

7 Kilduff, "Combat Fliers of Baden" in *Over the Front*, pp. 324-325.

8 Kogenluft, op.cit.

9 Born on 30 July 1894 in Totschen, Silesia, Schönfelder earned DLV License 634 on 27 December 1913 [Ref: Supf, *Das Buch der deutschen Fluggeschichte*, Vol. II, p. 666].

10 Kogenluft, *Nachrichtenblatt der Luftstreitkräfte*, Vol. I, No. 25, p. 157.

11 Kofl 4. Armee, [Weekly] *Meldung Nr. 26095/19* dated 26 July 1917, p. 7.

12 Henshaw, *The Sky Their Battlefield*, p. 200.

13 Hobson, *Airmen Died in the Great War 1914-1918*, p, 60.

14 Kofl 4. Armee, *Meldung*, op.cit., p. 9.

15 Revell, *High in the Empty Blue*, p. 104.

16 Haehnelt, *Ehrentafel der im Flugdienst während des Weltkrieges gefallenen Offiziere der Deutschen Fliegerverbände*, p. 73.

17 Puglisi, 'Jacobs of Jasta 7' in *Cross & Cockade Journal*, Vol. VI, pp. 307-308.

18 Cron, 'Organization of the German Luftstreitkräfte' in *Cross & Cockade Journal*, Vol. VII, p. 55.

19 Loewenstern & Bertkau, *Mobilmachung, Aufmarsch und erster Einsatz der deutschen Luftstreitkräfte im August 1914*, p. 119.

20 Quoted in Puglisi, op.cit., p. 308.

21 Ibid., p. 309.

22 Liddell Hart, *The Real War 1914-1918*, p. 329.

23 Ibid., p. 332.

24 Quoted in Puglisi, op.cit., p. 310.

25 Kofl 4. Armee, *Wochenbericht Nr. 158 op.*, 6 September 1917, p. 11.

26 Kogenluft, *Nachrichtenblatt der Luftstreitkräfte*, Vol. I, No. 33, 11 October 1917, p. 306.

27 Kofl 4. Armee, *Wochenbericht*, op.cit., p. 8.

28 48 Squadron, RFC Combat Report, 3 September 1917.

29 Grosz, *Albatros D.III – A Windsock Datafile Special*, pp. 10-11.

30 Puglisi, op.cit., p. 310.

31 Grosz, *Pfalz D.III Windsock Datafile 107*, p. 13.

32 Puglisi, op.cit., p. 313.

33 Ibid., p. 314.

34 Ibid.

35 Ibid.

36 RFC, *War Diary* entry, 8 December 1917.

37 Royal Naval Air Service, *Communiqué No. 11*, n.d., p. 3.

38 Puglisi, op.cit., p. 315.

39 RNAS, *Communiqué*, op.cit., p. 5.

40 Ibid., p. 6.

41 Franks, Bailey & Guest, *Above the Lines*, p. 74.

42 Franks, *Albatros Aces of World War I*, pp. 68, 93.

43 English translation by this author.

CHAPTER SIX
THE WHITE STAG FLIES

Year's end 1917 and early 1918 marked a winter of discontent for Jagdstaffel 7. Thursday, 18 December began with freezing weather and, during the afternoon patrol Carl Degelow became puzzled when Josef Jacobs suddenly disappeared from sight after scoring his twelfth aerial victory.[1] Had the Staffel-Führer been hit or wounded in the fight? He was nowhere to be seen.

The Fog of War

None of his men could have helped Jacobs after the event that he described:

> '[A] British scout came see-sawing toward me. I did a wing-over and went after him when I felt shots clattering on my Pfalz. I started to grab onto the control stick when a large shadow loomed over me. [There was a] terrible crash and I was hit severely in the head. I felt that I was dreaming. Suddenly, water was streaming over my face and, when I opened my eyes … I realized that another aeroplane had collided with mine. A quick glance at my altimeter told me I was at 200 metres' altitude. A part of my upper centre wing section with the radiator was gone. The propeller along with part of my engine was missing. The left aileron had disappeared. My machine did not fall vertically, but slowly went into a flat spin.'[2]

Unteroffizier [Corporal] Jupp Böhne was the only member of Jacobs' flight to witness the incident. When it was clear that his leader still had some control over the stricken aeroplane, Böhne flew at top speed back to the airfield to alert frontline ground units that Jacobs would surely be down in no-man's-land. Indeed, the Staffel-Führer was later rescued by advance elements of a German infantry battalion only 100 metres from Belgian lines.[3] The split-second accident did not leave a clue as to the identity or fate of the other aeroplane and its pilot; Jacobs and Böhne had other concerns at that moment and did not look for the other 'plane.

Jacobs learned the rest of the story some fifteen years later in Breslau, Germany in July 1933, when he met the other pilot involved. Jacobs recalled:

> 'Leutnant W. of my former neighbouring Jagdstaffel … assured me it had not been his intention to cause a collision. His landing gear and left lower wing had been torn away from behind the strut. He had assumed, wrongfully, that he had collided with a British fighter.'[4]

After the accident, bad weather kept Jasta 7 on the ground – and scoreless – for the last thirteen days of 1917. Then, after Jacobs recovered from minor injuries sustained during his harrowing experience, he was ordered to attend the aeroplane type tests at Adlershof airfield outside Berlin from 20 January to 12 February 1918.[5] The facility was well named, as *Adlershof*, which literally means 'court of eagles', was used by the Inspektion der Fliegertruppen [Inspectorate of Military Aviation, abbreviated *Idflieg*] to put competing manufacturers' aircraft through their paces to assure that construction contracts were awarded for the most suitable aeroplanes. And, just as Oswald Boelcke had once been a central figure in developing combat aircraft and tactics, in January 1918 his star pupil, Manfred von Richthofen, was the motivating force behind this first fighter competition. As one of the Red Baron's subordinates wrote:

'Richthofen was of the viewpoint that not just any home-front pilot, most of all [not] one working for one of the aeroplane companies, should be the man who determines what [aeroplanes] will be flown at the Front. Thus, representatives from all of the Jagdstaffeln at the Front came to these tests. The individual types were test-flown, [and] then the gentlemen agreed amongst themselves on which types were best suited at the moment …'[6]

Among the aeroplanes tested were two prototypes of what would become Germany's best fighter aircraft of World War I: the Fokker D.VII.[7]

Meanwhile, in Jacobs' absence, Carl Degelow achieved a significant triumph: his first aerial combat success as a fighter pilot, an event eminently provable after the enemy pilot was taken into custody by Degelow and his comrades.

It was cloudy[8] on Wednesday, 23 January 1918, when Jasta 7 Pfalz D.IIIs took off to patrol the front lines. At about 4:00 p.m., they were attacked by British fighters, as reported by the Royal Naval Air Service:

'Eight [Sopwith] Camels of No. 3 Squadron [RNAS] carried out an offensive sweep south of Ostende, Thorout and Roulers. When over Forêt D'Houthulst, our formation met seven enemy aircraft (four D.F.W. [two-seaters] and three Scouts, new type). Flight Lieut. [George B.] Anderson dived on one D.F.W., driving him down out of control. A general engagement ensued, in which many indecisive combats took place, and all the E.A. were driven down. One of our machines failed to return.'[9]

The missing airman was later identified as Flight Sub-Lieut. H.S.J.E. Youens,[10] whose loss was not mentioned in Flight Commander Frederick C. Armstrong's combat report. That document recounted only Anderson's 'decisive' victory and that 'all E.A. were driven down.'[11]

Carl Degelow told a different story:

'We were patrolling the area over Houthulst Forest, the scene of many, many aerial combats. On this day, however, the weather was not very inviting, as clouds and haze lowered visibility. For this reason the watchword from our flight leader was: "Keep a sharp look out!"

'We had already cruised over the "required" sector of the Front and were on our way home when, from out of the sun, a flight of British Sopwith Camels suddenly pounced on us. A number of individual battles soon developed and I found myself engaged with a fellow who had caught me by surprise. This pilot, who did not seem too well acquainted with the location of the frontlines, belonged, as we later learned, to a group of Dunkirk-based fighter pilots whom we called the "Armstrong Boarding School".

'The fellows were all young and inexperienced, having just arrived from England. To gain frontline experience, they were assigned to various sectors of the Front and indoctrinated in the manner of an English boarding school, hence the name we gave the group. They were always welcome adversaries, as their lack of experience allowed us to trick them into situations that made them easy prey for us.'[12]

'The Musical Tommy'

Degelow brought his fight to a satisfactory conclusion:

'Eventually, I forced my opponent to land on our side of the lines, near Dixmuide. As was our custom, we sent a car to pick him up and bring him to our airfield, where, in courteous fashion, he could spend the day with us as an honoured guest.

F/S/L Herbert Youens, a pilot of 3 Squadron, RNAS (fourth from right), posed for this photo with members of Jasta 40 at Aertrycke airfield after he was brought down by Carl Degelow on 23 January 1918. Others in the photo are (from left): Uffz Jupp Böhne, Fwbl Paul Hüttenrauch, Degelow, unknown, Youens, Ltn Otto Kunst, Oberflgmstr Kurt Schönfelder, and Fwbl Alfred Müller.

'The occupant of the downed Sopwith turned out to be Flight Sub-Lieutenant Youens,[13] a fine young man of twenty years who had his good looks temporarily marred by a bloody nose and a lovely pair of swollen black eyes caused by his rough landing. As soon as this son of Albion saw us approaching, he held out his hand in greeting and asked: "Was that you?" meaning the flyer who had forced him down. I confirmed his assumption and invited him to accompany us back to our airfield.

'On the trip back, our guest was visibly depressed by his misfortune. He mentioned something that many of his captured countrymen told us: "Your 'Archies' are awfully good." This statement led us to the conclusion that the British flyers had often felt the effectiveness of our anti-aircraft fire, which they nicknamed "Archie".

"Mr. Youens likewise expressed respect for our big bombers, one of which was at that moment passing overhead. He could not restrain his praise at the sight of this gigantic aeroplane, which, with others of its kind, nightly bombed British airfields along the English Channel. "Oh," he said, "That is a Gotha. I know its sound very well." He could not conceal the fact that he and his comrades, upon hearing the roar of our bombers, often wished they could make straight for their bomb-proof shelters.

'Meanwhile, we reached our airfield and took our guest to nearby Castle Wyndendaelsveld, which we had taken over to billet Staffel personnel. It was a beautiful structure, but difficult to heat, which is no doubt why its Belgian owners used it only during the summer months. In our Kasino the representative of the "Armstrong Boarding School" relaxed as he ate supper and drank a glass of wine. With the help of the wine we soon had a lively conversation going. My knowledge of English, which I had improved while in America a few years before the war, and a frequent *Pröstichen!* [Cheers!] appeared to help him forget the sorrow of defeat. The candles were lighted and soon no one could tell whether we were in a German Kasino or an English club.

'After the meal, our guest seemed at ease and a few shots of whisky completed the task of loosening his tongue. Mr. Youens then declared to us that he was musically inclined and performed rather well on the violin. So we had a violinist – but no violin.

'Just then, the cook, who had been following the conversation through the half open door, suddenly shouted that Monteur [mechanic] Schmitz had brought back a violin when he returned from leave.

'"Let's have it," I said and this "Stradivarius" was brought forth. It was in relatively good condition, except that it lacked an A string.

"Never mind," said the Tommy. "I have one right here." With that, he drew from his wallet at least two complete sets of strings for his favourite instrument. It seems that before taking off the Englishman had put these necessary parts into his pocket to be prepared for any eventuality. Mr. Youens busied himself stringing his fiddle and I took my place at the piano to assist him in tuning the instrument. Within ten minutes the international orchestra was ready to begin and as the opening piece we played the German national anthem, *"Deutschland über Alles"*. To the delight of all present, my partner played the song with as much intensity of feeling as if it were "God Save the King".

"Our guest gave us pleasure the entire evening and helped us pass the time with his musical entertainment. Eventually, we did play the British national anthem and every

German in the room stood at respectful attention as a sign of comradeship beyond the bounds of national or political affiliation. Thus, a battlefield defeat was transformed into a human victory.

'That evening at Castle Wyndendaelsveld was wonderful. It lasted until midnight and then our guest was shown to a one-bed room with the windows boarded up, both for protection from a sudden storm and to ensure that he would be with us long enough to partake of breakfast the following morning. As a final precautionary measure, Mr. Youens was politely asked to part with his braces and his boots temporarily, as running barefoot while holding one's trousers is a bit difficult.

'The following morning a car from an army interrogation unit came for our guest. He departed with fulsome praise and thanks for comradely hospitality, as well as good wishes for his conqueror and a flattering statement about the latter's gentlemanly manner of aerial combat. His visit was recorded in the annals of Jasta 7 as follows: "A double victory. On the one hand the hard-fought air battle that ended victoriously; and, on the other hand, the musical pleasure that the loser so bountifully and cordially provided us."

'Ours was not the only German Jagdstaffel to entertain an opposing flyer brought down without harm. Indeed, it was a custom all up and down our Front. As "lavish" as our brief ceremony was, however, it does not compare with that of an unnamed Staffel whose members captured a wonderfully gifted Irish tenor and had no desire to turn him over to those who would simply pack him off to a prisoner-of-war camp. So, to ensure the Irish flyer would not "fly the coop" while the Staffel was away at the Front, the German hosts arranged to get the Irishman so drunk every night that, the next morning, he would be in no condition to go anywhere. That little sojourn probably lasted about as long as did the Staffel's supply of alcoholic refreshments!'

A Tale of Three Dogfights

Despite obvious evidence that Carl Degelow brought down F/S/L Youens, his victory claim was officially disallowed. And, while the British pilot made an offhand reference to the accuracy of German anti-aircraft [*Flak*] fire, none of those units was credited with shooting down any Allied aircraft on 23 January.[15]

Operating far behind the lines, a month later the staff of the Air Force Commanding General (abbreviated Kogenluft) assigned credit for the day's two victories – both Sopwith Camels, downed at about the same time over the Flanders Sector – to twenty-six-year-old Ltn Gustav Wandelt of Jagdstaffel 36.[16] According to Jasta 36's war diary entry for the day:

'In the afternoon, Ltn [Heinrich] Bongartz with Leutnants [Max] Naujock and Wandelt took off for the Front. They were surprised by six Sopwiths coming down on them. Ltn Wandelt began to fight with one of [the attackers], got him in his field of fire, shot up his engine and was following him further. Suddenly, a new enemy was near him, a *Kurvenkampf* [dogfight] ensued, and a few moments later they crashed into each other. They plunged straight down in a tangled heap. Ltn Wandelt's body was found near Staden … [and on the following day his] body was transported to his hometown'[17] [of Alt Boyen/Schmiegel].[18]

The final action of that account bears little resemblance to the Jasta 7 and 3 Squadron, RNAS narratives. It does, however, correlate to the following report filed by another British naval air squadron that operated in the same area:

'While patrolling at 7,000 feet over Staden [Belgium], ten Camels of No. 10 Squadron [RNAS] observed three E.A. two-seaters and an Albatros Scout just above the clouds. These [E.A.] dived through the clouds and were followed by a part of our patrol. Below the clouds … [the E.A.] were joined by five more Albatros Scouts. In the general engagement which followed, one of the two-seaters was driven down out of control by Flight Commander [Wilfred A.] Curtis, and observed to break up in the air. An Albatros was driven completely out of control by Flight Commander [William M.] Alexander.

'Other indecisive combats took place, from which one of our machines failed to return; he was last seen spinning down with an E.A. scout, both machines being observed to crash simultaneously.'[19]

The pilot who fell in this fight was identified as F/S/L Ross A. Blyth.[20] The twenty-four-year-old Canadian's body was recovered by German troops and buried in a military cemetery in Zillebeke, Belgium.[21]

From these facts, it is clear that the Jasta 7 / Naval 3 fight took place over Houthulst Forest, a few kilometres east of Staden, where Jasta 36's Albatroses were attacked by Naval 10. But, while the Jasta 36 fight began at Staden, it drifted eastward. At about the same time, Degelow and his Jasta 7 comrades – whose Pfalz D.IIIs were identified by Naval 3 as 'Scouts, new type'[22] – headed northwest from Houthulst Forest and ended with F/S/L Youens' forced landing near Dixmuide. Thus, it can be reasonably concluded that Carl Degelow's first solo aerial victory was incorrectly assigned to Jasta 36's Ltn Gustav Wandelt, who came down some fifteen kilometres southeast of Dixmuide.

Degelow's disappointment in losing credit for his victory on 23 January was exacerbated by Kogenluft's administrative resolution of his victory claim in an air battle two days later. He claimed a Bristol Fighter shot down over Courtemarck on Friday, 25 January at 1:50 p.m. – German time, which was then an hour ahead of British time, and the importance of the time difference will soon become apparent. The Bristol F.2B that Degelow claimed reportedly left its aerodrome at St. Marie Cappel[23] at 11:54 a.m.[24] (British time = 12:54 p.m. German time), allowing plenty of time for the forty-five-kilometre flight to Courtemarck. Among the participants in that Bristol Fighter flight were Captain Robert B. Kirkman and Lieutenant A.D. Keith of 20 Squadron, RFC. Their combat report stated:

'At 12:50 p.m., ten Bristol Fighters engaged ten Albatros Scouts near Courtemarck. After fighting for five minutes, Capt Kirkman – pilot, and Lt Keith – observer, in [aircraft serial number] B.1156, noticed two Albatros Scouts diving on a Bristol Fighter beneath them. The pilot immediately dived on the [two] E.A. and brought one down.

'Capt [Frank O.] Soden of No. 60 Squadron, who was flying below Capt. Kirkman, observed the wings of the Albatros Scout fold back and saw an explosion in the machine, which he took to be the petrol tank, as the E.A. fell past him.'[25]

The squadron combat report made no mention of the loss of Sgt H.O. Smith[26] and 2/Lt H.S. Clemons[27] in Bristol F.2B number B.883 of 20 Squadron, RFC, which came down within German lines not far from Jasta 7's airfield. Subsequently, British authorities learned: 'Letters from Sergt. Smith's relatives stated that he is a wounded prisoner and getting on all right ... [and a] letter forwarded by the 2nd Brigade states that both are wounded prisoners of war. Information [also] received from relatives of 2/Lt H.S. Clemons.'[28]

British records indicate that one Bristol F.2B was lost in combat operations that day. Likewise, the German Air Force Commanding General's weekly summary showed only one Bristol F.2B as being downed on the Western Front on 25 January. The Kogenluft summary confirmed that F.2B as the nineteenth victory of Ltn Heinrich Kroll, the twenty-three-year-old commanding officer of Jasta 24, who was very close to attaining the twenty confirmed victories needed to earn the Pour le Mérite; he qualified for the honour on 29 March.[29] Interestingly, the Kogenluft report described the wreckage location as 'west of St. Quentin',[30] in the Aisne Sector, some 100 kilometres south of Courtemarck in Flanders. Equally of interest is the Jasta 24 war diary's recording of events:

> 'At 3:00 p.m. ... Ltn Kroll took off with three machines. North of St. Quentin he attacked one of two B.F. [Bristol Fighter] two-seaters and at 3:35 p.m. forced him to fall headlong, [and] in order to see where he crashed, Ltn Kroll spiralled down. When the enemy machine was about 400 metres above the ground, Ltn Kroll was attacked by a second British machine. After a short dogfight, Ltn Kroll had to break off [the fight] and go down in a dive ... [after which] he flew back to the airfield and made a smooth landing. The Staffel-Führer made his report by telephone ... to the Kofl [Officer in Charge of Aviation][31] for the 7th Army.'

Not surprisingly, Kroll received credit for shooting down an enemy aeroplane that was not seen to crash, and at a time and place far different from the only verifiable F.2B downing that day. Not yet worldly wise in the politics associated with aerial combat, Degelow submitted his claim up the chain of command and he received credit for it in the 4th Army's weekly summary six weeks later,[32] after which it was routed to Kogenluft in the normal scheme of things. By that time, Kroll had secured the credit he needed and, indeed, was awarded the Pour le Mérite just over two weeks after Degelow's claim was finally accepted by the 4th Army's officer in charge of aviation.[33]

A lesser man would have been disheartened or driven to prove himself through some rash act, but not Carl Degelow. He proceeded in his usual methodical fashion, performing his mission in his own particular way, which included a high regard for his British adversaries and a perverse desire to force (rather than shoot) down his opponents.

But it should also be mentioned that the records were adjusted after the war and the 25 January victory was rightfully credited to Ltn.d.Res Carl Degelow. Today, most post-World War I aviation history sources[34] acknowledge it as the White Stag pilot's first individual aerial triumph. Having received two half credits for his role in shooting down two Caudrons with Leutnant Kürten, Degelow could consider his bringing down Smith's and Clemons' Bristol Fighter as his second aerial victory. In light of the proof offered about F/S/L Youens above, this author contends that the Bristol Fighter should be counted as Degelow's *third* aerial victory.

The Tide of Events

Meanwhile, far from the Western Front, other events were having a profound effect on the war in France and Belgium. The Russian Revolution in October 1917 had led to a cessation of hostilities along the Eastern Front and provided German and Austro-Hungarian troops with a welcome respite. The subsequent Bolshevik take-over of the revolution and the attendant Russian surrender ensured a potential new source of men and materiel for Germany's spring 1918 offensive.

The official RAF historian described an ominous aspect of the situation:

'Russia had ceased to fight, and the bulk of the German and Austrian troops on the Eastern Front had become available for transfer to the west. [Chief of the German General Staff General Erich] Ludendorff had additionally at his disposal at least 4,000 guns taken from the Russians and 2,000 from the Italians, as well as great stores of captured war material of all kinds. The French armies were still suffering from the effect of the 1917 spring offensive and the British had been greatly weakened by the losses sustained in the costly battles that had been fought almost continuously throughout the year.'[35]

Consequently, British forces on the continent were primarily charged with watching and waiting for the coming German offensive. The best means to gather intelligence was by photographic reconnaissance, which revealed new airfield construction, troop and supply movements and other indications of impending hostilities to be launched by the Germans. But, as more missions were assigned to British aircrews, correspondingly more defensive measures were being taken by German air combat units.

The German High Command recognised that the spring 1918 offensive would be its last opportunity to seize a decisive victory in Europe. They had already ordered record-breaking war materiel production as part of the so-called *Amerika-Programm* in the face of exaggerated accounts of what US participation in the war would offer. The Kogenluft himself, General der Kavallerie Wilhelm von Hoeppner, appears to have been influenced by Allied newspaper accounts of American potential. 'According to them,' Hoeppner wrote, 'thousands of American aviators were going to swarm over Germany and force her to sue for peace.'[36]

General von Hoeppner was also concerned about developments in Britain that would present an even tougher challenge to the German aviation industry, still trying to cope with wartime shortages and lack of resources due to an effective British naval blockade in the North Sea. Later he wrote: 'The choice of such an energetic personality as [Winston] Churchill as Minister of Munitions (in July 1917), responsible among other things for the manufacture of airplanes, portended an increase in British aircraft.'[37]

As a direct response to the threat he perceived, Hoeppner directed his staff to create twice as many Jagdstaffeln – numbered from 40 to 81 – as well as seventeen more Flieger-Abteilungen primarily for artillery coordination missions. The escalation efforts were camouflaged as carefully as possible, but British reconnaissance aircraft continued to return home bearing photographs of new enemy airfields that were being prepared for new units arriving and for those expected to arrive at the Western Front. Meanwhile, many of the new units were being retained in Germany or in relatively safe rear areas to mask their existence from Allied reconnaissance and to allow for 'war games' to evaluate proposed tactics.[38]

Jacobs Returns to the Front

Ltn Josef Jacobs resumed command of Jasta 7 on 15 February 1918 and faced a serious situation. In addition to Degelow's two unresolved victory claims, the unit had only two other claims – both unconfirmed: one each by Leutnants der Reserve Martin Moebius and Paul Lotz on 24 January.[39] Jasta 7 had already bade farewell to its top performer, eight-victory ace Ltn Paul Billik, who in late December was assigned to command Jasta 52 and was allowed to take three experienced pilots with him.[40] More disheartening news followed. Jacobs recorded in his diary:

'I … learned that Ltn Moebius, who had been with the Staffel for only a few days, died in an air collision with his second adversary [on 24 January[41]]. Unteroffizier Paul Proske suffered a back injury and Uffz Paul Hüttenrauch crashed in the vicinity of our 'field and was slightly injured.'[42]

Consequently, Jacobs' work was made more difficult by having to identify potential new pilots from among students at the Jagdstaffelschule and help his current pilots improve their proficiency on the few days when they could fly.

On the very cold days, Carl Degelow exercised his own initiative to learn from his Staffel comrades or bundled himself up for a ride in the unit's little Opel runabout to visit nearby fighter units. He recalled:

'I was anxious to learn the best way to subdue a foe in the air. Of course, the fellow who relied on a telescopic gun-sight advised me to use that method. The stunt-flyer, who had shot down his opponent while executing a loop or while doing a tight turn, extolled the virtues of aerial skill. Seldom did anyone mention getting close to the enemy aircraft – "up to a metre's length", as it were – in order to shoot it down. In such reckless close-proximity fighting, one's destructive insight predominates, which certainly is not a humane sentiment, but the right one for a fighter pilot. When a man is called up to be a soldier, to defend his country, he has to agree with old von Clausewitz, who said: "In war, good-natured fools are the most disadvantaged." Hence, it was a spirit of grim determination that enabled the outnumbered German airmen to gain great victories over their British and French opponents.

'While we lacked the great numbers of aeroplanes that our opponents had, our fighters were generally equal to, or even better than, those of the enemy. That is why if, despite willingness and flying skill, a young fighter pilot did not conquer his opponent, we considered his failure to be primarily due to a lack of resolve. Such half-hearted measures would not bring success. We felt that people of that nature should face problems squarely and decide firmly, one way or the other. Many a fighter pilot involved in an aerial combat wanted to shoot down the enemy at no risk to himself. This desire came from opposing wills residing within the same soul. Success could only have been achieved by striking a deathblow to the faint-hearted side of one's nature. Only then would the fighter pilot have the self-assurance needed to defeat his opponent.

'In practice, this is what happens: To ensure his own safety while attacking, the faint-hearted fighter pilot put his aeroplane into a turn that placed him outside the accurate range of his opponent. In a tighter turn, he would have got behind and above the enemy, as he should have done. Obviously, the attacker's motive was dictated by the urge for self-preservation. Had the attacker been more resolute, the enemy, whose escape was due to the attacker's indeterminate action, would most likely have been defeated. If he wished to be a successful fighter pilot, he should not have taken as his guide the saying of one witty fellow: "Better five minutes a coward than your whole life dead." Such words, indicative of a faint heart, are alien to the feelings of an eager fighter pilot, who, free from all anxiety, is like the hunter who shoulders his gun and advances on the game. Just like Nimrod, the mighty hunter of Biblical times, the World War I fighter pilot felt excitement and the pleasure of the chase right down to his tingling fingertips; that feeling filled him with a great fighting urge as, prior to take-off, he slipped into his bulky but warm fur-lined flying boots.

'The technology that gave the pilot strength in his struggle with the forces of nature, while bringing disaster to his opponent, continued to progress and to give him greater psychological, as well as physical, comfort. The parachute, added to aircraft only late in the war, did more than ensure the physical safety of a fighter pilot. Just knowing that it was there in an emergency gave him a renewed and often more vigorous sense of boldness. He would then press home the attack with greater abandon, because there was less danger that, if his aeroplane caught fire, he would have to "ride it down" or simply leap into the air from a great height, filled with the awful knowledge that he was rushing to his doom. I have heard stories about fighter pilots who always kept a pistol on their persons for the express reason of administering their own quick *coup de grâce* in the event their aeroplanes were set afire at high altitude. One had only to see another aeroplane – friend or foe – roaring down on fire to appreciate fully what a horror that fate presented to pilots of World War I.'

1 A Sopwith 1F.1 Camel was brought down between Houthulst Forest and Dixmuide [Ref: Kogenluft, *Nachrichtenblatt der Luftstreitkräfte*, Vol. I, No. 47, 17 January 1918, p. 514]; possibly it was an aircraft of 65 Squadron, RFC [Ref: Henshaw, *The Sky Their Battlefield*, p. 262].

2 Puglisi, 'Jacobs of Jasta 7' in *Cross & Cockade Journal*, Vol. VI, p. 315.

3 Ibid., pp. 315-316.

4 Ibid., p. 316. It is highly likely that Jacobs encountered former Ltn Erich Weiss of Royal Württemberg Jagdstaffel 28, as that unit recorded Weiss' collision 'with a British fighter' on 18 December 1917 [Ref: Bock, *Jagdstaffel 28w Kriegstagebuch* abstract].

5 Grosz, *Fokker D.VII Windsock Datafile 9*, p. 4.

6 Wenzl, *Richthofen-Flieger*, pp. 46-47.

7 Grosz, op.cit., pp. 2, 4.

8 Weather report in Royal Flying Corps, *Communiqué No. 124*, 1 February 1918, p. 1.

9 Royal Naval Air Service, *Communiqué No. 14*, 4 February 1918, p. 2.

10 Ibid., p. 5.

11 3 Squadron, RNAS, *Combat Report*, 23 January 1918.

12 A reference to Fl.Cdr Frederick Carr Armstrong, DSO, officer in charge of a six-aeroplane flight of 3 Squadron, RNAS. German documents indicate that their intelligence apparatus was able to determine the identities of British officers at various levels of command. Hence, Fl.Cdr Armstrong's name would have been

known to Degelow and his comrades. It is unlikely, however, that only novices made up Armstrong's entire flight and there is nothing in the RNAS *Communiqués* to suggest that Armstrong's flight suffered inordinately high casualties. Therefore, Degelow's contention should be regarded as baseless rumour.

13 F/S/L Herbert St. John Edgerley Youens was born July/Sept 1898 in Buckingham, Buckinghamshire, England. He was appointed Probationary Flight Officer, RNAS, 6 May 1917, promoted F/S/L RNAS on 10 October 1917, assigned to 3 Squadron, RNAS, reported missing on 23 January 1918, and was repatriated 14 December 1918 [Ref: National Archives file ADM 273/13/112 Page 112].

14 Such hospitality appears to have been a German custom. During extensive research into many phases of World War I aviation history, this author has found mention of other instances of German-sponsored 'celebrations' of captured fliers. Reports of similar events for captured German aircrews have not yet come to the author's attention.

15 Kogenluft, *Nachrichtenblatt* Vol. I, No. 51, 14 February 1918, p. 586.

16 Kogenluft, *Nachrichtenblatt* Vol. I, No. 52, 21 February 1918, p. 601.

17 Reichsarchiv, *Kriegstagebuch der königlichen preussischen Jagdstaffel 36* (summary), p. 8.

18 Haehnelt, *Ehrentafel der im Flugdienst während des Weltkrieges gefallenen Offiziere der Deutschen Fliegerverbände*, p. 91.

19 RNAS, *Communiqué*, op.cit., p. 2.

20 Ibid., p. 5.

21 Hobson, *Airmen Died in the Great War 1914-1918*, p. 2.

22 RNAS, *Communiqué*, op.cit.

23 Aerodrome location noted in RFC, *War Diary* order of battle, 10 January 1918.

24 Royal Flying Corps, *Combat Casualty Report*, 25 January 1918.

25 20 Squadron, RFC, Combat Report by Capt Kirkman and Lt Keith, 25 January 1918.

26 Sgt. H.O. Smith, 20 Squadron, RFC, reported missing 25 January 1918, repatriated 1 December 1918.

27 2/Lt Harold Savigny Clemons was born in 1897 in Launceston, Tasmania. He arrived in Great Britain on 6 April 1914 at age seventeen, he was formerly Lt RASC Commissary, appointed Flight Officer Observer 20 Squadron, RFC, reported missing 25 January 1918, promoted Lt 1 April 1918, and was repatriated on 1 December 1918 [Ref: St Leonard's St Peter's Anglican Church and Cemetery records].

28 RFC, *Combat Casualty Report*, op.cit.

29 Zuerl, *Pour-le-Mérite-Flieger*, p. 293.

30 Kogenluft, *Nachrichtenblatt* No. 52, op.cit.

31 Reichsarchiv, *Kriegstagebuch der königlich preussischen Jagdstaffel 24*, pp. 93-94.

32 Kommandeur der Flieger der 4. Armee, *Wochenbericht* Nr. 1134 op., 14 March 1918, p. 6.

33 Zuerl, *Pour-le-Mérite-Flieger*, p. 293.

34 Among the most recent examples is Franks, Bailey & Guest, *Above the Lines*, p. 96.

35 Jones, *The War in the Air*, Vol. IV, p. 261.

36 von Hoeppner, *Deutschlands Krieg in der Luft*, p.140.

37 Ibid., p. 139.

38 Ibid., p. 276.

39 Kogenluft, *Nachrichtenblatt* No. 52, op.cit.

40 Puglisi, op.cit., p. 316.

41 Ltn Moebius collided with Lt Alan W. Morey, MC, of 60 Squadron, RFC, over Becelaere, Belgium; both men were killed [Ref: Franks, Bailey & Duiven, *The Jasta Pilots*, p. 216].

42 Puglisi, op.cit.

CHAPTER SEVEN
THE SPRING OFFENSIVE AND BEYOND

February 1918 was another 'dry' month for Carl Degelow. After three weeks of bad weather, there was a slight break on the 20th, and he was glad to be able to make two flights to the frontlines, even though one was during the morning mist and the other in afternoon rain. The flights were to no avail and Degelow's need to succeed in aerial combat remained unfulfilled, as he returned from both flights without sighting an enemy aeroplane. The time was so uneventful that his British counterparts reported 'no combats took place all day'.[1]

Fokker Triplanes Arrive

Indeed, Jasta 7's biggest event in February took place on the last day of the month, when Staffel-Führer Josef Jacobs flew from the Staffel's airfield at Aertrycke to the 4th Army Air Park at Ghent to trade his disappointing Albatros D.V for a Fokker Dr.I triplane fighter.[2] The pilots speculated – pro and con – about the new triplane, which had been in service since September 1917. In the hands of such skilled pilots as Rittmeister Manfred Freiherr von Richthofen and Leutnant Werner Voss the triplane gained a formidable reputation. Intended to replace the problem-laden Albatros D.V fighter, the Fokker triplane developed problems of its own. An example much discussed among German fighter pilots occurred on 3 February, when Degelow's erstwhile comrade from Flieger-Abteilung (A) 216, Ltn Hans Joachim Wolff, was flying a triplane in which the top wing collapsed. Fortunately for Wolff, by then a member of Jasta 11 in Richthofen's Jagdgeschwader I [Fighter Wing I], he made an emergency landing and saved himself and the aeroplane,[3] which was subsequently examined to determine the cause of the crash.

Adding to the bad situation, the Pfalz D.III was falling out of favour. Until the Fokker D.VII biplane could be made available in Staffel strength, however, further improvements to the Pfalz biplane and Fokker triplane fighters were the best immediate hope for German fighter pilots. These feelings were confirmed by a Pfalz pilot[4] who was captured in February and who admitted to a British interrogator that the 'Pfalz scout is not popular with pilots owing to its lack of speed and bad manoeuvrability; an improved type is expected. Richthofen's squadron is being equipped with a much improved aileron control.'[5]

According to the same captured pilot:

'Fokker triplanes have recently been received and are to take the place of the Albatros scouts; this [development] accounts for the high number of [triplanes then in frontline service] … the normal number being fifteen to sixteen machines [to a Staffel]. The strength of pilots [in a Staffel] is never more than ten to twelve on average, either in [the prisoner's] flight or in the majority of Pursuit flights …'[6]

During Jacobs' return flight from Ghent to Aertrycke, he flew into a hail storm and his engine quit. Fortunately, he was near Harlebeke, where Royal Württemberg Jagdstaffel 47 was based,[7] and made a safe landing.[8] Surely, he had to wonder whether this incident would foreshadow Jasta 7's future experiences with its latest replacement aircraft.

The Albatros and Pfalz fighters his men flew previously were powered by in-line stationary engines, while the Fokker triplane was equipped with a rotary engine; the entire engine spun, which created a gyroscopic effect of which pilots needed to be aware. Problems or not, Jacobs was determined to master the Fokker triplane and instruct his men to do the same.

The next day, after over five months of living on the comfortable grounds of the old château at Aertrycke, the officers and men of Jasta 7 packed up their equipment and began their first move southward in preparation for the German spring offensive. The objective of the 'Kaiserschlacht' [Kaiser's Battle], as it was called, was a massive Western Front assault to enable German land forces 'to separate the British from the French and drive them' to the English Channel.[9] But that action was three weeks away. Meanwhile, on Sunday, 3 March, low clouds and mist[10] covered Jacobs and his men as they made their way by car some twenty kilometres to their new airfield at Rumbeke. Covered with shards of tent fabric to ward off the effects of the weather, the aeroplanes were towed by automobiles and lorries to their new airfield.

The first day at the new 'field was not without incident, according to Jacobs: 'In the evening, I continued to fly my new triplane, but had to make another emergency landing [this time] at Courtemarck. The machine is all right, but it had to be transported back to the Staffel [being towed] by car.'[11]

Even equipped with Fokker triplanes, Jasta 7 was scoreless in March. The Air Force Commanding General's report acknowledged that, on the 6th, Oberflugmeister Schönfelder forced down a British Nieuport within its own lines.[12] His action was not a confirmed victory, but it provided some recognition for the Staffel.

Building on the success of the four-Staffel grouping of Manfred von Richthofen's Jagdgeschwader I, another preparation for the spring offensive called for more fighter units to be deployed as groups. Consequently, on 1 March, Jasta 7 was joined with Jastas 28, 47 and 51 to form Jagdgruppe 6 [Fighter Group 6], abbreviated JaGru 6.[13] Oberleutnant Hans-Eberhardt Gandert, leader of Jasta 51 and the highest ranking officer of the four Staffel-Führers, was appointed commander of the new Jagdgruppe.[14] Individual exploits of earlier days were being put aside to offer air units the strength of greater numbers and unified commands.

Jasta 7's lack of confirmed aerial victories was, very likely, due to the shift in aeroplanes and tactics. Carl Degelow, for example, slowed down and became more cautious in his mode of attack while learning to fly the Fokker triplane. This approach saved him from the embarrassment of his earlier recklessness, but it earned his Staffel-Führer's criticism. Commenting on an encounter on 13 March, Jacobs wrote in his diary: 'The flight spotted a Bristol Fighter north of Ypres, and Lotz, and Degelow went after [it]. Degelow got cold feet and dived away and, meanwhile, Lotz got his crate well plastered.'[15]

Degelow resented the implication that he had abandoned Ltn Paul Lotz, whose aeroplane was raked with machine-gun fire by the Bristol Fighter's rear gunner. Degelow contended that he had attempted to slip beneath the British two-seater when it eluded him. In any event, he said that he and Jacobs discussed the matter back at Rumbeke airfield. As is so often the case when two strong-willed individuals meet, neither really convinced the other of his point of view.

Members of Jasta 7 in front of that Staffel-Führer's Fokker Dr.I triplane. From left: Uffz Peisker, Fwbl Paul Hüttenrauch, Fwbl August Eigenbrodt, Fwbl Sicho, Ltn Willi Nebgen, Ltn Josef Jacobs (wearing his Pour le Mérite at the centre of his collar), Ltn Bannenberg, Uffz Jupp Böhne, Ltn Wirth, Ltn Rath and unidentified.

On 14 March, Jasta 7 changed airfields again, moving only a few kilometres west to Roulers. The short move seemed to have no practical purpose and may have been done to confuse British air units, whose reconnaissance activities intensified as the general feeling was that a massive German push was only days away. Jasta 7 made three flights on 17 March – one in the morning, afternoon and evening – and encountered enemy aircraft during all three missions. Again, however, the Staffel reported no aerial combat successes.

The following day a German two-seater was forced down over British-held territory and its pilot revealed during interrogation[16] that the anticipated offensive would begin on 20 or 21 March. This information caused British air leaders to intensify their efforts as Allied commanders sought to identify when and where the attack would take place. Meanwhile, German commanders prepared troops of their '17th, 2nd and 18th Armies (sixty-three divisions in all) on the forty-three-mile front [from] Arras … [to] La Fère, but its main force was intended to be exerted north of the Somme, and, after breaking through, the 17th and the 2nd Armies were to wheel northwest and oppress the British army against the coast, while the [Somme] River and the 18th Army guarded their flank.'[17]

If General Erich Ludendorff's plans were successful, German 6th and 4th Army forces (the latter including JaGru 6) would be heavily involved in the next phase. Hence, German ground and air units in Flanders awaited the call to arms amidst heavy fog covering most of the front on the morning of Thursday 21 March. The eerie silence was pierced at 4:45 a.m. by the hellish drumbeat of '6,000 cannons and 3,000 mortars'.[18] Barrages were directed at British positions from the most forward areas to zones as far back as twenty miles. The heaviest concentration was directed at the centre of the British line to force a split in the positions held by the British Third and Fifth Armies. The German attack was also very heavy north of Arras, at Ypres and Messines, and against French positions at Reims. But the main thrust was the Somme Front, the scene of some of the bloodiest battles of World War I in 1915 and 1916.

German air units claimed mastery of the air on the offensive's first day,[19] but they had little to show for it: only ten victories and one enemy aircraft forced to land[20] versus nine German air fatalities.[21] The German offensive was considered 'a brilliant tactical success, having achieved an advance of about forty miles in eight days',[22] but it did not succeed in splitting the British force in Flanders or in capturing Paris, an apparent objective of the opening hard push.

On 29 March, Jasta 7 moved further south, this time to an airfield at St. Marguerite, north of Lille. It was the only unit of JaGru 6 to advance at this time and, like other German Jagdstaffeln, remained on the offensive. During the early evening of 11 April, Jacobs scored his thirteenth victory,[23] thereby ending a long dry spell for his Staffel 7. He had a long and winding fight with a two-seater, according to his combat report:

'[Eventually] we had come down to about 200 metres' altitude, and the R.E.8 pilot had given his 'plane full throttle … He would try to side slip or dive each time I opened up with my guns.

'It was evident that the pilot had lost his way by manoeuvring to get out of the way of my guns …

'Because I had only a few cartridges left, I decided to get him with the burst and fired a deflection shot slightly ahead of his nose. He immediately hit the ground and flipped over on his back.[24] I believe that my last burst destroyed his propeller …'[25]

21 April 1918: Victory and Loss

Ten days later, Carl Degelow shot down his first enemy aeroplane since the end of January. At 10:35 a.m. on Sunday, 21 April 1918, Jacobs led a flight out of St. Marguerite airfield. The Jasta 7 aircraft were soon joined by aeroplanes from another JaGru 6[26] unit and, together, they headed southwest toward Armentières. The flight was brief, ending a little over an hour later, but it allowed enough time for the German airmen to spot two flights of hostile single-seat and two-seat aircraft heading west from Armentières at 2,000 metres' altitude. Before any of the German fighters could take action, however, a flight of British fighters caught them by surprise.

Unteroffizier August Eigenbrodt was attacked by a Sopwith Camel and sustained hits in the engine and gas lines. He was forced to land in a ditch near Waasten, close to the road to Comines. Eigenbrodt's attacker, meanwhile, was pursued by Ltn Paul Lotz, who drove his quarry down to ground level behind British lines west of Armentières. As the wild fray continued, with aircraft flying east and west, Jacobs was momentarily distracted from a Camel he was chasing by the sight of Carl Degelow diving after another Camel. Yet another Camel was being hotly pursued by Uffz Paul Hüttenrauch and Oberflgmstr Kurt Schönfelder.[27]

After it was all over, Jacobs was credited with shooting down a Camel, which was credited as his fourteenth victory. Degelow also received confirmation for downing a Camel,[28] thereby marking his third official aerial victory[29] – which, of course, implied that one of his previously unconfirmed claims had been valid, after all.

About an hour and a half after this fight took place in Flanders, what would become one of the most controversial air combats of World War I occurred near Corbie, farther south, on the Somme Sector. Rittmeister Manfred Freiherr von Richthofen, leader of Jagdgeschwader I and Germany's highest scoring ace, was in a fight with Sopwith Camels from 209 Squadron, RAF. In circumstances still disputed, Richthofen received one bullet through the heart and was killed instantly. His aircraft came down behind British lines and his body was buried with full military honours in a French cemetery.

Richthofen's death ended the last vestige of any implied German superiority in the air. If he could be shot down and killed – if even by some fluke – then any German pilot was vulnerable. Moreover, Richthofen provided the German war machine with an important source of propaganda and moral support. No other German ace (or any other World War I pilot, for that matter) equalled his eighty-victory score and no other German ace attained his level of recognition. Richthofen's successes inspired most German fighter pilots of the time and, even in death, he remained a role model for generations to come.

Lessons from the Red Baron

Shortly before his last fight, Manfred von Richthofen completed writing an aerial combat operations manual, which was distributed by the office of the Air Force Commanding General (Kogenluft) on 26 April 1918. The manual became required reading, not only because of Kogenluft's imprimatur, but because recipients understood it contained a distillation of the experiences and views of Germany's highest ranking fighter pilot and developer of its first Jagdgeschwader. Richthofen's legacy to his fellow fighter pilots contained his views on aerial combat operations and covered subjects ranging from individual air combats to deployment of groups of units – such as Jagdgruppe 6 – and to instructing German pilots on ways to attain mastery of the air as a means of assuring more success for German ground units.

In the area of leadership, Richthofen wrote:

'Everyone must show absolute trust in the leader in the air. If this trust is lacking, success is impossible from the outset. The [leader] gains trust by [his] exemplary daring and the conviction that [he] sees everything and shows himself to be up to every situation.

'The Staffel must develop diversity, i.e., not become accustomed to one position or another; rather, each individual must learn to work together… [Thus,] each man recognizes from the movement of the [next] aeroplane what the man at the joystick wants to do, above all, when the leader proceeds to attack or [makes a] tight turn alerting his fellow flyers to an enemy attack from above…

'Within the Staffel, each [pilot] has a special distinguishing emblem on his machine, best [applied] on the rear part of the tail above and below. The leader takes off last, gathers his Kette [flight] at low altitude, [and] makes allowance for the worst [performing] machine. At the approach to the Front he becomes oriented to the overall flight operation, the enemy's and his own. At this time he may never let his Staffel go unobserved. There will always be this one or that one turning off course. They must be guided back by turning and throttling down.

'The flight to the frontlines is no fighter mission; rather, one flies to the frontlines, best up the centre of his sector, and satisfies himself about enemy flight operations. Flying away from the frontlines, he seeks to attain the altitude of his opponents and tries, this time from out of the sun and over the lines, to attack the enemy. Thus, the fighter mission consists of thrusts over the lines and back again. When there is no enemy to be seen over there, then these thrusts over the lines have no purpose.'[30]

In the use of Staffel groupings operating together:

'During a defensive battle, I maintain that it is best that each army group is assigned a Jagdgruppe. This Jagdgruppe is not bound strictly to the army group's sector, but … its main purpose [is] to enable the working aircrews to do their function and, in exceptional cases, to provide them with immediate protection.

'Moreover, the Armee Oberkommando [individual army group command] has at its disposal a large number of Jagdstaffeln, which by all means must be allowed to hunt freely and whose mission throughout is dedicated to [stopping] enemy flight operations. With the help of air defence officers and a large telephone reporting network and radio-telegraphy they will catch the enemy air operations in progress.'[31]

Richthofen's own speciality, of course, was individual aerial combat. He recognised that, while it had become necessary to field larger forces of aeroplanes in the air, to counter ever-growing numbers of enemy aircraft being deployed in 1918, it was essential for individual Jagdflieger [fighter pilots] to know what to do in a variety of situations:

'Every [group] battle breaks up into individual combats. The theme "Air Combat Tactics" can be covered with one sentence and that is: "I approach the enemy until [I am] about fifty metres behind him, take aim at him carefully, [and] then the opponent falls." Those are the words with which Boelcke … [informed] me when I asked about his trick. Now I understand that it is the whole secret to shooting down [another aeroplane].

'One does not need to be an aerobatic artist or a trick shooter; rather, [one has] to have the courage to fly right up to the opponent.

'I make only one distinction between single-seaters and two-seaters. Whether the two-seater is an R.E.8 or a Bristol Fighter, the single-seater an S.E.5 or a Nieuport, it is all the same to me.

'One attacks the two-seater from behind at great speed, in the same direction he is going. The only way to avoid the adroit observer's field of machine-gun fire is to stay calm and put the observer out of action with the first shots. If the opponent goes into a turn, I must be careful not to fly above the enemy aeroplane. A long aerial combat with a completely combat-ready, manoeuvrable two-seater is the most difficult. I fire only when the opponent flies straight ahead or, better yet, when he starts into a turn. But never right from the side or when the aeroplane is tilted on one wing. It is then that I try to harass him by firing warning shots (streaks of phosphorous ammunition). I consider it to be very dangerous to attack a two-seater from the front. In the first place, one seldom encounters the opponent [this way]. One almost never makes him incapable of fighting [this way]. On the contrary, first of all I am within the field of fire of his fixed [forward-firing] machine and then in the observer's [flexible gun's field of fire]. If I squeeze through below the two-seater and then want to make a turn, while in the turn, I offer the observer the best target.

'If one is attacked from the front by a two-seater, that is no reason for one to have to pull away; rather, in the moment when the opponent flies over and away, one can try to make a sudden sharp turn below the enemy aeroplane. If the observer has not been careful, one can pull up and easily shoot down the opponent. But if he has been careful and, while making the sharp turn, one [realises that he] lies well within his field of fire, it is often advisable not to fly further into the observer's range; rather, to turn away and make a new attack.

'Individual combat against a single-seater is by far the easiest. If I am alone with an opponent and on this side [of the lines], I can shoot [him] down … unless I am hampered by a gun jam or an engine defect.

'The simplest thing is to surprise a single-seater from behind, which very often succeeds. Then the main point is to make tighter turns and to stay above the opponent.

'Whether the battle is on this side or the other, with a favourable wind an aerial combat like that will end with the opponent on this side until he is brought down to the ground. Then the opponent must decide whether he wants to land or risk flying straight ahead in order to make it to his own Front. If he does the latter, I sit behind the enemy flying straight ahead and …easily shoot him down.

'If I am attacked by a single-seater from above, I make it a point never to let up on the throttle; rather, to make all turns and dives at full speed. I turn toward the opponent and try by pulling up in each turn to attain the enemy's altitude and get the better of him. At the same time I never let the enemy get at my back. When I get the better of him, then the course of the battle is as it was during the first one. One can attack a single-seater calmly from the front. In spite of that, I believe that shooting down from in front, even a single-seater, is rare, as the moment in which one is at the right distance for combat is only a fraction of a second.'[32]

Degelow's Fourth Aerial Victory

Degelow carefully considered Richthofen's advice and – aside from the comment about shooting at the airmen, rather than the aeroplanes – obviously took it to heart. In the coming months, his own skills showed improvement and his victory score rose accordingly.

Additionally, the spirits of German fighter pilots rose with rumours (that turned out to be true) that the Fokker triplane's replacement – the Fokker D.VII – was being prepared for Staffel service in May.[33] The top-scoring units would receive them first, but eventually Fokker D.VIIs would be distributed among all Western Front units.[34] Also that month, Staffel-Führer Jacobs was temporarily detached from his duties to work with the commanding officers of two other units – Jastas 40 and 49 – to help bring them up to a more suitable level of proficiency. Both units had enjoyed only moderate success. Jasta 40, for example, had logged three aerial victories during nine months at the Front. Jacobs was unhappy about the assignment,[35] since he preferred to remain in action at the Front, but he also recognised the need to provide seasoned instruction to newcomers who would eventually fly with JaGru 6.

Still flying Fokker triplanes and Pfalz D.IIIs, Jasta 7 made good gains in May: two more victories – captive observation balloons this time – for Jacobs on the 14th, and a balloon for Uffz Max Mertens the same day. Two days later, when Jacobs' guns jammed in a fight, Carl Degelow moved in and claimed an R.E.8 two-seat reconnaissance aeroplane brought down over Vlamertinghe within German lines; he duly received confirmation for his fourth victory.[36] Once again, however, the validity of such claims must be examined. In this case, there is some question as to whether Degelow shot down this aeroplane or only

The eighth iteration in the Royal Aircraft Factory's series of 'Reconnaissance Experimental' aeroplanes, the R.E.8 was an important artillery-spotting and photo-reconnaissance machine. Over 4,000 examples were produced and they performed most of their work in the last eighteen months of World War I. Two of Carl Degelow's thirty aerial victories were against R.E.8s.

disabled it. British records show only one R.E.8 'incident' for this day: an aeroplane from 7 Squadron, RAF, in which one crewman, 2/Lt R.C. Mais, was reported as wounded in action.[37] The putative crash site at Vlamertinghe is less than fifteen kilometres due east of 7 Squadron's aerodrome at Droglandt.[38] Even swooping low over the ground, the R.E.8's pilot could have made it back to his own lines, if not to his aerodrome.

Carl Degelow was transferred to Jagdstaffel 40 on 17 May and, as he noted:

> 'Although we were reluctant to admit it at first, from that point on, Germany was losing the war. The rate of attrition among German combat pilots rose steadily. To keep the frontline air units up to a reasonable level of success, only men with proven combat records were given positions of command. Amongst the Jagdstaffeln this meant that almost any pilot who shot down five enemy aircraft could count on becoming either the commanding officer or at least the second in command of a frontline Staffel. Many non-commissioned officers were promoted to commissioned status (in the Reserves, not the Regular Army) when their victory scores were impressive enough. Experience had shown that tenacity in the air was a better quality of leadership than formal education and "class" background. As there were ultimately eighty-one German Jagdstaffeln, the need for such an expedient was obvious.

> 'My own career as a fighter pilot had made good progress in Jasta 7 under Jacobs' tutelage. When my victory score approached the "magic" number of five, I was informed that I would most likely receive my own command. Hence, in mid-May I was transferred to Jasta 40 to be second in command under Ltn.d.Res Helmuth Dilthey, a six-victory ace from Jasta 21. Jasta 40 was then based at a small airfield outside the town of Mouscron, which was also used by Jasta 7. Indeed, the two Staffeln often flew together during joint operations.'

By the time Degelow reported to Jasta 40 – a walk across the airfield – the war had taken several dramatic turns. Certainly, one of these was the arrival in France of fresh and well-supplied American troops. They were accompanied by pilots and observers, who were subsequently equipped with some of the best of the British and French aircraft. Finally, Germany's position on the Western Front was weakened by the eventual failure of the German offensive to divide British and French forces.

Jagdstaffel 40 Background

Degelow's new unit was formed nearly a year earlier. The German War Ministry had authorised the formation of a second large group of Jagdstaffeln on 26 June 1917[39] and the first of that number, Royal Saxon Jagdstaffel 40, was established at Flieger-Ersatz-Abteilung 6 in Grossenhain four days later.[40] The new Staffel was organised by an aviation service veteran, Oberleutnant Arthur Schreiber, who left Hessian Fuss-Artillerie-Regiment Nr. 3 in November 1913 to join the Fliegertruppe and initially trained as aviation observer at FEA 3 in Darmstadt. Later posted to Flieger-Abteilung (A) 205, he was shot down and wounded near Verdun on 22 July 1916.[41] After recuperating from his wounds, Schreiber was posted as Adjutant to FEA 7 in Braunschweig. Then he was transferred to Grossenhain to become *Offizier zur besonderen Verwendung* [officer seconded for special assignment] of Jasta 40.

Ltn.d.Res Helmuth Dilthey in the green-and-white-striped Albatros D.V he brought with him from Jagdstaffel 27 when he was appointed commanding officer of Jasta 40.

After several weeks of preparation, Jasta 40 deployed to the Western Front on 15 August 1917. To avoid drawing attention to its trucks and personnel, the Staffel entourage was despatched by diverse routes through Germany and rendezvoused at the main train station in Metz, a former French fortress city then in German hands. While Oblt Schreiber handled transportation arrangements, Staffel-Führer Eilers was already at Metz, where he arranged for billeting and preparation of an airfield near the village of Montey, east of Metz. Meanwhile, at Armee Flugpark C, a nearby aviation supply depot, the Staffel's motor vehicles and aircraft, mostly single-seat fighter biplanes – Halberstadt D.II, L.F.G Roland D.II and Fokker D.IV types – stood ready. By the end of the month, Oblt Eilers reported the unit's battle readiness to the area army aviation command centre.

Jasta 40 was assigned to patrol the Southern Front from Ronnvaux to Hennement and Cambrai to Noncourt, as well as the Woëvre plain in northeastern France. That behind-the-lines region was a 'quiet' area, but mishaps still occurred and, on 8 September 1917, the Staffel suffered its first casualty when twenty-four-year-old Ltn.d.Res Wilhelm Neumann was killed during a training flight over Montey. Later that same day Jasta 40 moved to a new airfield at Mars La Tour, site of a famous battle during the Franco-Prussian War of 1870-1871. The new airfield was closer to the Front and from that location Jasta 40 launched the patrol during which the Staffel's first aerial victory was scored. On 30 October 1917, Ltn Alfred King[42] shot down a French-built Nieuport 27 over Savonières.[43] It was King's second victory, but the only one credited to Jasta 40 in 1917.

Oberleutnant Arthur Schreiber, an early member of the German Fliegertruppe, organised Jagdstaffel 40 and led it to its first combat operational site. He remained with the unit for a time as its officer seconded for special assignment, his assignment being to serve as adjutant.

The year 1918 began with uncertainty. On 21 January, an otherwise fruitless encounter with a large enemy formation over Longuyon resulted in the death of Ltn Gunther Gellenthin[44] at age twenty-one. That score was evened by Ltn King, who was credited with shooting down a Spad over Pont à Mousson on 11 February.[45]

Following a change of airfields on 15 March, during which Jasta 40 left the Armee-Abteilung C Sector to become a unit of the German 17th Army, the Staffel's third victory was recorded. Once again, Ltn King received credit, on this occasion for shooting down an Airco D.H.9 two-seat bomber between Dickebusch and Reninghelst on the afternoon of 25 April. The crew of Lieutenants C.J. Gillan[46] and W. Duce[47] of 98 Squadron, RAF, were taken prisoner. But that fight also ended King's blossoming career with Jasta 40, as he was hit by phosphorous bullets (so-called tracer rounds) and severely wounded. Combined with complications from earlier wounds, his condition was enough effectively to keep him away from the frontlines for the rest of the war.

Most of the members of Jasta 40

Ltn.d.Res Alfred King scored Jasta 40's first aerial victory. For this formal view, he wore all of his awards (from left): Iron Cross Second Class, Württemberg's Knight's Cross of the Military Merit Order and Saxony's Knight's Cross Second Class of the Albert Order. Below his medals bar is the Iron Cross First Class and further below the Wound Badge in Gold (signifying five or more combat-related injuries) and the Military Pilot's Badge. King's early wounds left him unfit for infantry service, which led him to transfer to the Luftstreitkräfte in April 1916.

were in their early twenties and hardened beyond their years by wartime experiences and hardships. But these 'old veterans' must have been surprised on 22 April 1918 when a very youthful looking Regular Army Leutnant reported for duty. Young in years, nineteen-year-old Hans Jeschonnek[48] had as much combat experience as anyone else in the unit. Educated in the Prussian cadet system, he applied for active duty aged just fifteen. Jeschonnek gained his Leutnant's shoulder boards[49] within the year and, by age seventeen, he was in charge of a machine-gun company. In the summer of 1917, he followed the example of his older brother, Kurt,[50] and transferred to the Luftstreitkräfte. Upon completion of training at Jagdstaffelschule I in Valenciennes, Hans Jeschonnek was posted to Jasta 40, where he would meet Carl Degelow, under whose tutelage he would become a successful combat pilot.

The factory-fresh French-built Nieuport 27 seen here was an example of the Royal Flying Corps' last V-strut biplane fighter. Assigned only to 1 and 29 Squadrons, RFC in 1917, the Nieuport 27 was later used as a fighter trainer by the US Air Service.

1   Royal Flying Corps, *Communiqué No. 128*, 27 February 1918, p. 2.

2   Puglisi, 'Jacobs of Jasta 7' in *Cross & Cockade Journal*, Vol. VI, p. 319.

3   Bodenschatz, *Jagd in Flanderns Himmel*, p. 168.

4   Most likely Uffz Hegeler of Jasta 15, who was captured on 26 February 1918 after being forced to land in Pfalz D.III 4184/17; his aircraft was assigned the British captured aircraft number G.141 [Ref: Puglisi, 'German Aircraft Down in British Lines' in *Cross & Cockade Journal*, Vol. X, p. 162].

5   RFC, *Summary of Air Intelligence No. 17*, 1 March 1918, p. 1.

6   Ibid., *Summary No. 18*, 2 March 1918, p. 1.

7   Franks, Bailey & Duiven, *The Jasta Pilots*, p. 59.

8   Puglisi, 'Jacobs', op.cit.

9   Esposito, *A Concise History of World War I*, p. 108.

10 RFC, *Communiqué No. 129*, 6 March 1918, p. 3.

11 Puglisi, op.cit.

12 Kogenluft, *Nachrichtenblatt der Luftstreitkräfte*, Vol. II, No. 16, 13 June 1918, p. 233.

13 Puglisi, op.cit.

14 Hildebrand, *Die Generale der deutschen Luftwaffe 1935-1945*, Vol. I, p. 346.

15 Puglisi, op.cit.

16 Jones, *The War in the Air*, Vol. IV, p. 269.

17 Liddell Hart, B. *The Real War 1914-1918*, p. 370.

18 Esposito, op.cit., p. 108.

19 Kogenluft, *Nachrichtenblatt*, No. 5, 28 March 1918, p. 57.

20 Kogenluft, *Nachrichtenblatt*, No. 17, 20 June 1918, p. 250.

21 Franks, Bailey & Duiven, *Casualties of the German Air Service 1914-1918*, p. 255.

22 Esposito, op.cit., p. 110.

23 Kogenluft, *Nachrichtenblatt*, No. 19, 4 July 1918, p. 280.

24 Henshaw, *The Sky Their Battlefield*, p. 309 identifies the crew as Capt Thomas B. Jones, aged twenty-six, and Lt Vernon King, thirty-one, of 16 Squadron, RAF in R.E.8 B.6522; both men were killed [Ref: Hobson, *Airmen Died in the Great War 1914-1918*, pp. 157, 159].

25 Quoted in Puglisi, op.cit., p. 321.

26 Most likely Jagdstaffel 51, then based on Iseghem, but about to join Jasta 7 at St. Marguerite [Ref: *The Jasta Pilots*, op.cit., p. 62.

27 Puglisi, op.cit., pp. 321-322.

28 Henshaw, op.cit., p. 314 identifies Lt Robert J. Marion, nineteen, of 54 Squadron, RAF in Sopwith Camel 1F.1 B.9315 as perishing in a fight over Estaires, some ten kilometres from Armentières, which would have put him well within Degelow's operational range at that time of day [Ref: Hobson, op.cit., p. 167].

29 Kogenluft, *Nachrichtenblatt*, No. 19, 4 July 1918, p. 281.

30 Kogenluft, *Richthofen-Bericht*, p. 8.

31 Ibid., p. 14.

32 Ibid., pp. 12-13.

33 Grosz, *Fokker D.VII Windsock Datafile 9*, p. 5.

34 Ibid.

35 Puglisi, op.cit., p. 322.

36 Kogenluft, *Nachrichtenblatt*, No. 22, 25 July 1918, p. 329.

37 Henshaw, op.cit., p. 325.

38 At the time the most recent aerodrome of 7 Squadron, RAF [Ref: Royal Air Force, *War Diary* entry, 23 April 1918, p. 2].

39 Neumann, *Die deutschen Luftstreitkräfte im Weltkriege*, p. 68.

40 Kriegsministerium (organisational manual), *Teil 10 Abschnitt B, Flieger-Formationen*, pp.238-239.

41 Supf, *Das Buch der deutschen Fluggeschichte*, Vol. II, p. 482.

42 Alfred Karl Theodor King was born on 20 May 1897 in Stuttgart. He was a Fahnenjunker [officer cadet] with Royal Württemberg Infanterie-Regiment Nr. 125 when the war began. He was promoted to Fähnrich [army ensign] on 26 March 1915 and to Leutnant on 2 August. During combat in Serbia, King was severely wounded on 19 October 1915. Following lengthy hospitalisation, King transferred to the Fliegertruppe and, on 25 April 1916, reported to FEA 2 in Schneidemühl for pilot training. Assigned to Kampfgeschwader 5 on 29 August, he completed qualifications for his pilot's badge on 5 October 1916. King scored his first confirmed aerial victory on 2 November 1916 and received his *Ehrenbecher dem Sieger im Luftkampf* [Honour Goblet for the Victor in Aerial Combat] the following day. Within a week of his victory, he was assigned to Kampfstaffel 28 and then, on 4 April 1917 to Flieger-Abteilung (A) 279. On 23 April he reported to Jagdstaffelschule I in Valenciennes and on 11 May to Jasta 20. With no further air combat successes and wracked by physical problems, he was transferred to the home defence unit Kesta 4a on 28 July 1917. On 13 September he was transferred to Jasta 40 and scored his second victory on 30 October 1917, his third on 11 February 1918 and his fourth and final victory on 25 April. Following hospitalisation, King was transferred to FEA 1 at Altenburg and then to FEA 10 at Böblingen. He was promoted to Oberleutnant on 5 July 1920 and was killed in a civilian air crash on 4 February 1931 [Ref: Personal-Bogen].

43 RFC, *War Diary* entry reported the loss/death of 2/Lt Eric D. Scott, nineteen, of 1 Squadron, RFC, a unit in the vicinity equipped with Nieuport 27 scout (fighter) aircraft [Ref: Hobson, *Airmen Died in the Great War 1914-1918*, p. 91].

44 RFC, *War Diary* entry reported: 'Enemy aircraft activity was slight all day, a few indecisive combats taking place' and no RFC victory claims were filed. Similarly, the French *Résume des Operations Aériennes* for 21 January recorded no French victory claims along the entire Western Front, leaving unclear the circumstances of Ltn Gellenthin's death.

45 No RFC or French casualties are listed in official records for this date.

46 Lt Charles John Gillan was born in 1897 in Lambton, Québec, Canada. He was commissioned T/2Lt RFC 22 September 1917, joined 42 Squadron, RFC 12 March 1918, then transferred to 98 Squadron, RAF, captured 25 April 1918, promoted Lt 26 April 1918, repatriated 1 December 1918 [Ref: National Archives file WO 339/129960].

47 Hon. Lt William Duce was born in India (?). He served in the Indian Army 12 October 1912 - 4 July 1915, transferred Artists Rifles 16 August 1915 - 6 January 1916, then 7 January 1916 20 Bn. London Regiment, was promoted 2/Lt (T.F.) Observer Officer, promoted Lt 30 December 1917, assigned to 98 Squadron RFC, promoted Hon. Lt 24 April 1918, captured 25 April 1918, repatriated 1 December 1918 [Ref: National Archives file WO 374/20898].

48 Hans Jeschonnek was born on 9 April 1899 in Hohensalza in the Prussian province of Posen. He was accepted as a Fähnrich in the 3. Niederschlesisches [Lower Silesian] Infanterie-Regiment Nr. 50 on 10 August 1914 and rose to *Leutnant ohne Patent* [Second Lieutenant without a commission] almost seven weeks later, on 26 September. He served with the infantry until 19 July 1917, when he was posted to the German 3rd Army Air Park. After receiving basic aviation training at schools in Braunschweig and Travemünde, Jeschonnek was trained as a pilot at the flight school in Schwerin and, after completing his qualifications, on 9 April 1918 was transferred to the 18th Army Air Park. After a short time – 13 to 21 April – at Jagdfliegerschule I in Valenciennes, on 22 April, Jeschonnek reported for duty to Jasta 40, where he remained for the rest of the war. He remained in German military service through the 1920s and 1930s and, once World War II began, he advanced quickly in rank. On 1 March 1942, he was advanced to Generaloberst [Colonel-General] at age forty-two. Hans Jeschonnek served as Chief of Staff of the Luftwaffe from 1 February 1939 until 19 August 1943, when he committed suicide at the Führer-Headquarters in Rastenburg, East Prussia [Ref: Hildebrand, *Die Generale der deutschen Luftwaffe 1935-1945*, Vol. I, pp. 138-139].

49 Deutscher Offizier-Bund, *Ehren-Rangliste des ehemaligen Deutschen Heeres*, p. 207.

50 Ibid., p. 571.

CHAPTER EIGHT
COMMAND IN THE AIR

By the time Carl Degelow arrived at Jagdstaffel 40, the new commanding officer, Leutnant der Reserve Helmuth Dilthey[1] had scored his first (and only) victory with the unit on 5 June – thus bringing the Staffel's total score after ten months in service to four enemy aircraft downed. A victory claimed by Ltn.d.Res Hermann Gilly on 24 May was not officially confirmed.

As Degelow recalled:

> 'There were, of course, the usual rumblings from the Army Group Command, wondering when our Staffel's performance would improve. We could not convince these fellows that our opponents did not simply come along like ducks in a row and wait for us to pop them off, one by one. Indeed, although I joined Jasta 40 in May, I did not attain my first victory with the unit until 18 June.'

Given the choice of aeroplanes available at the time, Degelow selected a Pfalz D.IIIa, a type he had flown in Jasta 7. He had his White Stag personal battle emblem painted on a black fuselage and, to distinguish it from his earlier 'plane, Degelow had the entire tail section of the newer Pfalz painted white. Unlike many of his peers, Degelow did not feel comfortable flying the Fokker Dr.I triplane when it replaced his Albatros biplane. He noted:

> 'The Pfalz was somewhat underpowered and did not climb as well as the Albatros, but I felt it was a safer aeroplane. For some time the Albatros D.Va had a structural problem with the lower wing spar, which had a tendency to break under stress, causing the bottom wing to part company with the rest of the aeroplane. The defect was eventually corrected by encasing the spar in a metal sleeve, but pilots were instructed to avoid going into a very stressful dive, which was one of the best ways to save our own hides when we were on the losing end of an aerial combat. Suffice to say, this information did little to instil confidence in the Albatros fighter 'planes. So, I took the second-rate Pfalz and, having learned its limitations, made the best of it.'

Dilthey proved to be more than a good instructor; he became Degelow's new mentor. Having flown since 1914, Dilthey had experience in a variety of single- and two-seat aircraft and was well disciplined and incredibly brave. While serving under Oberleutnant Hermann Göring in Jasta 27 a year earlier, Dilthey often engaged Royal Naval Air Service

Sopwith Triplane fighters in air combat. He acknowledged that the RNAS three-winged fighter was faster and had better climbing ability than his Albatros D.V but, by his actions, he showed that he would have questioned the Royal Air Force historian's contention: 'The sight of a Sopwith Triplane formation, in particular, induced … enemy pilots to dive out of range.'[2]

Dilthey Fearless in Battle

Helmuth Dilthey did not feel such fear, as seen in his description of a July 1917 encounter with a Sopwith Triplane fighter:

> 'I set myself behind him and, when I had him in my gun-sight, I pushed the firing button, but not a shot came out. Nonetheless, I remained behind the Triplane and tried again and again to force him down, whereby he went into steep dives to try to get away from me. He also tried suddenly to pull up to get up and behind me. But he was not able to do this, despite his greater climbing ability, because I paid close attention even as I tried to clear my jammed gun. Then in the blink of an eye he slipped below me and I lost sight of him.
>
> 'But in that moment I saw that he was already above me and firing away to knock me down. I tried to get away from him by going into a steep upward spiral in an attempt to climb above him. Of course, at first this manoeuvre did not work, but then another aeroplane of my Staffel appeared and engaged the Triplane for a while … From 5,000 metres I was now down to only a few hundred metres … and I noticed I could no longer fire my gun, so I gave my machine the gas and flew home …'[3]

While commanding Jasta 40, Dilthey demonstrated the same coolness under fire on the evening of 5 June 1918, when he and Ltn.d.Res Hermann Gilly targeted British observation balloons raised above Poperinghe, just west of Ypres. Tethered by steel cables, the balloons rode high in the sky so their observers, in wicker baskets beneath the hydrogen-filled 'envelopes' could use telescopes to spot their opponents' artillery and other emplacements. With telephones linked to their own gun batteries, the observers directed – and corrected the range of – the batteries' guns. The balloons seemed quite vulnerable in the air, but due to the importance of their mission, they were ringed by anti-aircraft guns that often put up a murderous 'cone' of protective fire to fend off enemy fighter aeroplanes.

Despite those dangers, Dilthey approached one balloon with the setting sun at his back and shot it down at 8:50 p.m. As the flyers encountered no anti-aircraft fire at this time, Gilly remained vigilant for enemy fighters. After Dilthey's balloon went up in flames, Gilly went after the second one in the same manner as his leader,[4] while Dilthey covered him.[5] In addition to receiving official credit for his first aerial victory,[6] Gilly was awarded the Iron Cross First Class on 25 June.[7]

Six days later, on 11 June, the teenage pilot Ltn Hans Jeschonnek proved himself by shooting down an R.E.8 over Vlamertinghe. Recorded as his first victory, it was confirmed in the Air Force Commanding General's listing.[8]

The next Jasta 40 aerial victory was Degelow's. On the morning of 18 June, his flight engaged a number of S.E.5 fighters over Vieux Berquin, in a hotly-contested area about fifteen kilometres west of Armentières. Amidst heavy ground fire in all directions, Degelow took a chance and slipped in behind one of the British fighters; he shot it down and watched it crash in no-man's land. Witnesses corroborated his claim. However, the pilot of S.E.5a C.8870, Lt R.G. Pierce of 29 Squadron, RAF, managed to get clear of his wrecked 'plane near Vieux Berquin and make it back to his own lines. He contended that he had been brought down by German anti-aircraft fire.[9] In any event, Degelow was credited with his fifth aerial victory.[10]

The Sopwith Aviation Company of Kingston-on-Thames provided initial examples of its revolutionary triplane design to Royal Naval Air Service squadrons and then to the Royal Flying Corps. The success of the Sopwith Triplane led to several German attempts to copy the design and the most successful was the Fokker Dr.I triplane.

The Fokker D.VII comes on the Scene

When Carl Degelow arrived at Jasta 40, the Staffel was still equipped with Albatros D.Va and Pfalz D.IIIa aircraft. Both were quite different from the Fokker Dr.I triplanes that he had flown in Jasta 7, as they were biplanes powered by stationary in-line engines, rather than with rotary engines as with the triplanes. At Jasta 40, however, he was pleasantly surprised to receive the vastly superior Fokker D.VII biplane. He described the evolution of the Staffel's equipment:

'A soldier never failed to receive a new steel helmet or a new uniform, when the quartermaster deemed it necessary. The soldier received his new equipment without ever knowing – or even asking – why it was issued. So, too, the pilot flew his missions

The Royal Aircraft Factory's S.E.5a became one of the best fighter aircraft of World War I. It was superior to Albatros and Pfalz fighters, as well as Fokker Dr.I triplanes, and performed well against Fokker D.VII biplanes. Even though Carl Degelow shot down nine S.E.5s, he also had some hair-raising experiences while in combat with this rugged fighter.

in whatever type of aircraft was assigned to his unit, until such time as the gentlemen "upstairs" decided he should receive a different or, hopefully, newer and better type of aircraft.

'A month or so passed in my service with Jasta 40 and, failing to take due note of the passage of time and the advances being made in aviation technology, I had neglected to requisition a new "crate". Therefore, I was surprised when I was summoned to the nearby aircraft depot to receive not only a new aeroplane, but the very latest type of German fighter: the celebrated Fokker D.VII biplane.

'I believe that the Fokker D.VII was the best German fighter aeroplane developed during World War I. Unlike the wooden-frame aircraft produced by most other manufacturers, the Fokker D.VII employed a welded tubular steel frame that enabled it to take much more stress than most other aircraft of the period. Its six-cylinder 180-horsepower Mercedes engine provided the power and speed required of a good, hard-hitting fighter aircraft.

'I could sing endless praises of the Fokker D.VII, but, instead, I will simply point out how impressed the victorious Allied powers were by this aeroplane. Under the terms of the armistice agreement, the Fokker D.VII was the only aeroplane specifically mentioned by type to be forbidden to Germany. A wide range of other aircraft were allowed – including some of the big two-engined bombers, which in the post-war period became the predecessors of modern airliners – but not the Fokker D.VII.

Americans, Belgians, British, Canadians, French and Italians all took D.VIIs to their own countries to test-fly them and thereby derive points to incorporate into their own new aeroplanes. But they definitely did not want Germany to have any of them.

'In the mid-1960s, I visited the Deutsches Museum in Munich, and was very pleasantly surprised to see a Fokker D.VII on display. A colleague of mine reminded me of the dictate of 1919 and I pointed out that the machine on display in this fine museum carried no machine guns, had no fuel in the tank and was no doubt generally inoperable – thus being in the only condition acceptable to the victors of World War I.

'In any event, on the fine summer day of 25 June 1918, I brought my new Fokker D.VII back to our airfield [then at Lomme, at the western edge of Lille] and had it thoroughly checked by our mechanics. Once it was approved by them and ammunition was loaded into the twin machine guns, I decided to take the Fokker up for a test flight. I had no intention of extending the flight to the Front, especially since it did not take long to notice a slight leak in the radiator. But the lovely weather tempted me to continue this maiden flight. So, at 5,000 metres altitude I steered toward Ypres, where, on the enemy side of the lines, I saw a dozen Sopwith single-seaters, gathered like a swarm of dragonflies playing in the fading hours of daylight.

'From our side of the frontlines a flight of Fokkers approached and placed itself right on a point we laughingly referred to as the "meeting place of the world's gentry", over Houthulst Forest, near Ypres or a bit southward. As I was about 1,000 metres higher than the two flights which had joined the battle, I could oversee the fighting and observe the outcome of the engagement.

'The British were soon forced to their own side of the front and only one brave pilot of this swarm tried again and again to take on the German single-seaters that were chasing his friends. The fellow flew very skilfully and smartly and, in so doing, got himself into a very advantageous position behind one of the Fokkers. This seemed to be the proper time for me to give up my spectator's role. Diving steeply, I came down on the back of the daring Tommy and, with the first burst of fire from my machine guns, I set fire to him. Turning over and over, he crashed into the shell-holed Flemish terrain.

'The victory was confirmed as Jasta 40's eighth and my sixth.'[11]

Degelow's likely victim was Lt O.J.F. Jones-Lloyd[12] of 54 Squadron, RAF, who came down in a Sopwith Camel at about 8:25 p.m. (German time) near Zandvoorde, some forty kilometres north of Ypres. Apparently, prevailing winds carried his and Degelow's aeroplane fairly far afield. In any event, nineteen-year-old Jones-Lloyd came down uninjured and was taken prisoner. The earlier portion of the fight, over Ypres, was described by one of Jones-Lloyd's squadron-mates, Captain R.A. James, who wrote in his combat report:

'During an offensive patrol Fokker Biplanes and Triplanes were observed among the clouds and were attacked by four Camels. [A] general engagement ensued, towards the end of which Capt R.A. James fired on one [Enemy Aircraft] and fired a good burst at [another] E.A. at about 100 yards range. E.A. started going down vertically, but the result was not observed owing to proximity of other E.A.'[13]

James' report was amended by his commanding officer, the nine-victory ace[14] Major Reginald S. Maxwell, MC, who wrote: 'This [enemy] machine was reported by A.A. [anti-aircraft unit] as having burst into flames.' No German sources reported fighter casualties in the Flanders Sector for that day, which again raises the issue of accurate reporting of aerial combats and their conclusions. Having studied literally thousands of American, British, French and German combat reports, this writer concludes that definitive answers are less common than the 'absolutes' ascribed to the majority of aerial victory claims on all sides in World War I.

Occasionally mistaken for its predecessor, the 1F.1 Camel, the Sopwith 5F.1 Dolphin was also a small, tough, versatile fighter. It appeared later in the war and was encountered by Jasta 40, which claimed to have shot down two of them. The Sopwith Dophin seen here was from a batch of 500 aeroplanes (serial numbered E.4629 – E.5182) built by Sopwith.

Hermann Gilly led the scoring in Jasta 40's next fight, on the morning of 26 June. The Staffel's airfield was just minutes away from Armentières. When German forward air observers noticed British fighters heading for that town, several Staffeln responded to the call and Degelow led Jasta 40's flight against the attackers. In fact, three British flights had converged on the area, and Gilly was in a position to go after the advance flight of new Sopwith 5F.1 Dolphin biplane fighters. Equipped with a more powerful stationary engine than 'its stumpy little predecessor',[15] the rotary-engined Sopwith 1F.1 Camel, the Dolphin was a rugged and worthy adversary in any fight. But Gilly managed to out-manoeuvre his adversary and at 9:30 a.m. sent him down. Two Dolphins went down over Armentières at this time and it is uncertain which one[16] was Gilly's victim.

Gefr Eduard Hellwig was twenty-four years old when he arrived at Jasta 40 in the early summer of 1918. He was wounded in aerial combat on 27 June and died on 7 July. Native of Grebendorf, Hesse he was buried in a small churchyard outside Lille.

German records show only one loss in the 27 June fight. Jasta 40's Gefreiter Eduard Hellwig,[17] was severely wounded in a Pfalz D.IIIa and came down near Ploegsteert, east of Bailleul. Two Dolphin pilots of 79 Squadron, RAF claimed to have shot down a Pfalz, but each was at a different altitude, which serves as further proof of how multiple claims were made for the same downed aircraft.

Lt Vernon G. Snyder, flying at 14,000 feet at the beginning of the fight, wrote:

> 'While on Offensive Patrol we met fifteen [Enemy Aircraft] west of Armentières. I dived on one and opened fire. I observed smoke issuing from the fuselage of this E.A. The E.A. then burst into flames and I followed him down to 3,000 feet. I fired about 100 rounds. Capt [H.P.] Rushforth observed this machine to burst into flames and crash.'[18]

Lt H.L. MacDonald, flying at 11,000 feet, wrote:

> 'I fired about 125 rounds into one Pfalz Scout from about fifty feet. At the time he was on the tail of one of our machines. He went down in a right hand side-slip with his engine on fire and his guns blazing. He crashed about half a mile from Neuve Eglise [east of Bailleul]. This E.A. was seen going down by Lt Lang.'[19]

Five minutes later, as the fight drifted westward, Vizefeldwebel Rausch shot down a Sopwith Camel near Bailleul. And, at 9:40 a.m., Carl Degelow despatched an S.E.5 fighter over Le Leuthe, just outside Bailleul. His opponent was most likely Lt F.R. Brand,[20] of 29 Squadron, RAF, who was reported to have left his aerodrome at 8:00 a.m. (British time) and was 'last seen southeast of Bailleul at 8:45 a.m. going down in a *vol plane* [French for 'glide']'.[21]

Jasta 40's good news about this air battle was that Degelow was credited with his seventh victory, Gilly his second and Rausch his first.[22] The bad news was that Gefr Eduard Hellwig was so severely wounded – having flown through a hailstorm of over 200 bullets – he died on 7 July.

Carl Degelow's score now equalled that of his Staffel-Führer and on 2 July, he surpassed him. While leading an early morning patrol east of his usual hunting ground, he spotted a group of enemy aircraft and went after them, with his men following. Degelow got behind an S.E.5 of 29 Squadron, RAF, and sent it crashing down near Kruistraat, thereby scoring his eighth victory.[24] Although the pilot[25] came down well within German-held territory, he was listed in the squadron's daily reports as having been 'shot through [the] head and killed'.[26]

A Famous Flyer Joins Jasta 40

The other big event of 2 July 1918 was the arrival of a member of Jasta 40 whose fame preceded him, Ltn.d.Res Willy Rosenstein.[27] A pre-war student of flight pioneer Edmund Rumpler's flying school at Johannisthal, near Berlin, Rosenstein became associated with early military aviation. After qualifying for Deutsche Luftfahrer Verband (DLV) private pilot's licence 170 on 14 March 1912,[28] he was hired by Dr. Rumpler to teach small groups of military officers how to fly and he joined them in such prestigious events as the national competition in Berlin in 1912.[29] 'Of all of us, Willy was one of the few really professional pilots,' Carl Degelow wrote.

Rosenstein was a highly capable, tough, experienced pilot. Despite wounds received flying over Verdun in April 1916, he continued to fly regularly while convalescing. He flew with the early single-seat fighter Fokkerstaffel attached to the German 3rd Army and went on to serve with Jastas 9 and 27. While with the latter unit, he scored the first of his nine confirmed aerial victories on 21 September 1917.[30] But, while serving with Jasta 27, commanded by Oblt Hermann Göring, he felt the sting of what would become that Staffel-Führer's notorious anti-Semitism. Rosenstein later wrote:

> 'I had a personal quarrel with Göring, caused by an anti-Semitic remark [he made] in front of all comrades in the Officers' Mess at Iseghem, Flanders. I had been compelled to demand its retraction. These circumstances caused me to apply for… transfer to a Home Defence unit, which was granted after a short time …'[31]
>
> Göring covered his tracks by giving Rosenstein a favourable recommendation on the transfer form: 'Ltn.d.Res Rosenstein … has won the confidence of his Staffel-Führer due to his aggressiveness in air combat and the affection of his Staffel-mates because of his fine comradeship …'[32]

Willy Rosenstein was well rid of the acid-tongued Hermann Göring and was back in a frontline unit, where he found a much friendlier environment. Given a better opportunity to prove himself, he ultimately became Carl Degelow's second-in-command. At that point, the Staffel needed experienced pilots such as Rosenstein to raise the unit's victory score, which was considered a direct reflection on its leadership.

Degelow recalled the problem that faced Jasta 40 at the time of Rosenstein's arrival:

> 'Dilthey and I led many flights over the lines, but often we came back empty handed. Indeed, his dedication to his work led to his own demise. We were attacking a formation of D.H.9s heading for the Lille railway station on 9 July when our own anti-aircraft batteries opened up and, instead of hitting the British aircraft, struck a mortal blow at Dilthey. His machine immediately caught fire and fell to the ground.'

A British report noted that a flight of Airco D.H.9s of 107 Squadron, RAF dropped eighteen 112-lb bombs on the Fives Railway Station in Lille. It further stated: 'While machines of 107 Squadron were releasing their bombs in formation, three hostile machines attacked them in the rear. 2/Lt J.R. Brown and Aviation Mechanic J.P. Hazell fired forty rounds at one of the enemy aircraft, which burst into flames.'[33]

Degelow Takes Command

Brown and Hazell almost certainly were firing at Dilthey's aeroplane when it was hit by anti-aircraft fire and exploded. The fight's implications for Degelow were obvious:

> 'Dilthey's death meant that I was now in command of Jasta 40. In view of the Staffel members' varying experiences and overall lack of success, I was convinced that the unit

Ltn.d.Res Willy Rosenstein in the cockpit of an Albatros D.III he flew while assigned to Jagdstaffel 27.

needed more training.

'Consequently, I instituted a rigorous flying schedule. In addition to our daily missions over the lines, we spent considerable time flying safely behind the lines, where we could practice what I felt to be the tactics needed to defeat the enemy. No doubt, the 4th Army staff must have wondered why we were consuming so much precious fuel, but no official objection to these activities was registered. We proved the value of this practice in the final months of the war by doubling and then quadrupling our score of enemy aeroplanes brought down.

'The unity of purpose necessary to a Jagdstaffel's efficiency depended greatly on the confidence its members had in their leader. Manfred von Richthofen understood this fact of life and set an example of bravery and excellence that his subordinates followed keenly. He was well remembered for flying the same type of aircraft issued to other pilots and squadrons up and down the Front, but he displayed a certain intangible spirit of victory that contributed greatly to the success of his *Staffel-Kameraden* [squadron-mates]. Richthofen knew how to arouse enthusiasm in his men and, above all, how to inspire new members of his famed Jagdstaffel 11.

'In the spirit of Richthofen, from before dawn until the last rays of twilight, I led the zealous neophyte fighter pilots on flights to airfields all along the Front. The new men who had not yet gone up to trade shots with the enemy could be found in the company of their more experienced comrades, studying with the aid of the telescope the traits of various enemy aircraft. By such observation, which often lasted for hours, we fighter pilots studied the manoeuvres needed to shoot down an enemy airplane. This form of military training – first practised by Richthofen's mentor, the celebrated ace Hauptmann Oswald Boelcke – was the elementary education of the young fighter pilots, during which time, with the coaching of their more experienced comrades, they prepared to enter the great and deadly tournament in the skies.'

Then on the rainy morning of Saturday, 13 July, Degelow led a flight of Fokker and Pfalz biplanes the short distance to Armentières to let them watch 'the master' at work. And they were not disappointed. He sent down an S.E.5 over the town of Erquinghem, a few kilometres from the city. The pilot,[34] later identified as Lt W.S. Robertson of 85 Squadron, RAF, was recorded as having 'left aerodrome [at] 7:15 a.m. Last seen in combat southeast of Armentières. German message received 30.9.18 states [he was] killed.'[35] Robertson was Degelow's ninth victim, although – due to the rapidly changing situation – the Air Force Commanding General's victory list showed Degelow as having attained his tenth and twelfth victories on 13 July.[36]

The following day, Degelow gave his men a lesson in capitalising on their opponents' limitations:

'During the German Army's last offensive in Flanders, British single-seat fighter squadrons were very busy, not only in their normal offensive role, but often coming over our lines in another capacity, namely as bomb-haulers. Indeed, each aeroplane carried enough 12.5-kilo bombs so that, when dropped by large groups simultaneously, they caused great anxiety amongst our troops, especially those recuperating in the rear areas.

Comradeship irrespective of rank was important to the success of German air units and this photo is a good example. From left, unidentified Jasta 40 enlisted man, Uffz Werner Hertel, Ltn.d.Res Hermann Gilly and Ltn.d.Res Anton Raab strike a casual pose in front of Gilly's Fokker D.VII with the reverse swastika emblem. The aeroplane to the left is Raab's D.VII bearing his white cat individual marking.

'The British fighter pilots' collateral duty presented a great difficulty for them, as their aeroplanes were overburdened by the weight of the bombs. In aerial combat with them, we could more easily deal with these otherwise fast and manoeuvrable aeroplanes. Loaded with their dangerous cargo, their manoeuvrability was hampered and their aircraft controls responded much differently – to their disadvantage.

'During our flight on 14 July, we encountered a pack of these mischief makers and used their handicap in our favour and chased them home.

'We were flying over Lys when I became aware that far behind the British lines a big formation of enemy machines was approaching our positions. Even at this great distance I could make out that the enemy force consisted of about twenty single-seat fighters. That number of fighters in one formation appeared to me to indicate nothing less than a bombing mission bent on attacking our artillery emplacements.

'I said to myself: "Just walk this way, you Tommy gentlemen, and we will make it hot for you!" With that thought in mind, I held back our attack until the enemy flight made

Following a large-scale aerial combat southeast of Vieux Berquin on 14 July 1918, Jasta 40 pilots brought home two captured British airmen. Seen here, standing from left: unidentified Jasta 7 pilot, Ltn Frodien, Ltn Willy Rosenstein, Uffz Ebert, 2/Lt Brewster Garrett (wearing RAF jacket) of 64 Squadron, Ltn Hermann Gilly, 2/Lt Nelson H. Marshall (wearing older type RFC tunic) of 85 Squadron, and Ltns Degelow and Jeschonnek. Degelow brought down Marshall and either Rosenstein or Gilly shot down Garrett. The two enlisted ground crewmen below the standing figures are unidentified.

a turn. Then we could hit the gentlemen on the outermost flank, who were straining to keep up, while the aircraft forming the inner flank would have to expend less effort, as they were sort of shoulder-to-shoulder. At my signal – waggling my wings – Jasta 40 charged into the crowd of S.E.5 fighters and each man picked out an adversary.

'I side-slipped down with my "dancing partner", who, as the first shots hit his aeroplane, was forced out of the fray. Apparently the Englishman had hopes of gliding back to his own lines, but that was something I did not care for, as I always enjoyed personally meeting an opponent after an aerial contest. I made my viewpoint known with a burst of machine-gun fire just ahead of him. The Tommy, impressed by the grey smoke trails neatly woven across his intended escape route, turned in a direction more to my liking and then landed. On greeting the soft earth of Flanders, however, his aeroplane turned over. Then – slowly, cautiously and somewhat exhausted – the pilot crawled out from beneath the wreckage. I immediately spotted him from the air, as he was wearing a marvellously stylish bright yellow leather coat. With raised hands and the resigned air of a man who had just received his draft notice, he quickly left the theatre in which he had for the present concluded his flying career. After I concluded that Lieutenant Marshall,[37] as my opponent introduced himself during the handshake that followed his unplanned arrival, had been taken into protective custody by some of our artillery soldiers, I flew off on a homeward course.

'Along the way I made a heart-stopping discovery: during my last round of "persuasive" firing, my machine gun had jammed. Immediately, I went to work on the ammunition belt – holding the control column steady between my knees, while I tugged on the ammunition belt to get it to clear the gun breech. Just then I was taken by surprise when a series of shots came up from the ground. I could not understand why our own troops were firing at me this far behind our lines. Then, looking around and below, I spotted the object of the ground gunners' attention: a single British gentleman far below me, dropping bombs. "Just wait, fellow, you shall pay for that." Having cleared the jam in my guns, I went after him with a roar.

'But this fellow was no weakling. Indeed, he was what our English–speaking colleagues characterised as a "tough guy" or as we would say in the *Plattdeutsch* [low German] dialect: *"Datt ist ein ganz togen!"* I then underwent what was perhaps the most intense dogfight of my life. This Tommy was so wild that, whenever we flew toward each other, he tried to ram me. We repeatedly whizzed past each other with only metres to spare. Unfortunately, he wore a face mask; otherwise, I would surely never forget the face of my able opponent.

"Now each of us tried to overtake the other in a turn and then get the opponent in his gun-sight. I must have done this last manoeuvre a bit more frequently and better, as, after a quarter of an hour of fighting, my partner then tried his utmost to disappear from the scene. His withdrawal, however, proved to be his undoing. I got right onto his tail. During the ensuing chase, ever closer to the ground, as my opponent tried every trick to shake me off, I succeeded in bringing him down with a well-placed stream of fire. We were just within the advanced British lines when, from about fifty metres altitude and with the engine going full out, the enemy aircraft dived furiously into the ground and on impact was smashed to pieces. The flight back to my own airfield was then undisturbed.'

The Jasta 40 pilots did not know it, but they had encountered a flight of S.E.5s led by one of the top British fighter aces, Major Edward (Mick) Mannock, commanding officer of 85 Squadron, RAF, who had been motivated to 'join the fighting services and start 'destroying Germans'.[38] There is no doubt as to which German air unit he and his men encountered that morning over Merville, some eighteen kilometres west of Armentières. Mannock's combat report describes his attack on a 'Fokker biplane marked thus 卍 ... with white tail and black fuselage ... swastika in white'. His report continued:

'Dived with patrol from 10,000 feet over Merville on leader of two scout E.A. Disengaged owing to observing a Fokker biplane [as noted above] on tail of an S.E.5. Brought this machine down to 1,000 feet and observed it crash northeast of Merville (one mile approximately). This machine confirmed by Capt [Arthur C.] Randall. Patrol of S.E.5s unfortunately split up at this juncture.'[39]

1/Lt John C. Rorison, an American pilot attached to Mannock's squadron, also claimed to have brought down a 'Fokker Scout [with] planes and tail white', as follows:

'Diving with Capt [George C.] Dixon's patrol on E.A. patrol, I got into position on the tail of one Pfalz Scout and fired several bursts. In the general combat which followed I lost sight of this E.A.; meantime another E.A. dived on me from above, whereupon I turned and engaged this E.A., which was [a] Fokker Scout, getting in several good bursts at very close range at [a] height of 1,000 feet, whereupon E.A. dived steeply away and I saw the debris on the ground in a field southwest of Estaires, [my] being then at 500 feet.

'Just before engaging this E.A. I observed Capt Dixon firing at close range at a white-tail Pfalz Scout which appeared to be completely out of control.'[40]

The Fokker D.VII with the black fuselage decorated with a white reverse swastika was flown by Ltn.d.Res Hermann Gilly, who returned from this flight safely. In fact, while Mannock, Dixon and Rorison[41] were credited with downing black aeroplanes with white tails – Jasta 40's battle colours – German records show no comparable losses. On the other hand, three of the four S.E.5s claimed by Jasta 40 are verified by British records: Lt N.H. Marshall of 85 Squadron, 2/Lt B.N. Garrett[42] of 64 Squadron, and Lt H.A. Whittaker of 29 Squadron. The latter was very likely piloting the S.E.5 that Degelow sent down within British forward lines; Whittaker was wounded, but made it back to his own lines, where he reported being shot down by anti-aircraft fire.[43] However, German records show no S.E.5s shot down by Flak that day.[44] Ltn Gilly claimed an S.E.5 near Vieux Berquin, but British records show no matching RAF casualty. The Kogenluft aerial victory summary credited their day's work.[45] As Degelow later wrote, 14 July was very successful for the Staffel:

'Immediately after landing, two gentlemen of my Staffel – Leutnants Gilly and Rosenstein – reported to me that each had caught one of the members of the bombing formation. Our six aircraft had, therefore, brought down four enemy aeroplanes within a short time, an achievement with which we could be quite satisfied. All four aircraft were of the S.E.5 type, an outstanding British single-seater with a 220-horsepower stationary engine and with good diving ability and great speed.

'As two of the S.E.5s had come down within our own lines, we fetched the pilots, the previously mentioned Lieutenant Marshall and a Lieutenant Garrett. We heard from their own mouths the particulars of their misfortune. Right at the beginning, Marshall had received a shot through his control column, while further damaging shots went into his wing, causing the whole sheet of fabric to come loose from the wing framework, thereby forcing him to land. Both men assured us that they had been badly handicapped in having to carry bombs and only for that reason had we been able to be victorious over them.

'Suffice it to say that Gilly, Rosenstein and I fancied that our flying ability had contributed "somewhat" to the Englishmen's misfortune.'

Other Issues

Individual aerial combat victories were small matters. The larger issue on 14 July was that Général (later Maréchal) Ferdinand Foch, commander of all French forces, appealed to Britain's Field Marshal Sir Douglas Haig, for ground and air units to reinforce French

The Sopwith 1F.1 Camel was an iconic World War I aeroplane. Once its very sensitive controls were mastered, it was a first-rate dog-fighting machine. Carl Degelow received confirmation for shooting down eight of these fast and versatile craft, and maintained a healthy respect for the rotary-engined biplane. The Camel was widely used by the RNAS, RFC and RAF. The example seen here was built under license by Boulton & Paul Ltd.

positions in the Champagne Sector. That day Haig acceded to Foch and transferred nine squadrons of aircraft to the headquarters of the French *IXéme Brigade*. The transfer was marked by rainstorms, but the British air units forged southward and arrived to strengthen the French line. Despite his giving the order, Haig was apprehensive, as he expected a German offensive to be launched on the Flanders Sector between Ypres and Hazebrouck about 15 July.

His fears were somewhat allayed when, at midnight on Sunday, 14 July, a massive German bombardment farther south heralded the beginning of the second battle of the Marne. Four hours later, German infantry moved forward. This activity created a more favourable combat environment for German units in northern France and Belgium. Consequently, German Jagdstaffeln were out in force, taking advantage of British fighter

Line-up of Jasta 40 Fokker D.VIIs in summer 1918. Pilots' markings that can be discerned are (from right): white stag of Carl Degelow, white heart of Willy Rosenstein, rampaging bull of Hans Jeschonnek and reverse swastika of Hermann Gilly.

aircraft that were forced to double up as bombers due to the transfer of other RAF units to the Champagne Sector.

On the morning of 22 July, Degelow led a flight due west from his airfield at Lomme to the Merville area and this time caught a flight of Bristol F2.B two-seat fighters returning to their base. The Staffel-Führer achieved his twelfth victory by sending down one of the Bristol Fighters, which was recorded as having 'left aerodrome [at] 7 a.m. Last seen [at] 8:30 a.m. over Laventie engaging three E.A. at about 16,000 feet.'[46] Laventie is only five kilometres from Lestrem, which indicates the fight must have been brief. The two RAF crewmen[47] were uninjured and taken prisoner.

Three days later, Degelow shot down his fourth Sopwith Camel (and thirteenth victory overall) near Wytschaete, north of Armentières. The pilot,[48] Canadian Lt Walter Carveth, was taken prisoner and later told a harrowing tale:

'At this time we were being heavily "archied" [fired on by anti-aircraft guns] and all at once I found myself going down out of control … [with] petrol streaming all over me. I had been hit by an anti-aircraft shell which pierced my main petrol tank. I immediately righted my machine and got my engine going again by switching … on my spare petrol tank…

'Suddenly I heard that well known sound behind my machine – put, put, put, put – and on looking around I saw two Fokker Biplanes making for me. One quite a piece behind the other …

'I decided to give this Hun a crack [at me] and take my chances on my petrol lasting. In the middle of the fight my engine cut out and, being unable to continue the scrap, I was forced to land about two miles west of Armentières, which was done in a half-dazed condition in [amongst] old German trenches.

'The next thing I remember [was] some German soldiers were pulling me out of my machine, from which they took me to a dug-out … I remained [there] for about twenty minutes until the battery commander, Capt von Hulmann, arrived, he being the commanding officer of the battery … [that] had been lucky in hitting my machine …'[49]

Degelow was confirmed as shooting down Carveth's Sopwith Camel. The only aircraft of that type brought down by anti aircraft fire was credited to Offizierstellvertreter [Warrant Officer] Sach, leader of K-Flakbatterie 123; no mention was made of a Hauptmann von Hulmann in the Air Force Commanding General's weekly summary of air combat events.[50]

Battle Colours and Symbols
As Jasta 40 turned in its less-desirable Pfalz D.IIIa fighters for newer, better Fokker D.VIIs, the unit took on a more uniform look. That development served a purpose, as Degelow explained:

'World War I brought on changes in battle dress for differing reasons. The gaily uniformed French Zouaves exchanged their bright red pants for the more sombre tones of the earth as a means of camouflage. We in the air, however, went from subdued paint schemes for our aeroplanes to conspicuous colours, easily seen from a distance. Since we could not hope to "blend in" with the sky, the thought was to paint the aircraft in colours befitting their use.

'Night-time aircraft such as our Gotha bombers, which so often disturbed the sleep of Londoners, made their nocturnal visits cloaked in shades of dark blue or even black. Likewise, the daytime aircraft first appeared over the Front in various modes of camouflage that, from above, made them hard to distinguish from the earth. Although this appearance protected the flyers, like the mimicry of many insects that protected them from preying birds, fighter pilots gradually went to the other extreme and, by painting their aircraft in gaudy colours, challenged and even provoked the enemy. Manfred von Richthofen, whose all-red aircraft earned him the appellation "The Red Baron", and the Bavarian ace Hauptmann Adolf Ritter von Tutscheck, known for his all-black aircraft, are two examples.

'Aeroplanes of German Jagdstaffeln were usually of one colour or a colour combination chosen by the commanding officer. Within each Staffel, however, each aeroplane bore a particular symbol as a means of identification during aerial combat. These symbols were not added merely for amusement, or as a reversion to the tactics of American Indians, who painted their faces and bodies with hideous designs in order to frighten their enemies. It was of the greatest importance in a flight for a Staffel-Führer to know at every point which of his 'planes were attacking and which were hard-pressed and needed support.

'Thus he saw, perhaps by the symbol of the attacker, that the object of that man's attention was "in good hands", while, conversely, he may have seen one of his men in a predicament that demanded help from himself or another of his fighters, who could have been alerted by the sight of different colour flares being fired by the leader. For this reason, every individual battle symbol gained a certain combat value, which in a capably-led Staffel was a great influence in the mounting number of victories. It was very interesting in this regard to hear from British fliers taken prisoner about the different symbols they had encountered in their aerial battles.

'As long as it was not expressly forbidden, we often conducted these "retired" enemy fighter pilots around our airfield and showed them our aeroplanes so that we could hear from their own mouths what they thought about the efficiency of our machines. One such visitor, a Mr. Smith, stopped and pointed to one of our Fokker D.VIIs and said: "We know this one very well. We call him the 'double lucky stick', meaning that the aircraft bearing the Hindu swastika good luck sign had often been met in aerial combat and had instilled deep respect in its opponents. The prisoners had good reason for that remark, as the pilot of that machine [Ltn.d.Res Hermann Gilly] was someone in whom burned the spirit of the Staffel's motto: "Ever closer, metre by metre!"

'Battle symbols came from many sources, including zoology; one man in Jasta 40 [Ltn Frodien] used a hawk's head, another [Ltn Hans Jeschonnek] a rampaging bull. An exception to this custom was the Fokker decorated with a white heart [Ltn.d.Res Willy

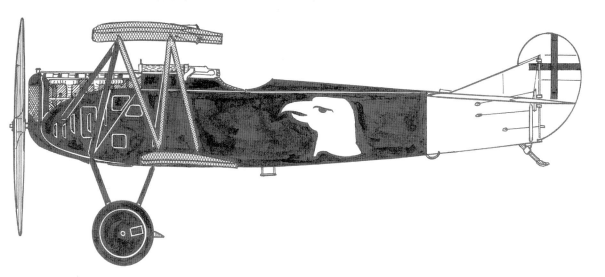

A hawk's head insignia applied to the fuselage of the Jasta 40 Fokker D.VII flown by Ltn.d.Res Frodien. *(Original artwork by Greg VanWyngarden)*

When Ltn.d.Res Willy Rosenstein joined Jasta 40, he selected a white heart for the personal emblem of his Fokker D.VII. *(Original artwork by Greg VanWyngarden)*

Uffz Werner Hertel flew in a Fokker D.VII decorated with his flaming sword insignia while with Jasta 40.

Rosenstein], which clearly indicated a good relationship with the eternal woman. If we had to forgive him for this, we did it gladly, for he was our "patron saint", performing for us the essential duty of keeping the rear free of our enemies, as he flew last and highest in our formation.

'Our British opponents used large capital letters to identify their aircraft. I remember bringing down one gentleman whose plane bore a large white "Y" on the top wing. Then there was one shot down with a "V" and still another with an "S" who, after a lengthy aerial combat, had to admit defeat.

'Once, while we were attacking some captive balloons, we came upon a Belgian single-seat fighter that had joined in the air battle; it bore as its symbol the victorious emblem of the laurel branch. With his comrades, the laurel-bedecked pilot intended to deal us a shattering blow. This I deduced not only from his glorious symbol, which was very decoratively painted on his aircraft, but also from the very energetic manner in which he repeatedly attacked us.[51] The laurel alone did not make a victor and our

Belgian friends, even though they outnumbered us, did not cause any damage to our Staffel. Reaching our airfield after the successful retreating fight with the laurel flier, we concluded that the frustration of our enemy raised serious doubts in our minds as to the appropriateness of his vainglorious symbol.'

As the German Army's spring 1918 offensive failed to make the dramatic impact on the war that the Kaiser's generals had anticipated, German strategists planned a second all-out offensive for the late summer. But this move was expected by the Allies, who began preparations to seize the initiative from German forces.

Hence, the furious air activity in Flanders – during which Carl Degelow's victory score more than doubled, rising from six to thirteen aeroplanes brought down – was in reality a diversion intended to draw the Allies' attention from the primary German target: the Marne Front.

Before the German Army could follow up with plans for a Flanders offensive, however, Général Foch launched a counter-offensive on 18 July. That attack on the front between Château Thierry and Soissons gained enough momentum to dissuade plans for a German offensive to the north. It also marked the beginning of the end of German gains in France. Five days later the Allied counter-attack on the Marne was assured of success and the Allies began to regain ground taken by the Germans during their July offensive. Indeed, German gains were quite modest; despite the planning and sacrifices made, German troops moved about six miles from the offensive staging areas. The next offensive would be launched by the Allies.

1   Helmuth Dilthey was born on 9 February 1894 in the Rhineland city of Rheydt. Aged twenty, in November 1914, he enlisted in the Fliegertruppe and began training at the school run by the Rumpler Luftfahrzeugbau Johannisthal, near Berlin. Upon completion of his pilot's qualifications, Dilthey was transferred to the German 10th Army's air park on the Eastern Front. Assigned to Flieger-Abteilung 50, he flew many bombing missions against Russian troops. In view of his aggressive nature, Dilthey was transferred to Jagdstaffelschule I in Valenciennes in March 1917. He was assigned to Jasta 27 a month later. After attaining his sixth confirmed victory, on 5 February 1917, Dilthey was appointed to lead Jasta 40 [Ref: von Langsdorff, *Flieger am Feind* pp. 214, 340].

2   Jones, *The War in the Air*, Vol. III, p. 364.

3   Dilthey, '*In der Staffel Göring*' in von Langsdorff, op.cit., pp. 212-213.

4   Dilthey and Gilly very likely shot down balloons from the 2nd Balloon Wing, 5th Company, which reported losses by its 2nd and 25th Sections on that evening [Ref: Bailey, 'German Balloon Claims During 1918' in *Cross & Cockade Journal*, Vol. XXIV, p. 231].

5   *Kommandeur der Flieger der 6. Armee Wochenbericht Nr. 1716 op*, 20 June 1918, p. 3.

6   Dilthey received credit for his seventh aerial victory and Gilly his first [Ref: Kogenluft, *Nachrichtenblatt der Luftstreitkräfte*, Vol. II, No. 24, 8 August 1918, p. 366].

7   Gilly, *Personal-Bogen*, p. 3.

8   Kogenluft, *Nachrichtenblatt*, No. 24, 8 August 1918, p. 364.

9   Henshaw, op.cit., p. 343.

10 Ibid., p. 365.

11 Kogenluft, op.cit.

12 Lt Owen John Frederick Jones-Lloyd was born October-December 1898 in Pembroke, Pembrokeshire, Wales. He joined 54 Squadron, RAF as Lt 1 April 1918, was reported missing 25 June 1918, and repatriated 13 December 1918 [Ref: National Archives file WO 339/97952].

13 54 Squadron, RAF, *Combat Report*, 25 June 1918.

14 Shores, Franks, & Guest, *Above the Trenches*, p. 263.

15 Bruce, *British Aeroplanes 1914-1918*, p. 600.

16 Capt William A. Forsyth, twenty-three, fell in Sopwith 5F.1 Dolphin C.3806 of 79 Squadron, RAF [Ref: Hobson, *Airmen Died in the Great War 1914-1918*, p. 141].

17 Franks, Bailey & Duiven, *Casualties of the German Air Service 1914-1918*, p. 282.

18 79 Squadron, RAF, *Combat Report* by Lt Snyder, 27 June 1918.

19 79 Squadron, RAF, *Combat Report* by Lt MacDonald, 27 June 1918.

20 Lt Francis R. Brand, nineteen, in S.E.5a C.9573 of 29 Squadron, RAF was listed as killed in action [Ref: Hobson, op.cit., p. 120].

21 Royal Air Force, *Combat Casualty List*, 27 June 1918.

22 Kogenluft, *Nachrichtenblatt der Luftstreitkräfte*, Vol. II, No. 24, 8 August 1918, p. 365.

23 Zickerick, *Verlustliste der deutschen Luftstreitkräfte im Weltkriege* p. 32.

24 Kogenluft, *Nachrichtenblatt*, No. 29, 12 September 1918, p. 451.

25 Lt Wilfred E. Durant, twenty-three, in S.E.5a B.8524 of 29 Squadron, RAF was listed as killed in action [Ref: Hobson, op.cit., p. 136].

26 29 Squadron, RAF, *Squadron Record Book*, 2 July 1918.

27 Willy Rosenstein was born on 28 January 1892 in Stuttgart. He began flight training on 15 August 1911 and, at age twenty, was certified as a pilot on 14 March 1912. He was decorated by early aviation supporter Carl Eduard, Duke of Saxe-Coburg-Gotha, on 7 August 1913 and a year later, repaid the Duke's generosity by enlisting in the 6. Thüringisches Infanterie-Regiment Nr. 95 in Gotha. On 24 August 1914, to gain his military indoctrination, Rosenstein was posted to the Militär-Fliegerschule in Gotha. Rosenstein completed his military aviation requirements at Flieger-Ersatz-Abteilung 5 at Hannover, where he was promoted to Unteroffizier on 18 October and received his Military Pilot's Badge on 22 October. He was promoted to Vizefeldwebel and appointed Offizierstellvertreter [Warrant Officer] on 24 November. Rosenstein was posted to the German 5th Army's air park at Montmédy on 11 January 1915 and then to Flieger-Abteilung 19, where he flew combat missions in Fokker and Pfalz Eindeckers. Commissioned Leutnant der Reserve on 17 February 1916, he was wounded in aerial combat in April and then posted to training duties at FEA 10 at Böblingen on 31 May 1916. He was returned to combat flying on 17 September and posted to the German 5th Army's air park. Rosenstein was posted to Jasta 9 on 7 October 1916 and remained there until 13 February 1917, when he was transferred to Jasta 27, where he scored his first two aerial victories. Assigned to an aviation observer school on 10 December 1917, he was reassigned to the Home Defence Command on 5 January 1918. He flew against enemy aircraft attacking the German homeland, first with Kampfeinsitzerstaffel 1a based in Mannheim and then Kest 1b out of Freiburg. During the latter assignment, on 31 May, he shot down an Airco D.H.4 attacking Karlsruhe, for which he was later awarded Grand Duchy of Baden's Knight's Cross Second Class of the Order of the Zähringer Lion. He was posted to Jasta 40 on 2 July 1918.

28 Supf, *Das Buch der deutschen Fluggeschichte*, Vol. I, p. 566.

29 Ibid., p. 499.

30 This victory, over an Airco D.H.4, is not listed in Kogenluft, *Nachrichtenblatt*, Vol. I, No. 34, 18 October 1917, p. 328. However, Rosenstein's *Personal-Bogen* [service record] lists the Kogenluft confirmation number Fl.IIIc 113092, which indicates the victory was, indeed, credited to him.

31 Quoted in O'Connor, *Aviation Awards of Imperial Germany and the Men Who Earned Them*, Vol. IV, p. 181.

32 Gill, R. 'The Albums of Willy Rosenstein' in *Cross & Cockade Journal*, Vol. XXV, p. 311.

33 RAF, *War Diary* entry, 9 July 1918.

34 Lt William Scott Robertson in S.E.5a C.1818 of 85 Squadron, RAF, was killed in action and later buried in Armentières [Ref: Hobson, op.cit., p.183].

35 RAF, *Combat Casualty List*, 13 July 1918.

36 Kogenluft, op.cit.

37 2/Lt Nelson Hepburn Marshall was born on 11 May 1899 in East Retford, Nottinghamshire. He enlisted as Private. No. 2996, 1st Training Reserve Battalion on 12 June 1917, was promoted T/2Lt on probation on 2 July 1917, promoted Lt on 1 April 1918, assigned to 85 Squadron, RAF, captured 14 July 1918 and repatriated 14 January 1919 [Ref: U.K. National Archives files WO 339/124135 and WO 339/122169].

38 Bowyer, *For Valour – The Air VCs*, p. 157.

39 85 Squadron, RAF, *Combat Report* by Maj Mannock, 14 July 1918.

40 85 Squadron, RAF, *Combat Report* by Lt Rorison, 14 July 1918.

41 RAF, *Communiqué* No. 15, 17 July 1918, p. 3.

43 2/Lt Beverley Noble Garrett was born on 6 January 1897 in Canada. He joined the RFC in Canada, was promoted 2/Lt on 27 November 1917, assigned to 92 Squadron, RFC, on 7 January 1918, appointed Flying Officer on 12 March 1918, captured 14 July 1918 and repatriated on 16 January 1918 [Ref: U.K. National Archives files WO 339/116325, WO 339/118543 and WO 339/134115].

43 RAF, *Combat Casualty List*, 14 July 1918.

44 Kogenluft, *Nachrichtenblatt*, No. 28, 5 September 1918, p. 438.

45 Kogenluft, *Nachrichtenblatt*, No. 29, 12 September 1918, p. 451.

46 RAF, *Combat Casualty List*, 22 July 1918.

47 Lt W.E. Coulson and 2/Lt W.H.E. Labbett in F.2B F.5810 of 62 Squadron, RAF; both men were taken prisoner.

48 Lt Walter Alva Carveth was born in York, Canada on 31 December 1897. He was a student at the University of Toronto when appointed T/2Lt RFC on 1 August 1917, promoted Lt in the RAF on 1 April 1918, posted to 208 Squadron, RAF, reported missing on 25 July 1918 in Sopwith Camel D.1889 and was repatriated on 13 December 1918 [Ref: U.K. National Archives file WO 339/128376].

49 Carveth, Personal summary, p. 1.

50 Kogenluft, *Nachrichtenblatt*, No. 28, op.cit.

51 Most likely a formation from the Belgian *1ère Escadrille* commanded by *Chevalier* [Knight] Willy Coppens de Houthulst, who, with thirty-seven victories to his credit, was the highest ranking Belgian air ace of World War I. The laurel was his squadron's emblem.

CHAPTER NINE
THE TIDE OF WAR TURNS

Late July and early August 1918 were hard times for Jagdstaffel 40. Following Carl Degelow's thirteenth victory on 25 July, the unit remained scoreless for seventeen days. Not for lack of trying, to be sure, but air fights on 31 July and 7 August resulted only in casualties; two new men, Leutnant Erichson on the former date and Vizefeldwebel Prinz on the latter, were wounded and wrecked their aeroplanes in trying to land.

Even the weather was against flyers on both sides of the lines. Clear skies that inspired so much air activity in July gave way to a week of cloudy, rainy and misty conditions beginning on Saturday, 3 August 1918. But the weather was a blessing to Allied ground commanders who were preparing for a dramatic counter-offensive in the wake of the failed fifth (and final) German offensive in mid-July.

The German Army's 'Black Day'

The Allied offensive began at 4:20 a.m. (British Time) on Thursday, 8 August, with the thundering fire of over 2,000 artillery pieces. Under cover of darkness, rain and fog the British Fourth Army (augmented by American, Australian and Canadian forces) and the French 1ère and 3ème Armées attacked the German 2nd and 18th Armies.[1] The Amiens Salient, about forty kilometres from Morlancourt south almost to Hangard, was hit by 'tanks, armoured cars, armed lorries, and infantry … [and] the enemy was taken completely by surprise and at the end of the day the British troops had advanced about seven miles … The whole German army was shaken by the rapidity and by the extent of the success, as is clear from [General Erich] Ludendorff's description of August the 8th as the "black day" of the German army in the war …'[2]

British troops captured some 16,000 prisoners and 200 field guns within the attack's first two hours. Badly demoralised retreating German soldiers are said to have shouted out to their replacements: 'You are prolonging the war.'[3] From that point forward, the German Army fought a series of holding actions, designed to allow for as orderly a retreat as possible to within German borders with as many men and as much equipment as could be saved. If successful, such forces might have been a positive factor in the armistice negotiations that were as inevitable as the coming winter.

While Allied ground fighting advances were made on the Somme Sector, British air units were in the air as soon as the weather began to show some improvement. Despite taking heavy losses that day, Royal Air Force units were active along most of the Western Front. Previous opponents of Jasta 40 – 29, 48, 54, and 98 Squadrons – all reported successful air combats on the counter-offensive's opening day.[4] The German

Luftstreitkräfte claimed to have brought down thirty-three enemy aeroplanes (including seventeen by anti-aircraft fire) and listed these casualties: 'three aircraft [lost] in aerial combat, one forced to land on the other side of the lines, four aeroplanes missing [and unaccounted for], five observation balloons shot down, [and] nine damaged.'[5]

British air activity was also high on 9 August and the only bright spot on that otherwise dismal day for Carl Degelow was receipt of news that he had been awarded the Knight's Cross of the Order of the House of Hohenzollern with Swords. A high decoration from Germany's monarchy, it 'was sometimes referred to as the *Orden Pour le Mérite des kleinen Mannes* (literally the "Order of Merit for Lesser Men") in World War I … [and] came to be the customary intermediate award for officers between the Iron Cross 1st Class and the *Orden Pour le Mérite* itself.'[6]

Almost as if to celebrate Staffel-Führer Degelow's high honour from the Kaiser's royal house, on 10 August, Jasta 40's Vzfw Paul Groll shot down an S.E.5 over Swartenbrouck. It was confirmed as his second victory.[7]

Carl Degelow's position as the ranking ace of Jasta 40 was emphasised in joking fashion during a celebratory occasion at the Staffel's pilots' mess. His comrades and the ubiquitous Staffel dog are pointed toward him. Sitting are (from left): Leutnants Auer, Degelow, Hans Jeschonnek, Rosenstein and Frodien. Standing are (from left): two unidentified Jasta 7 pilots, Leutnant Kurt Jeschonnek (pointing an empty flare pistol), and three other unidentified airmen. Kurt Jeschonnek, the older brother of Hans, was a former sapper officer who became an observer with Flieger-Abteilung (A) 281. He was killed in combat on 23 August 1918, shortly after this photo was taken.

Enduring a 'Lukas'

A week later, a member of Jasta 40 shot down a Sopwith Camel, but under unusual circumstances, as Degelow related:

'During the last months of the war, the British carried out surprise air attacks against our airfields with increased frequency. For such raids they consolidated many air units so that the total number of aeroplanes participating in such an undertaking often exceeded eighty. To warn airfields that such an attack was imminent and that we should prepare to repel it, German observation posts were set up in the forward areas. Once they spotted an enemy formation heading for any of our airfields, they would call the 'field involved and simply transmit the code word "Lukas", which had the sobering effect of a dash of cold water on all those who knew the danger it represented.

'As "polite people" – and who will dispute that the English have not been so numbered since time immemorial? – they saw fit on the morning of 17 August to pay such a visit to our airfield at Lomme. It was about 9:00 a.m. and I had just given orders to have our aeroplanes made ready for a flight over the lines. I was discussing with my pilots the manner of beginning the attack, when fierce anti-aircraft fire in the direction of the Front attracted our attention. Then, our forward observation posts called in: "Here come the British, they want a Lukas."

'The strong west wind drove the formation with great speed toward our airfield. With the naked eye alone we could make out over fifty enemy aircraft. The airfield was quickly alerted by the wail of sirens and, since taking off was now out of the question, I promptly had carbines passed out and ordered everyone into covered trenches – which were far too close to our own hangars. They were to hinder the British by taking pot shots at them. Among the workers at our airfield were groups of Belgian civilians, who, at the approach of this danger, escaped as quickly as their feet would let them. They had nothing on their heads, so, to find better protection, they threw themselves in pairs into a flooded trench in which the water came up to their knees. With furious curses directed at the Tommies, they cowered in their uncomfortable hiding place and awaited the manifestations of a Lukas.

'Shortly before reaching our airfield, the lower swarm of the enemy flight dived in a left turn. This was a trick, intended to divert our machine-gun protection; for, simultaneously, out of the great formation of scattering single-seat units came one squadron in a dive down on our hangars. At the same moment, two-seat Bristol Fighters flying above the single-seat fighter squadron dropped their bombs in order to render our defence powerless, while British Sopwith single-seaters attacked our hangars at low altitude with concussion bombs. They flew the length of the sheds, which were all in a row, dropped their high-explosive bombs and then split up, half wheeling into a left turn, while the others turned right.

'The Sopwiths that led the attack flew in a continuous circle above and then tried through the use of incendiary ammunition to set fire to the hangars and tents. More violent explosions followed and, shortly thereafter, two of the smaller sheds were in flames. We could not extinguish them or even get to them; for, as soon as one of us dared to come out of the covered trenches, a Tommy would come down and "spray" us, his hammering machine gun making it necessary to take cover as quickly as possible. Almost a quarter of an hour was sufficient for the British to vent their destructive fury all across our airfield. Thick smoke from the oil of aircraft that had been set afire spread over the airfield. This spontaneous fogging was indeed the reason why the enemy squadron leader finally gave the signal to withdraw.

'At his flare signal, all of the British aeroplanes re-grouped and flew off on a westerly course. Only one British Sopwith Camel pilot, a pennant fluttering from his wing, pursued his special ambition in using his incendiary ammunition to set fire to the remaining hangars during the attack. Again and again he flew at the hangars, coming in at rooftop level, and in so doing missed joining up when his comrades moved on.

'When he finally realised that his earnest efforts were unsuccessful, he pulled up in order to reach the main body, which was already on the flight home. To his misfortune after this display of bravery, he flew into the line of fire of a ground machine gun and through a well-sighted series of shots by a skilled ground gunner. The Sopwith pilot learned that one may not take part in a Lukas unpunished. Decidedly, he was the bravest of the whole Lukas group. Later, we found him dead from many chest wounds, amidst the wreckage of his machine. According to his identification, he was an Australian.

'The attack caused all manner of damage to us and to the other Staffeln located at Lomme. Mechanics were wounded or killed by concussion bombs and machine-gun fire, and four of Jasta 40's best Fokkers were burned up in the aeroplane sheds.'

The RAF *War Diary* entry for 17 August, 1918 notes that the raid on Lomme airfield was carried out by elements of 2 and 4 Squadrons, Australian Flying Corps (S.E.5s and Sopwith Camels, respectively), and 88 and 92 Squadrons, RAF (Bristol Fighters and S.E. 5s). The entire force of sixty British aircraft was led by Lieutenant Colonel Louis A. Strange, commander of the 80th Wing, RAF. According to the *War Diary*:

'One hundred and four 25-lb and two 40-lb bombs were dropped from an average height of 200 feet. Some pilots, who dropped them from fifty feet, had their machines damaged by their own bombs. Many direct hits were observed on sheds, hangars and huts. From photographs taken during the raid, two sheds can be seen burning fiercely and from the strength of the wind it is probable that others also caught fire, but the sheds to the leeward were obscured by smoke. A large number of rounds were also fired and casualties [were] inflicted on personnel on the aerodrome, and on a party of mounted troops who made for Lille at full gallop.'

The attackers' lone casualty was corroborated by the official Australian history:

'The German anti-aircraft gunners stuck gamely to their work, despite furious attack from the raiders, and their fire hit Lieutenant E.P.E. McCleery's machine in the Camel formation.[8] It crashed … on the aerodrome floor, and McCleery was killed. Photographs disclosed that heavy damage was done to hangars and workshops during the raid, and prisoners subsequently taken stated that seventeen Fokker biplanes were destroyed in the wreckage.'[9]

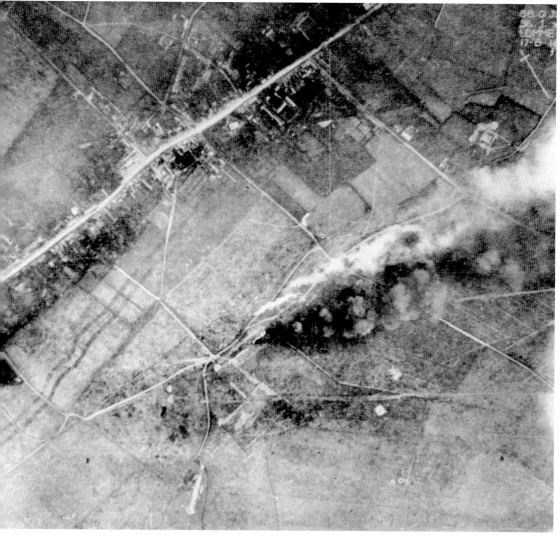

Four Jasta 40 Fokker D.VIIs were destroyed when 80th Wing, RAF bombed Lomme airfield on 17 August 1918. This aerial photo was taken by the observer in a Bristol Fighter of 88 Squadron, RAF.

Degelow added:

'A similar visit was paid by the British "travelling circus", as we came to call this particular unit, to a neighbouring airfield early one morning. In so doing, the Flight Start Officer, who slept in the Starter's Hut at the edge of the field, was frightened from his resting place by machine-gun fire. Clothed only in a nightshirt, he sought to avoid the embarrassing effects of the Lukas by escaping across the airfield. One British single-seat fighter was attracted to the gentleman with the fluttering white banner and did not recognise this improvised sign of capitulation. Instead, the British pilot fastened like fury onto his quarry's tracks and chased the poor man with machine-gun fire back and forth across the field.'

Left: Ltn.d.Res Adolf Auer was Carl Degelow's wingman during much of autumn 1918. For this formal post-war photo Auer wore the ribbons of his Iron Cross Second Class (centre, above) and the Grand Duchy of Hesse's General Honour Decoration for Bravery. On the left side of his tunic he wore (above) the Iron Cross Second Class, (below at left) the Wound Badge in Black earned during his last air combat on 28 October 1918, and the Military Pilot's Badge.

Above: Early in Adolf Auer's time in Jasta 40, he was assigned to fly a hand-me-down Fokker D.VII, seen here, previously flown by Willy Rosenstein. Auer was too new to the unit to understand that he could have selected his own personal combat insignia and so this 'plane was arbitrarily redecorated with a Star of David.

Following the devastating air raid on Lomme airfield, Jasta 40's loss of four (out of ten) aeroplanes severely impaired its operational ability. Carl Degelow anticipated a lull in activity until repairs were made to the damaged facilities and replacement aeroplanes arrived. The pause provided a rare break for Degelow, who went on his first leave in over a year, thinking that, after the air raid, it would be weeks before the unit was ready for full frontline service. During his absence, Ltn Willy Rosenstein was in charge of the Staffel.

Serving Under Rosenstein

A few days before the raid, a new pilot, Stuttgart native Ltn.d.Res Adolf Auer, had arrived at Jasta 40. Degelow thought that, since Rosenstein was also born in Stuttgart, the two Württembergers would get on well together and assigned Auer to work with his valued deputy. Degelow required all new pilots to make practice flights over a rear area before going over the battlefront. Hence, Auer spent most of his first full day in Jasta 40 studying a map and aerial photos of the area he would patrol. The next day, he and Rosenstein went up in a pair of old Albatros fighters to practice air combat tactics. Auer remembered the lessons of his fighter pilot training and constantly turned his head, scanning the sky for the mock opponent who seemed to be able to disappear into the clouds. Time and again, however, Rosenstein made a tight turn or dived out of sight and re-emerged on Auer's tail in the classic 'kill' position. A careful balance of speed, audacity and caution were the keys to survival. At the end of the session, Rosenstein promised that Auer would soon fly a Fokker D.VII.

Due to the losses suffered during the air raid, Auer thought it would be some time before he would fly in a Fokker. But, a few days later, four new Fokker D.VIIs arrived from the 4th Army's air park. Auer's hope of being assigned one of the new aeroplanes faded when Rosenstein used his seniority to claim one of the new machines. Auer recalled:

'After the catastrophic air raid I received Rosenstein's old aeroplane. The silver outline of a heart, which was his battle symbol, was painted over and replaced with a six-pointed star. At the time I was unaware of the religious significance of the symbol and took it to be the commonly-seen beer brewer's emblem. In my first days with the Staffel, Rosenstein drank a special toast of brotherhood with me. Probably because of the star.[10]

'I made my first combat patrol, from Lomme to Ypres, on the evening of 21 August. Despite previous training, a pilot making his first combat flight over the lines felt like a child learning to walk. It was such a totally new experience.

'We flew toward the Front in an arrow-like formation, with the leader at the point and others spreading out behind him, left and right. It was relatively quiet that day and so we tried to attain the highest altitude possible. We got as high as 5,500 metres without having to use oxygen. Fortunately, at Jasta 40 it was customary to have beginners fly in the middle of the formation. That was fine with me; if an enemy formation got above us and, as usual, attacked from out of the sun, the man flying at the end of our formation would be the first target. The farther back a pilot flew, the more life-threatening his situation became.'[11]

Auer was fortunate in that his early combat flights were without incident. For several weeks his flight spotted – or was observed by – British fighters at great distances, but both groups carried out their missions, without deviating course to encounter the distant opponents.

Jagdgruppe 6's four Staffeln were very active over their sector, but had little success for their efforts, as reported in 4th Army weekly activity overviews:[12]

Week of	Missions Flown	Victories	Casualties	Deaths
22 August	252	2	1	1
29 August	345	0	0	0
5 September	72	0	1	0
12 September	191	0	2	2
19 September	215	7	1	1

These reports trailed actual activity by a week; hence, the late recording of what Adolf Auer recalled as the Jagdgruppe's fuel shortage at the end of August. Due to the low fuel supplies and success of the British advance, in early September the units were transported by lorry from Lomme to a small airfield at Reckem, northeast of Lille.

Shooting Down a Balloon

By the time Carl Degelow returned from leave, Rosenstein had overseen the move of men and equipment to Reckem. Jasta 40 had its full complement of aeroplanes and the orientation and operational flights had taken place – but there were no new aerial victories to report. Degelow had hardly unpacked his bags at the new airfield when he was informed of work yet to be done. He recalled:

'Among the items that came to my attention after I returned to the Staffel was news of a particularly bothersome British captive balloon unit outside Poperinghe. It provided excellent observation service for British forces assaulting our lines near Ypres and beyond. We received a special request from Hauptmann Wilberg, Kommandeur der Flieger for the 4th Army, to put the balloon out of business. I was not particularly keen about going after a captive balloon as, shortly after returning from leave, my machine-gun synchronisation gear failed during a flight over the frontlines and I literally shot off my own propeller. After a beautiful glide to the pitted Flemish terrain, I landed my Fokker in a shell crater, where it turned over. This unpleasant incident remained in my thoughts for a long time and it required great willpower and military discipline for me to overcome the chilling feeling that such a memory evoked. Considering the request from the 4th Army, my mind formed an image of a bad end to my diving on an enemy gas bag, after which I would be the captive and be done for, rather than the balloon.

'On the other hand, I found it more difficult to delegate the task to one of our other pilots, or even to ask for a volunteer. One of the obligations of leadership is not asking a subordinate to do what you yourself would not be willing to do. Hence, Staffel-Führer Degelow appointed Jagdflieger [fighter pilot] Degelow to do the job.

'In attempting to shoot down captive balloons, wind conditions were of great importance, as was ably demonstrated by Oberleutnant Fritz Röth, Germany's greatest "balloon-killer". Of his twenty-eight aerial victories, twenty were scored against enemy balloons, which he sent down in flames. For his achievements, this mild-mannered air-fighter received almost every award bestowed by his native Bavaria, as well as the German Empire. After his death, Bavaria made him a *Ritter* [Knight] of the *Militär-Max-Josef-Orden*, that kingdom's highest bravery decoration which carried with it elevation to the nobility and the addition of the prestigious "von" before the recipient's family name. Of course, Röth also became a Knight of the Order Pour le Mérite.[13]

'As we learned from his widely-circulated reports, before every attack, Röth spent many hours peering through a telescope, watching the manoeuvres of the aeroplanes protecting his intended targets. Most important of all, he devoted considerable time to the weather forecast charts. He would wait for a favourable day on which the wind was somewhat parallel to the Front and to the row of balloons. Then he would go up to a very high point and dive straight down on the carefully arranged row of British gas bags.

By this tactic, Röth initially achieved a quick and almost unnoticed approach to the balloons. Secondly, the speed of his single-seat fighter, aided by the speed of the wind, enabled him to fly so swiftly through the curtain of protective anti-aircraft and machine-gun fire that he was too fast-moving a target to hit.

'Having been made aware of Röth's tactics, I spent the better part of two days observing this particular balloon through a telescope. It was only some twenty kilometres away from us and mounted high enough in the sky to be visible for miles around. Having decided on a course of action, based on my observations, I ordered my armourer, Unteroffizier [Corporal] Schmitz, to make special preparations. Very carefully, he loaded my gun bullets with a combination of regular bullets, incendiary phosphorous bullets to ignite the balloon's hydrogen gas, tracer bullets to guide my stream of fire, and armour-piercing rounds to ensure the balloon was punctured in case my other bullets glanced off a steel cable holding the balloon.

'I could not take up a normal flight of four or six Fokkers, as that would arouse too much suspicion. Therefore, one September evening, I chose my most successful colleague, the able Willy Rosenstein, already the victor in four combats, to accompany me. It was a beautiful day, with large, billowing cumulus clouds drifting low across the bright blue sky.

'No sooner were we over Reckem than we could see the *Himmelswurst* [sky sausage] up at about 1,000 metres, just below the cloud cover. That was perfect. I looked over at Rosenstein and he nodded, already perceiving that we should go up another 200 metres or so and, dodging in and out of the clouds, sneak up on the tethered gas bag.

'Then, through a hole in the clouds, we saw the monster, for that is what it looked like when viewed at close range. Rosenstein stayed above, to keep any would-be intruders from thwarting my mission, and I went into a steep dive, pouring bullets into the balloon as fast as my machine gun would allow. The balloon swung merrily on its cable, as if nothing were happening. Then I had to pull up from the dive or risk colliding with the big, rubber-skinned behemoth. An incredibly tight, corkscrew turn, during which negative gravitational forces threatened to push my stomach up through my rib cage, put me back on an even plane with the balloon. Again I opened fire. Again, the damned thing continued to swing in the wind. This swinging motion often brought destruction to a pilot and therein lay this aerial giant's strength in a fight; the movement back and forth caused by the air currents could easily put the balloon on a collision course with the attacking aeroplane.

'Once, twice, three times I tried to woo the inflammable soul of my opponent – but all in vain. I could not understand how it could survive such an assault of incendiary bullets, most of which were right on the mark. Now, the Himmelswurst was being zealously hauled down by a motorised winch on the ground. British gunners from all directions turned their attention to my frail Fokker. The balloon went lower and lower and yet showed no sign of burning. Ultimately, it was obviously within metres of being saved, so I could do nothing but give up the fight and go home. All the way back to Reckem I reviewed the situation in my mind. It was unbelievable that I could fire over 250 incendiary rounds into a balloon filled with the most highly volatile gas and not set the damned thing on fire. I was almost tempted to believe it was indestructible.

'Back at our 'field, I was still shaking with rage over the events of the last hour when I was summoned to the telephone. It was some "mole" of an officer from 4th Army Headquarters, who, by his obvious insensitivity to the work of flyers, proved that he had never been more than a metre off the ground.

'"Why didn't you set fire to that balloon near Poperinghe?" he demanded to know in a shrill voice.

'"I don't know," I replied in as calm a tone as I could manage. "'Why don't you tell me after you have found the answer?"

'With that, our telephone link to 4th Army Headquarters "suddenly" went silent. A few days later, on the afternoon of 18 September, I sought my revenge. The insouciant British balloon had to go down. Again, Rosenstein and I flew over the lines, this time assisted by rain and cloud cover. I vowed to myself that the gas bag would burn this time, even if I had to land alongside it and personally light a match to it. While Rosenstein waited amidst the clouds, I began my first attack. Then, to my surprise and delight, my first burst of fire produced the most brilliant pyrotechnic display I have ever seen. Before he even had a chance to warm his limbs in the "pleasant" heat, the balloon observer jumped over the side. His parachute opened and he fluttered down like a leaf in the summer air.[14]

'Hurrah! It was such a joy to see the vertical smoke column, rising skyward like a burnt offering on the Flanders plain. As I soon found out, such joyful feelings are better indulged in after one has safely returned to his own airfield. Suddenly, bullets came crashing into my crate – Pitsch! Pitsch! Pitsch! – and then I noticed two British aeroplanes apparently intent on avenging my little exercise in arson. But good old Rosenstein was on them in a second, firing away. Since the Englishmen did not know whether he was alone or leading an entire swarm of Fokkers, they cautiously pulled away for a moment to assess the situation. That was long enough for Rosenstein and me to seek the safety of our own lines. We had done a good day's work; we would catch up with these fellows another time.'

Observation balloons were very difficult targets. Hence, this first and only balloon 'kill' brought Carl Degelow firmly to the attention of achievement-driven staff members of the Air Force Commanding General. For morale-building and propaganda purposes, Degelow had become an airman worthy of note. If he were to shoot down increasing numbers of enemy aircraft, he would become a valuable motivational resource for the Kogenluft. Even with the war all but lost, General von Hoeppner and the other top leaders still needed examples of German superiority to hold up as examples of combatants ready and willing to risk everything for the Fatherland. Consequently, the eagerly awaited opening narrative of the 26 September 1918 issue of the Kogenluft weekly summary of information, *Nachrichtenblatt der Luftstreitkräfte*, made reference to Degelow's fourteenth victory (the British balloon) and his fifteenth and sixteenth air combat triumphs, which occurred shortly thereafter.[15] And, of course, his triumphs were included among the overall aerial victory tallies published weeks later.

A Caquot R captive observation balloon of the type shot down by Carl Degelow on 18 September 1918. Designed by the Frenchman Albert Caquot, who improved on the German Parseval Sigisfeld ballon, the type R was in common use by American, British and French observation units. The example seen here bears a US Air Service cockade, painted on a square piece of fabric which was glued to the balloon.

Increasing the Score

For the next ten days, Carl Degelow became Jasta 40's principal air combat victor. Flying a superior aeroplane – the Fokker D.VII – and employing proven tactics, while showing dogged determination and great personal courage, he raised his score from fourteen to nineteen confirmed aerial victories. He described his winning streak, beginning with his fifteenth victory, on 20 September thus:

'My encounter with the British captive balloon and its defenders was not without consequence. Back at our airfield I discovered that I had taken a hit in the radiator. Of course, our very able mechanics immediately set to work to find the trouble spot and repair it. One would think that a radiator leak would be an easy thing to find and fix, but that was not the case. We were just beginning to be affected by the lack of so many small items that we had taken for granted and, in this case, the problem was that we did not have suitable material to make an effective weld over the hole in the radiator. Consequently, our mechanics had to work for almost two days to make a repair that would last. Knowing how badly I wanted to get back into action, they stayed up the whole night of 19/20 September working on my Fokker.

'Early on the morning of the 20th, just after I had awoken from a fitful night's sleep and was walking around the field to build up an appetite for breakfast, I was greeted by Feldwebel [Sergeant] Heinrich, my leading mechanic. As tired as he obviously was, he still had a cheerful way about him when he reported that my aeroplane was again fit for service.

'"Wunderbar!" I replied and told him to have it brought out onto the 'field so I could take it up immediately for a test flight. Within five minutes, I was in the cockpit, listening to the steady roar of the Mercedes engine and watching the temperature gauge with a careful eye. Everything was running smoothly, so I waved away the chocks from beneath the wheels and raced across the 'field and into the air.

'I had no sooner got up to about 3,000 metres over Reckem when I spotted three British two-seaters in the distance. Despite my initial disinclination, due mainly to the erratic wavering of the needle on the temperature gauge, it seemed like a good idea to bring down one of these Tommies before breakfast.'

As a result of his efforts, two of the Bristol F.2Bs flew off and Degelow forced the third to land north of Annappes. He thereby gained the capture of a perfectly intact aeroplane and two prisoners from 48 Squadron, RAF: Lt M.R. Mahony and 2/Lt J.N. Kier (as is recounted in greater detail in Chapter One of this book).

The following day, Degelow led four Jasta 40 comrades against a more typical British two-seat reconnaissance aeroplane. He spotted a big, ungainly-looking R.E.8, bucking strong winds as the pilot tried to stay on a course to enable his observer to photograph ground positions north of Ypres. The aeroplane's inherent instability[16] required the full attention of the pilot, twenty-year-old Lt Wilfred Allanson[17] of 7 Squadron, RAF. The backseat man, 2/Lt William Anderson, aged twenty-one,[18] was so occupied with his camera that only the ominous grey threads of Degelow's incendiary ammunition alerted him to danger from above.

Quickly, Anderson stowed the camera and swung his single Lewis machine gun toward his attacker. But, the black Fokker leader was too quick for his adversary and, after a brief exchange of fire, had triumphed again. The R.E.8 caught fire and smashed into the ground. Both crewmen in Degelow's sixteenth victory[19] perished.

The Staffel-Führer could only take cold comfort in having destroyed whatever revealing photos Lt Anderson may have taken of German positions. Like many other combatants, Carl Degelow sought to de-personalise his actions, which meant in this case that, by denying British intelligence officers of the information, the lives of German infantrymen would have been saved – if even for one more day of the hard-fought rearguard action needed to salvage and consolidate ever more demoralised German army units.

Three days later, on the early evening of Tuesday, 24 September, Degelow led his entire Staffel in interdicting a flight of bomb-laden S.E.5s. He recalled:

'Toward evening the Staffel started out on patrol. We knew from experience that at this time of day British bombing squadrons would cross our lines in an attempt to saturate strategic points in the army sector with their dangerous cargo. To stop them, we would have to catch them unawares and our approach to them was arranged accordingly. We knew they expected us to attack from above, so we alternated our plan and put off "making altitude", as we called it whenever we tried to reach great heights of 5,000 metres or so, and catch them from below.

'Such flights during clear weather were always a pleasure, offering the best sport. We could fly a wide course, looking for our prey. Coming over Lille at a relatively low altitude, we could see on the edge of the fortification the outlines of the city's famed citadel, whose angular lines were a welcome point of orientation even during poor visibility. The big northern train station of Lille passed beneath us like a black blur, from which thin, fine tracks branched out in all directions. The white highways, glistening in the landscape with their characteristic forking, led the eye on a northeasterly course toward the industrial city of Tourcoing and to the suburban Roubaix. Both of these towns, with their gleaming red roofs whose rows of houses grew into each other, were good reference points for fliers moving endlessly in the sea of air. To make it from here to the Front, which was our duty, we simply followed the course of the Lys River. With an easy left turn we reached our goal.

'Then came the moment when the seeker of beauty, searching for scenic pictures and the geographic peculiarities of Mother Earth, had to be supplemented by the devoted fighter pilot. Profound contemplations were replaced by a readiness to react to whatever the enemy might do. We reconnoitred and searched the heavens for enemy aircraft. Puffs of anti-aircraft smoke in the distance were enough to tell even the novice that intruders were over our territory.

'We came upon an enemy bombing flight near Menin. It consisted of ten bombing aeroplanes protected by eight single-seat fighters. Our tactic was first to attack the fighters, since they flew higher than their bomb-carrying companions. We gained altitude and caught the British S.E.5s from the least expected point: right below their floorboards.

'I closed in on a fellow with a big white letter "Y" painted on his top wing. "Mister Y" was a very skilful flyer and avoided my attack through a series of very deft turns. His higher altitude worked to his advantage, as he could move faster on his own level than I could in a climbing position. Nothing I did could entice him to come down to my level. So, after we had wildly stormed round and round each other a few times, I tried to bluff him. I pulled my Fokker straight up and for one supreme moment I had the S.E.5 squarely in front of my guns. I pressed the buttons of my machine guns, really only to intimidate my partner by the fire and hopefully get him to give up his advantageous altitude and dive for the ground. But, in so doing, some of my shots, which were surely accidental hits, went into the S.E.5's reserve fuel tank.

'Bright flames immediately burst from the aeroplane's top wing, where the tank was located. I was very pleased by my tactic and believed the enemy was finished. "Mister Y" had, however, pulled far away, as there was no way for him to bring the aerial battle to a favourable end. Then, with his machine glowing with fire, he dived right at me, all the while maintaining a murderous stream of fire from his machine guns. I must say that this unexpected attack upset me, to put it mildly; but at the same time the fellow's foolhardiness aroused my fighting spirit.

'The Englishman suddenly dived violently, during which the rush of air almost snuffed out the inferno over his head. But, as soon as he resumed level flight, the fire became even more intense.

'After a last futile attack, he must have recognised the hopelessness of carrying on the fight. He withdrew from the encounter and tried to slip away from me. But I was not yet ready to give up the fight. I pursued him doggedly and was soon joined by another gentleman of my Staffel who added a few shots to the effort to ensure that "Mister Y" did not reach his lines intact. Severely battered by our attack, the enemy aeroplane exploded at low altitude and broke up close to the edge of Zillebeke Lake.'

On this occasion Jasta 40 apparently also encountered a flight of Armstrong Whitworth FK 8 two-seaters from 82 Squadron, RAF being escorted by S.E.5s of 41 Squadron, RAF. In his combat report, the flight commander, Captain William E. Shields, DFC, of 41 Squadron, wrote:

'... [A]fter dropping bombs on Comines at 5:50 p.m., our formation was attacked by fourteen Fokker Biplanes painted black with white tails. I immediately climbed and turned on one E.A., which had started down on an A.W. [Armstrong Whitworth], and fired two good bursts into E.A., which went down with smoke coming from it. I followed [the] E.A. and saw it crash a little northwest of Comines.

'I saw Lieut [H.C.] Telfer attack another ... E.A., which went down vertically.'[20]

Capt Shields received credit for shooting down one of the Fokkers, but it is unlikely that his victim was from Jasta 40, which reported no losses that day. The pilot of the lone S.E.5 casualty – confirmed as Degelow's seventeenth victory – was twenty-two-year-old Capt Charles Crawford[21] of 41 Squadron, who was reported as 'last seen in combat [at] 6 p.m. northwest of Lille'.[22] He survived the destruction of his aeroplane and was taken prisoner by German ground forces.

During a pause in the ground fighting, Degelow inquired about this opponent:

'The next morning a search party was sent out to the crash site, which I had indicated on a map. I did not go with them. While I liked nothing better than to shake the hand of a captured foe and to have a drink or two with him in our Kasino, I did not care at all to visit the scene of a fatal crash or the wreckage of an opponent who was mortally wounded by my guns. I had no desire to see the bone–smashing effect of my bullets. War is a gruesome business. No apology was ever made for killing an opponent – because no apology could be acceptable. So, the soldier simply pushed on, trying to the best of his ability to achieve the objectives set forth for him by that ever elusive presence: The High Command.

'Not far from Zillebeke Lake our men found pieces of S.E.5 wreckage. The serial number of the engine was noted for our records. The body of a British pilot was found nearby. In his coat pocket, the mechanics found a cigarette case bearing the inscription: "Bennett to his Brand." Later, I tried to return this memento to a British aviation facility, but could find none to accept it. During the Allied night bombing raids on Germany in World War II, this relic of World War I was lost amidst the witches' dance of destruction.

'In the silence of my quarters at Jasta 40 I rendered to Mister Brand the last honour by saying a special prayer. He was a brave and worthy opponent, who, despite overwhelming adversity, fought to the very end.'

New research by this author shows that Carl Degelow was incorrect in his assumption that he had killed his opponent. And, while his comrades may have located the wreckage of Captain Crawford's S.E.5 near Zillebeke Lake, the body they recovered must have been a casualty from a different fight. Previously,[23] that body was identified as that of twenty-eight-year-old Lt Harry J. Bennett, an Airco D.H.9 pilot from 49 Squadron,[24] who perished on the morning of 24 September while attacking the Aulnoye railroad junction, east of Cambrai. But Bennett's fatal crash in a two-seater was too early in the day and at a location too far south to be related to Degelow's evening aerial combat in Flanders. However, the Jasta 40 Staffel-Führer could not have known those facts and, in any event, was focused on keeping Allied aeroplanes away from German combatants on the ground:

'Following my victory over the S.E.5 on Tuesday evening, there was an unusual calmness over our sector of the Front. We made routine patrols over the lines, but could not seem to interest our British friends in any aerial encounters. Such an unusually quiet period could indicate only one thing: the enemy was preparing for a massive offensive.

'Just that suspicion alone was enough to make me even more tense than usual, for such an undertaking was always carried out by a vastly superior force that made us fight harder than ever. The enemy was smart; he saved his valuable aircrews for the bigger job yet to come.

'Consequently, it was a refreshing sight that Friday afternoon, 27 September, to spot normal British air activity over our lines. It was partly cloudy as my Staffel passed over Armentières on the way to the frontlines. Down below and completely unaware of our presence was a flight of three Bristol Fighters, no doubt loaded with bombs, in addition to the combined firepower of the pilot and observer.'

Two of the Bristol F.2Bs eluded the black Fokkers and the Jasta 40 flight's extended chase of the remaining two-seater finally ended over Valenciennes (as more fully related in Chapter One). Degelow had fired enough bullets into the stubbornly flown Bristol Fighter to cause structural failure in the aircraft, causing it to crash to the ground, killing the crew of Lt Cuthbert Foster and Sgt Thomas Proctor of 88 Squadron, RAF.

The event was officially logged in as Degelow's eighteenth victory. While he did not discuss such matters with his pilots – not even his closest associate, Willy Rosenstein – Degelow knew that he had become a serious contender for the coveted Pour le Mérite. To be sure, the war was all but lost – but personal honour remained achievable.

1   Esposito, *A Concise History of World War I*, p. 118.

2   Jones, *The War in the Air*, Vol. VI, p. 437

3   Esposito, op.cit., p. 119.

4   Royal Air Force, *Communiqué No. 19*, 14 August 1918, p. 2.

5   Kogenluft, *Nachrichtenblatt der Luftstreitkräfte*, Vol. II, No. 25, 15 August 1918, p. 368.

6   O'Connor, *Aviation Awards of Imperial Germany and the Men Who Earned Them*, Vol. II, p. 132.

7   Kogenluft, *Nachrichtenblatt*, No. 33, 10 October 1918, p. 528.

8   Lt Edgar Percy Everard McCleery was born in 1893 in Moss Vale, New South Wales, Australia. Assigned to 4 Squadron, AFC, he was flying Sopwith Camel 1F.1 D.1961 when he was killed during the raid on Lomme [Ref: Cutlack, *The Australian Flying Corps in the War of 1914-1918*, p. 349]. He was buried at Ration Farm, La Chapelle-d'Armentières, France [Ref: Hobson, *Airmen Died in the Great War 1914-1918*, p. 211].

9   Cutlack, op.cit.

10   According to his *Personal-Bogen* and comments he made to this author, Adolf Auer followed the Lutheran faith, but it seems that Rosenstein thought him to be a Jewish co-religionist. Having been subjected to anti-Semitic remarks by Hermann Göring, Rosenstein naturally sought the companionship of a kindred spirit. In any event, the men became lifelong friends and, prior to his death on 23 May 1949, Rosenstein wrote a favourable recommendation for Auer, who, like so many German officers and officials, had to undergo denazification proceedings after World War II.

11   Kilduff, *Over the Battlefronts*, p. 136.

12   *Übersicht über die Tätigkeit der Fliegerverbände* in Kommandeur der Flieger der 4. Armee, *Wochenberichte Nrn 2215* (29 August 1918), 2277 (5 September 1918), 2326 (12 September 1918), 2430 (19 September) and 2492 (26 September 1918).

13   Zuerl, W. *Pour-le-Mérite-Flieger*, p. 396.

14   The balloon was very likely from the 2nd Balloon Wing, 17th Company, 36th Section, RAF, as it was 'the only [balloon] claim and loss reported in this sector' [Ref: Bailey, 'German Balloon Claims During 1918' in *Cross & Cockade Journal*, Vol. XXIV, p. 246].

15   Kogenluft, *Nachrichtenblatt*, No. 31, 26 September 1918, pp. 471-473.

16   Bruce, *British Aeroplanes 1914-1918*, p. 426.

17   Hobson, Airmen Died in the Great War 1914-1918, p. 112.

18   Ibid.

19   Kogenluft, *Nachrichtenblatt*, No. 31, 26 September 1918, p. 473.

20   41 Squadron, RAF, *Combat Report* by Capt Shields, 24 September 1918.

21   Capt Charles Bois R. Crawford was born on 25 December 1895. He served as Lt in the Army, was posted to 22 Squadron as Hon. Capt, and then as Capt to 41 Squadron, RAF. He was reported as missing on 24 September 1918 and repatriated on 29 November 1918 [Ref: U.K. National Archives files WO 339/65552 and 339/132328].

22   RAF, *Combat Casualty List*, 24 September 1918.

23   Kilduff, *Germany's Last Knight of the Air*, p. 162.

24   Hobson, op.cit., p. 117.

CHAPTER TEN
FINAL GLORY OF THE JAGDSTAFFELN

The Last Flanders Offensive Begins

Carl Degelow's suspicions of an impending Allied offensive in Flanders became a reality on 28 September 1918, when forces directed by Belgian King Albert I initiated a vigorous artillery barrage to drive German forces from Belgium. The RAF historian wrote:

'The front of attack extended from Dixmuide to St. Eloi, and the forces involved were from the Belgian army, some French divisions and the British Second Army under General Sir Herbert Plumer …

'As secrecy was essential there was no abnormal air activity before the attack was launched at 5:30 a.m. on the 28th of September …'[1]

The Allied plan had the desired effect, as Degelow related:

'Drowsily I rubbed my eyes, trying to snap myself out of my dream-like stupor. The barrage increased in intensity, the windows clattered and the wooden barracks that served as our shelter vibrated to the tune of the hellish music that was hitting us from the Front.

'In this twilight condition, there was a feeling of our senses being numb and it was no figment of imagination, no illusion. We clearly heard the rumbling and grumbling of the artillery barrage. The British and their Allies had begun their last big push. Our 4th Army, which formed the right angle of the line of withdrawal on the Western Front, was supposed to close in with great forces, for which reinforcements of aerial observers had already been brought in. Our submarine bases at Zeebrugge were in danger of being cut off by this Allied drive, thereby paralysing our submarines operating in the Atlantic and in the English Channel. The withdrawal of our southern armies would collapse if the Allied breakthrough were successful. In rapid succession orders came from the Kommandeur der Flieger for the 4th Army (Kofl 4):

'"Large-scale British and French aircraft squadron operations are expected to begin at daybreak. Jagdstaffel 40 should prepare immediately for the highest state of readiness: Aeroplanes in front of the hangars, pilots in their cockpits, engines ready to start. Further orders will follow."

'The cannon thunder rolled on uninterrupted and the heavy artillery muzzle flashes blazed across the Front like bolts of lightning. A fine mist drizzled down incessantly. It was not a hopeful outlook for the coming day of battle. The wide-ranging aerial battles

142

we had known before were scarcely to be expected during such weather conditions. But then hunting fever gripped our bodies. The time spent waiting for the mission made us nervous – each of us wanted to be "after the Tommy", but in the heavy rain, there was little prospect of activity.

'Usually, the first day of a great offensive was full of encounters with our cockade-bedecked opponents. But just waiting was exhausting. Morning had dawned, the artillery became weaker – but our Divine Confederate allowed it to continue raining. Muffled in their flight suits, my pilots stood by their machines, shrouded by a hopeless greyness. Then there was always the uncertainty: what could we do when the Tommy came? Or had the heavy rains and clouds made orientation impossible? Up front in the mud-filled shell holes along Zillebeke Lake, the battle of man against man raged on. And we – we sat on alert!

'No report about the situation at the Front was received from Kofl 4. The staff-types sat at different levels far to the rear and they were entirely dependent on reports from the reconnaissance and infantry-liaison aircrews. But those crews could similarly not take off under such weather conditions. We flyers could only wait and drink tea.

'Several nerve-wracking hours passed. The dark clouds in the sky moved a little. The British were better off with the prevailing west wind than we were; their patrol vessels at sea could promptly pass along by radio every change in the weather.

'The rain-heavy clouds passed and soon we were aware of the roar of engines in the sky. Every pilot eagerly thought about catching a Tommy. Then an S.E.5 emerged through a break in the clouds and disappeared in a gust of hail and rain. We took off after it, but lack of visibility was the stumbling block; any sort of normal aerial battle was no longer possible. The rain became more furious; our goggles were blurred by the driving torrents of water. Our overly-eager flight into this mess could not continue. We had no choice but to land quickly and then take our water-logged "birds" into the hangars to dry out.

'It was not until afternoon that there was a significant improvement in the weather. The rain stopped and the blue of the sky smiled. Our mood improved. We were all set to take off and head for Ypres when our spirits were dampened by this order from Kofl 4:

'"Jagdstaffel 40 is to remain in reserve and may take off only on my express orders. But, when British squadrons attempt to reconnoitre the important replacements in our rear areas, they are to be immediately forced away."

'Yes, the old adage was certainly true: for half of his life the soldier waits in vain. What bad luck! While the other Staffeln of our Jagdgruppe [fighter group] danced with Tommy, we were playing the game called "Hans, watch the sky".

'Finally, at about three in the afternoon, the long-awaited order came. As there was no clear idea of the army's situation at the Front, an especially experienced infantry-liaison aircrew was sent out to determine how far the British had pushed the forward-most points of their front line. Kofl 4 would at last see what was taking place amidst the fiercely contested trenches. But we knew the British would oppose this mission with as many aeroplanes as they could muster out there to greet us.

'The infantry-liaison crew passed over our field at Reckem in an "old hare" of a two-seat reconnaissance plane. The observer made their presence known by firing a red signal flare. Our Staffel responded by taking off and, once in the air, surrounding him on all sides. We immediately headed for the frontlines.

'Once there, we saw that we had company and that they all bore the blue, white and red cockades of England, which we called *Portwein-Augen* [bloodshot eyes]. Our flight of fighters closed around our two-seater crew, which was busily communicating with the infantrymen by a series of flashing light signals. White cloth panels were spread out on the ground to mark the positions of our troops, while Sopwiths and S.E.5s scurried about at 1,000 metres altitude. My fighter pilots did not like such a defensive role, but that was what the tactical situation called for. This time a precise knowledge of our most forward lines was much more important than shooting down an Englishman or two.

'Our two-seater repeatedly criss-crossed the frontlines. We could see very distinctly how the observer worked on his notes in his cramped cockpit space. Then a swarm of twelve British fighters tried to block our way. Like a wedge, our tightly-led flight dived on the loose formation of Tommies. They wanted to play with us – now we would play with them.

'Soon, I was on the tail of a Sopwith Camel and, due to his lack of experience, the pilot did not see me until I was only two aeroplane lengths behind him. With one burst from my machine guns, he was on fire. He plunged into a water-filled shell hole. I turned to get his companion in my sights, but he was luckier and was able to bring his stricken machine down onto the muddy ground.

'Then I fired off a flare to signal my Staffel that it was time to go back home.

'But back at Reckem there was no calmness. We were ordered to move back again, this time a few kilometres northeast to Bisseghem. For the pilots the move was easy; each of us simply loaded our belongings into his aeroplane, behind the seat. The ground crews, however, had to make their way by cars and lorries over clogged, poorly maintained roads. It was all very depressing.

'As the Allied offensive wore on, the aerial battles between ever larger groups of aeroplanes became more frequent. The struggle for a swift, decisive victory by the Allies was countered by our hopes of holding the line until winter allowed us to consolidate our position. These opposing goals led to battles of increasing severity and, I may say, with greater bitterness.'

While Carl Degelow claimed to have shot down two Sopwith Camels that day, he was credited with only one, which was listed as his nineteenth victory.[2] That one – and possibly even two – aircraft most likely came from 70 Squadron, RAF, which was active in a broad area northeast and southeast of Ypres for much of the day. As 70 Squadron lost four Sopwith Camels[3] during those encounters on 28 September, it was nearly impossible to tell who fought with whom on a day when abundant cloud cover offered an easy escape. One of the Royal Air Force participants, Lt Oscar A.P. Heron, described his encounter with Fokkers with black fuselages:

'While on Low Flying Patrol, I encountered three Fokker Biplanes at about 1,200 feet. They dived on me and I did a climbing turn, got on the tail of one and he went into a spin when I had fired about 100 rounds. The other two continued the attack until a French Spad joined the scrap … [after which the Fokkers] climbed into the clouds.'[4]

The sparse 'office' of a Sopwith 1F.1 Camel, a frequent opponent of Jasta 40.

The following day, the activity was just as hectic, but Jasta 40 returned to Bisseghem airfield with only one aerial victory to show for their efforts. The deputy squadron leader, Leutnant der Reserve Willy Rosenstein, had claimed a Bristol Fighter, which was credited as his sixth victory.[5] However, as no Bristol F.2B was listed as lost in Jasta 40's operational area that day,[6] it is more likely that Rosenstein was part of a JaGru 6 force mentioned in reports filed by 211 Squadron, RAF, a unit equipped with similar-looking two-seat Airco D.H.9 aircraft and assigned to bomb Ypres and Courtrai on the early afternoon of 29 September.

The RAF formation leader on that raid, Lt. H. Axford, DFC, described the fight – which had all of the hallmarks of an aerial shark attack – in which he and his observer, Sergeant Mechanic Fred Williamson, DFM, encountered 'forty to fifty enemy aircraft, Fokker Biplanes [and] Fokker Triplanes':

'Just before reaching the objective, we saw about twenty E.A. climbing to attack. After bombing the objective, we turned to come back. Almost immediately, about eighteen E.A. attacked from the front, apparently endeavouring to break up the formation; we, however, kept straight on firing with the front guns. The E.A. then split up to the sides of the formation and attacked from the rear. Shortly afterwards twenty more E.A. attacked the right side of the formation and attempted to break it up. This manoeuvre again failed, 'though two of our machines were shot down in flames and two [were sent down] absolutely out of control and several others driven down. The E.A. continued the attack across our lines until we were almost over Ypres; they then retired. There were apparently no Allied scouts in the vicinity at the time.'[7]

Given the number of aeroplanes involved in this action, it is virtually impossible to identify who shot down which aircraft. But this massive attack in broad daylight is typical of furious German efforts to protect ground troops involved in the gradual withdrawal to the homeland.

Among the German casualties on 29 September was twenty-six-year-old Oberleutnant Hans-Eberhardt Gandert, who commanded both Jasta 51 and Jagdgruppe 6, to which Jasta 40 belonged. He was wounded and shot down over Langemarck, very likely by a Sopwith Camel of 210 Squadron, RAF,[8] and was taken prisoner.[9]

Gandert was succeeded as JaGru 6 commander by Erhard Milch,[10] who was the same age as his predecessor and also a career army officer with extensive aviation experience. Milch had been promoted to Hauptmann five weeks earlier and, while he had received both pilot and observer training, he spent most of World War I in two-seat reconnaissance units and aviation-related command and staff positions. A consummate organisation man (who, as a forty-eight-year-old Generalfeldmarschall, held one of the top positions in the Luftwaffe in World War II), Milch quickly took charge of his new command on 1 October and held it together during the chaotic remainder of the war.[11]

October Darkness

With fewer hours of daylight in the autumn, good flying weather on Tuesday, 1 October, brought out Royal Air Force units in great numbers from morning through late afternoon. Consequently, on that day, RAF bombers dropped 30 tons of bombs[12] over German-held territory. Within JaGru 6's operational area, according to one British report:

'A bomb raid of 109 Squadron, after dropping their bombs on Ingelmunster Station, [was] attacked by a large formation of thirty-three E.A. During a running fight, which lasted for over ten minutes, the [two seat] D.H.9s kept together in close formation and shot three of the hostile machines down in flames ... one was seen to crash near the railway line at Roulers ...'[13]

Jasta 40 suffered no casualties on 1 October and, indeed, had one confirmed air triumph – an S.E.5 fighter escort shot down over Menin[14] by Carl Degelow. It was recorded as his twentieth victory[15] and, the following day, Degelow scored his twenty-first,[16] a Sopwith Camel over Roulers.[17] The pilot was the only member of his eight-aeroplane flight to be lost, having been reported as 'gone missing' at 8:10 a.m.[18]

The following day, 3 October, brought Jasta 40 face-to-face with French Spad S.VII fighters. Degelow recalled:

'At this point in the war, our encounters were almost exclusively with British aeroplanes, as they were largely responsible for contending with us on the Flanders Sector. That was quite a change from a year earlier, when the celebrated French ace

Capitaine Georges Guynemer and his "Stork" Escadrille were part of the Allied air effort. At that time, French aircraft appeared in great numbers all along the Front. In 1918 we did not see the abundance of French aircraft that we had previously and so we tended to look down on the Frenchies. We felt they simply "lurked" along the frontlines,[19] while their cousins from across the Channel took the leading part in the attempt to achieve mastery of the air. As may be imagined, we were anxious to test our fine Fokkers against their vaunted Spads. Our opportunity came soon enough.

'Dark black shell bursts at about 1,000 metres altitude announced that our anti-aircraft batteries had sighted a pack of enemy fighters out hunting in the vicinity of the Belgian town of Roulers. At the time we spotted the enemy, our Staffel had reached an altitude of about 3,500 metres. Therefore, we had a good overview of the enemy situation and could calmly prepare the appropriate attack strategy. The man up high always had the advantage, as he could cut off the opponent's escape route. Right off, I took aim at the enemy formation leader, who, having spotted us, headed as quickly as possible for his own lines. But I was soon right on his heels and I clearly recognised the red, white and blue cockades of France on the wings of his Spad.

'The pilot suddenly turned around in his seat. Yet I still did not fire, remembering the rule: "You can never be too close." At this moment, his Spad and my Fokker D.VII were travelling at the same speed, quickly approaching the lines, where he might find salvation. The target filled my gun-sight. I fired both machine guns – tak-tak-tak-tak- – and in an instant the Spad caught fire. It quickly broke up along the way and crashed on the edge of Roulers.

'The next knight of the air tried to take his leave through aerial artistry, which did not work. He was sent spinning down out of control.

'One of my Staffel comrades, my left wingman, let the third one slip away. It was now left to the last man of the Spad formation to bring home the bad news about the ill-fated fight. But then I saw a Fokker chasing the badly smoking Frenchman, who crashed into a row of houses near Roulers. The fourth had also been attended to and now all four assailants lay scarcely a good stone's throw from each other in what was left of their machines.'

The four French Spads shot down on 3 October were credited to Jasta 40 as follows: one to Degelow, his twenty-second victory[20]; one to Ltn Rosenstein, his sixth; one to Ltn Gilly, his fourth; and one to Vizefeldwebel Paul Groll, his third. According to French records, the fighter unit Escadrille Spa 82 lost three pilots in that fight over Roulers: Caporal [Infantry Corporal] Henri Fouriex, Cpl Louis Rolland and Brigadier [Cavalry Corporal] Edmond Priolley; all three men landed within German lines and were taken prisoner.[21] There is no mention of a fourth loss and, once again, the hectic conditions of aerial combat most likely led to errors on the battle's tally.

Friday, 4 October, was a different kind of day for Jasta 40, as Degelow noted: 'We were not so lucky the following day, however, when we got into a low-level running fight with a squadron of Sopwith Camels. Even though Ltn Rosenstein and I each sent one down, one of the Englishmen managed to get above one of our newer pilots, Unteroffizier Paul Podbiol, and shoot him down.'

The fate of Degelow's twenty-third victory[22] (or Rosenstein's seventh) was noted in the records of 65 Squadron, RAF: 'A Camel thought to be [piloted by] 2/Lt Hill[23] [was] seen going down in flames near Lendelede at 17.50 [hours].'[24] And the Camel squadron's 2/Lt William H. Bland very likely shot down Uffz Podbiel near Menin.[25] Bland's combat report was not found in the squadron file, but his pursuit of his target was reported elsewhere to have been: '… in an engagement with several Fokker biplanes, [and] dived to within 100 feet of the ground at one of them, firing continuously, when he saw it crash a complete wreck. [Bland] was now so close to the ground that enemy infantry threw stones at him.'[26]

A day later, on the morning of 5 October, Jasta 40 was among fighter units trying to interdict a formation of Airco D.H.9 two-seat bombers heading for Roulers. Staffel-Führer Degelow shot down one of the intruders and it was credited as his twenty-fourth victory[27] – but British records show the aircraft made it back to British lines, with both pilot and observer being wounded in the fight.[28]

During the Battle of Flanders, squadrons of the 11th and 65th Wings, RAF were attached to the British Second Army, then leading the ground offensive.[29] Elements of those Wings, including 65 and 70 Squadrons, took advantage of a strong wind from out of the southwest at mid-morning of 7 October to launch bomb-carrying Sopwith Camels into JaGru 6's operational area. 65 Squadron, which contributed eighteen aircraft to the effort, reported: 'Forty-four twenty-five-pound bombs [were] dropped from 3,000 feet at 10:30 [a.m.] on Iseghem. No results were observed owing to bad visibility.'[30]

But the squadrons' actions were being watched by Carl Degelow, who recalled:

'We encountered about two dozen Sopwith Camels in the cloudy sky. The Englishmen were forming up on the other side of our frontlines. Here we used a clever strategy, namely deceiving the Tommies as to our nationality by making a broad arc that changed our direction of flight so the sun was now at our backs. That way, the Englishmen could not tell we were Germans until the last possible moment. Obscured by the cloud, we turned our ten Fokkers toward the west. Without being noticed by the enemy anti-aircraft batteries, we pushed far over the enemy hinterlands. All the while, the British squadron flew a straight course eastward, in the direction of the city of Ghent. Since we were flying higher than the British swarm, we could come right down on their necks.

'As we got closer to the enemy formation, we could see that it consisted of about thirty aeroplanes. The best plan of attack was for our flight of ten Fokkers to charge the main body of the swarm, coming in on an angle at one flank. The British, who were still not aware of our presence, were taken by surprise. At the very beginning of the attack the swarm to the right was forced away, while simultaneously there was great confusion in the enemy's centre and on his left flank. Two Sopwiths were sent down trailing ribbons of smoke right away. After a short battle, two more Sopwiths went spinning down in flames. Settling the fight was made easier when a German Marine-Jagdstaffel [naval fighter squadron] arrived on the scene and put three more Sopwiths out of action.'

Unconfirmed 'victories' were claimed by both sides. But Jasta 40 certainly suffered a casualty, when twenty-six-year-old Saxon Vzfw Paul Groll was shot down. A British report indicates the likelihood that Groll fell victim to the other Sopwith Camel unit in the RAF flight: 'Lieut. [Oscar A.P.] Heron, 70 Squadron, dived on one of fifteen Fokker biplanes, which broke up in the air after 100 rounds had been fired into it. He then attacked another which was on the tail of a Camel and shot it down in flames. Capt [Walter M.] Carlaw of the same squadron also brought down a Fokker biplane.'[31]

The German 4th Army air combat summary reported only that Vzfw Groll was 'missing' after this fight,[32] while a British source indicated only the loss of one Sopwith Camel from 65 Squadron's morning patrol, 'last seen flying east of Ypres at 11:30 [a.m.].'[33] Despite the disparity in numbers, confirmed victories for 7 October were assigned to Jasta 40 as follows: one to Ltn Degelow, his twenty-fifth victory[34]; one to Ltn Rosenstein, his eighth; one to Ltn Gilly, his fifth; and one to Vzfw Groll, his fourth and last.

Carl Degelow added:

'After the engagement, Jasta 40 re-formed for the flight back to our airfield at Bisseghem. Looking around, I could see only eight of my comrades. It was only after we had landed and got together to discuss the fight that we discovered that one of our more successful "hunters", Vzfw Paul Groll, had apparently been lost during the big fight over Ghent. He was last seen following a Sopwith, apparently in the process of shooting it down. There were no other pilots' reports. Likewise, there were no reports that he had made an emergency landing at any of our other fields in the area. We never learned what happened to Groll, as neither his body nor the wreckage of his aeroplane was ever found. Only his empty chair at the dinner table that night served as a haunting reminder of his absence.

'As for the Belgian inhabitants of Ghent, who were eyewitnesses to the great aerial struggle, the turn of events meant little to them. Their joy came a few days later, when German forces had to pull back ever further east, and their own tri-colour once again fluttered from the towers of the historic old city of art.'

Special Recognition for Willy Rosenstein

Now with eight confirmed aerial victories to his credit and over four years' service as a military flyer, Stellvertretender Staffel-Führer [Deputy Squadron Leader] Willy Rosenstein had earned special recognition. On the evening of 7 October, he was proposed for Prussia's second-highest bravery award: the Knight's Cross of the Royal House Order of Hohenzollern with Swords.[35] In his nominating letter to Hauptmann Helmuth Wilberg, the 4th Army's Kommandeur der Flieger, Degelow recounted Rosenstein's many aviation achievements and concluded:

' … In July 1918 Ltn Rosenstein came to Jasta 40, with which he attained five additional aerial victories. Since August 1911 he has been active uninterrupted as a pilot, and [the years] 1911-1913 as a military flight instructor at Johannisthal. With exceptional perseverance and tenacity he has been devoted to Jagdfliegerei [fighter aviation] and because of that during the last great attacks in Flanders has achieved the largest portion (four victories) of his successful battles with enemy flyers.'[36]

Between the Red and the Blue

On Tuesday, 8 October, Jasta 40 made a final – and brief – advance by relocating from Bisseghem about seven kilometres westward to Menin. Under cover of low clouds, the move positioned Jasta 40 closer to the fighting so as to distract Allied flyers from observing German ground forces making a deeper withdrawal eastward. While the Staffel's enlisted men transported the equipment, Degelow led all of the unit's aeroplanes on a frontline patrol:

'Wartime German Army maps always showed the enemy frontlines marked in red and our own in blue. On this particular day over the Flanders Sector, I forced a British pilot to land his aeroplane in the narrow space between the red and the blue: that desolate, bombarded section of contested territory aptly called no-man's-land.

'Nine of my comrades and I made an aerial tour of our forward lines. Our mission was to intercept any enemy aircraft attempting to cross our lines, or, if there was little activity in that regard, then we were to look for our own two-seater reconnaissance aircraft and protect them from attack by enemy fighters.

'We were over the lines only a few minutes when, from my vantage point at the head of the flight, I spotted a group of British single-seat fighters. They appeared to be heading for a row of German captive balloons which our artillery units had sent aloft with crews of observers to telephone to the ground the degree of accuracy (or inaccuracy) being attained by the big guns. Without the balloon observers' corrections, the artillery would be much less effective – and that's why the British fighters were on the scene. Their aim was to put the balloons out of business.

'I immediately fired off a bright red signal shell with my flare pistol and my comrades recognised the signal to follow me in attacking the enemy formation. We had two advantages: we were at a higher altitude than our opponents and, coming from an easterly direction, the sun was at our backs, making us a more difficult target to the enemy flyers, who had to squint into the bright sunlight in order to see us.

'Our Fokker D.VII fighters, which I consider to be the best German fighter aeroplanes of World War I, were also faster and more manoeuvrable than the Sopwith Camels flown by our adversaries.

'Thus, ready for battle, my comrades and I charged headlong at the enemy. But we did not catch them totally unawares. The British flight commander suddenly spotted us and, recognising our numerical superiority, fired off a flare to warn his comrades. The swarm began to turn away, heading back to its own lines and leaving our balloons unmolested. I realised their intention and was annoyed, as I was looking forward to bringing down some of these intruders.

'But then I saw the real plan. All of the Sopwiths turned back except one. While we were distracted by the main body of aircraft which only appeared to lope off in retreat, this fellow was going to slip by and pounce on our balloons. My Staffel-mates took care of those on the run. I dealt with the one sly fellow.

'He pressed on toward our balloons until the clatter of my machine guns suddenly forced him to change course. I whistled right through the clouds after him, firing away all the time, and the ribbon of smoke that his aeroplane left as it went was enough to tell me that I had hit his oil and fuel tanks. Becoming ever slower, the Tommy glided toward his lines – with me right behind him.

'I noticed that the Englishman's engine was badly shot up and had quit on him. He was helpless now and it would be only a matter of time before he had to attempt to land in the bombarded area that was wonderfully "levelled" for that purpose. I had to admire my opponent's skill, as he made what might almost be called a precision landing on a flat spot between two shell holes and managed to keep his aeroplane relatively intact.

'After that, I could no longer tell whether the pilot, who was probably wounded, was able to get out of his aeroplane. Enemy machine-gun fire from the ground made further observation impossible for me. Through our own aerial reconnaissance efforts later the same day, however, we determined that the downed aeroplane was exactly between German and British trenches on that sector of the Front and, therefore, was irretrievable by either side. I could only hope that advanced infantry patrols from one side or the other would rescue the pilot before the site was pulverised by artillery fire.'

Fortunately for the Sopwith Camel pilot,[37] he was taken prisoner by German ground troops before the next wave of artillery fire began. Credited as Degelow's twenty-sixth victory,[38] the pilot's squadron and its mission were described in an RAF report:

'210 Squadron low bombing patrol, after dropping bombs on Thourout, attacked formation of ten Fokker biplanes escorting a two-seater east of Staden. E.A. were at 3,000 feet and were surprised by the Camels diving down with the sun behind them. Lieut C.P. Pineau shot down one Fokker biplane in flames. Capt E. Swale and Lieut C.W. Payton each shot down a Fokker biplane which was seen to crash and Capt E. Swale and Lieuts Jenkins and Gyles each shot down a Fokker biplane out of control. In all we destroyed three and three others were [driven] down out of control. We lost one machine.'[39]

While there is some question about which side was first to attack out of the sun, it is certain that Jasta 40 reported no aircraft lost.

High Recognition for Degelow

Later that day, General der Infanterie Friedrich Sixt von Armin, Commanding General of the 4th Army, released a message of special praise for the fighter units in his sector:

'In the difficult battles of recent days, our Jagdstaffel have performed quite superbly. They intercepted and fell on the opponent wherever they found him. Entire [enemy] flights were destroyed. In striving to above all bring relief to the infantry, they did not avoid the difficult battle with enemy trench-strafers and sent many of them crashing down. In the first eight days of the battle Army and Navy Jagdstaffeln shot down 89 enemy aeroplanes and lost only five of their own – a visible sign of the German spirit of attack and the excellence of German-piloted aeroplanes.

'Gratitude and appreciation to the Jagdflieger of the 4th Army, especially the admirably proven Leutnants Jacobs (Jasta 7), Degelow (Jasta 40), Osterkamp (II. Marine-Jasta) who alone attained nine, seven and six victories, respectively.'[40]

Just over two weeks later, General Sixt von Armin's message also appeared in the second to the last issue of the Air Force Commanding General's weekly summary,[41] which was distributed to all German air units and organisations. Even this late in the war and under such hectic conditions, airmen and aviation staff members who followed reports of aerial victory scores and their links to high awards would have understood these basic facts: Ltn Josef Jacobs and Oberleutnant zur See [naval lieutenant, junior grade] Theodor Osterkamp had each been awarded the Pour le Mérite after their twenty-third aerial victories.[42] Therefore, with twenty-six victories to his credit, Carl Degelow could reasonably be expected to join their élite group.

1   Jones, *The War in the Air*, Vol. VI, pp. 531-532.

2   Kogenluft, *Nachrichtenblatt der Luftstreitkräfte*, Vol. II, No. 32, 3 October 1918, p. 494.

3   Henshaw, *The Sky Their Battlefield*, p. 425.

4   70 Squadron, RAF, *Combat Report* by Lt Heron, 28 September 1918.

5   Rosenstein, *Personal-Bogen*, 1919, p. 2.

6   Royal Air Force, *Combat Casualty List*, 29 September 1918.

7   211 Squadron, RAF, *Combat Report* by Lt Axford and Sgt Williamson, 29 September 1918.

8   Franks, Bailey & Guest, *Above the Lines*, pp. 113-114.

9   Hildebrand, *Die Generale der deutschen Luftwaffe 1935-1945*, Vol. I, p. 346.

10 Erhard Milch was born on 30 March 1892 in Wilhelmshaven. A product of the Prussian cadet system, he was a Fahnenjunker assigned to East Prussian Fussartillerie-Regiment von Linger Nr. 1 in Königsberg on 24 February 1910. Milch was commissioned Leutnant on 18 August 1911 and served with his unit until he began pilot training at the Artillerie-Fliegerschule at Jüterbog on 1 July 1915. Promoted to Oberleutnant on 18 August 1915, he went on to fly as an observer with Flieger-Abteilungen (A) 204 and 205. From 15 June 1916 until 3 July 1917, he was Adjutant at Artillerie-Fliegerschule Ost I in Gross Auz, Latvia. Subsequently, Milch was Deputy Leader of Flieger-Abteilung 5 and served on the 17th Army staff until he received his first command position with his old unit, Fl.-Abt (A) 204, which he held until he was assigned to command Jagdgruppe 6 [Ref: Hildebrand, *Die Generale der deutschen Luftwaffe 1935-1945*, Vol. II, pp. 394-395; Deutscher Offizier-Bund. *Ehren-Rangliste des ehemaligen Deutschen Heeres*, p. 535; Milch correspondence with this author, 1970].

11 Hildebrand, op.cit.

12 RAF, *Communiqué* No. 27, 9 October 1918, p. 1.

13 Ibid.

14 Henshaw, op.cit., p.430; Lt Albert Montague Sanderson fell in S.E.5a F.5464 of 74 Squadron, RAF and has no known grave [Ref: Hobson, *Airmen Died in the Great War 1914-1918*, p. 186].

15 Kogenluft, op.cit., p. 495.

16 Kogenluft, *Nachrichtenblatt* No. 33, 10 October 1918, p. 511.

17 Henshaw, op.cit., p. 432; Capt Maurice Lea Cooper, DFC, age nineteen, fell in Sopwith 1F.1 Camel F.3121 of 213 Squadron, RAF and has no known grave [Ref: Hobson, op.cit., p. 129].

18 RAF, *74 Squadron Record Book*, 2 October 1918.

19 Degelow's statement about the French position in 1917 is pure conjecture and not supported by any facts.

20 Kogenluft, *Nachrichtenblatt* No. 33, op.cit.

21 Bailey & Cony, *The French Air Service War Chronology 1914-1918*, p. 311.

22 Kogenluft, op.cit., p. 512.

23 2/Lt Samuel John Hill fell in Sopwith 1F.1 Camel F.1596 of 65 Squadron, RAF; he was buried in Harlebeke, Belgium [Ref: Hobson, op.cit., p. 151].

24 RAF, *65 Squadron Record Book*, 4 October 1918.

25 Ibid.

26 RAF, *Communiqué*, op.cit., p. 3.

27 Kogenluft, op.cit.

28 2/Lt V.G.H. Phillips and 2/Lt A.F. Taylor went down in D.H.9 E.8872 of 211 Squadron, RAF.

29 Jones, op.cit., p. 532.

30 RAF, *65 Squadron Record Book*, 7 October 1918.

31 RAF, *Communiqué* No. 28, 16 October 1918, p. 1.

32 Kofl 4. Armee, *Wochenbericht Nr. 2642* dated 10 October 1918, p. 6.

33 RAF, *Combat Casualty List*, 7 October 1918; 2/Lt Leslie Seymour Ross Jones, nineteen, went down in Sopwith 1F.1 Camel H.7001 of 65 Squadron, RAF, and was buried at Blankenberghe, Belgium [Ref: Hobson, op.cit., p. 157].

34 Kogenluft, op.cit.

35 O'Connor, *Aviation Awards of Imperial Germany and the Men Who Earned Them*, Vol. II, p. 132.

36 Königliche Sächsische Jagdstaffel 40, *Bericht Nr. 12781F*, 7 October 1918 [Ref: Rostenstein, op.cit., p. 6].

37 2/Lt R.W. Hopper went down in Sopwith 1F.1 Camel D.3382 of 210 Squadron, RAF; apparently he was uninjured and was taken prisoner [Ref: Henshaw, op.cit., p. 437].

38 Kogenluft, op.cit., p. 513.

39 RAF, 5 Group, *Dover Patrol Fortnightly Summaries*, 1-15 October 1918, p. 6.

40 Armee-Oberkommando 4, *Armeebefehl 287/Okt.*, 8 October 1918.

41 Kogenluft, *Nachrichtenblatt* No. 35, 24 October 1918, p. 550.

42 O'Connor, op.cit., p. 220.

CHAPTER ELEVEN
HOMEWARD, HOME AND REUNION

Another Black Thursday

With the war grinding to its inevitable end in the autumn of 1918, air units continued to be withdrawn to safer rear areas. Accordingly, Hauptmann Helmuth Wilberg, the 4th Army's Kommandeur der Flieger (Kofl 4), ordered Jagdstaffel 40 to leave Menin airfield at daybreak on Thursday, 10 October 1918. For reasons not made clear, Jastas 7 and 51 remained near Menin,[1] but, despite low clouds and rain, Carl Degelow had to lead his pilots on a flight to an airfield to the northwest.

Degelow waited for a break in the weather when he and his pilots could take off for the new airfield. And they could not wait long. Hptm Wilberg, a career army officer in the Prussian tradition, was known to have 'reined in' Germany's greatest air hero – Manfred von Richthofen – by enforcing an order limiting the Red Baron's flying while he convalesced from wounds,[2] and Wilberg was a firm leader and not a man to be ignored. The latest relocation order tested Degelow's mettle, whether to follow instructions rigidly or to exercise his own judgment.

After the war he wrote:

'As the British offensive thrust continued in the direction of Menin and Courtrai, there had been another massive attack further south, near Cambrai in France, designed to divert attention from Flanders. Our strategists recognised this tactic and began making appropriate plans to strengthen our lines. Hence, an officer was despatched from Kofl 4 to Menin to ensure that the Jasta 40 transfer order was carried out.

'All around us we could see the war effort collapsing. Although our ever-eastward trek was officially designated a "regrouping", I knew the end was coming and that it was a time when strict discipline had to be enforced to avoid total collapse. When Headquarters issued an order, unit commanders were responsible for carrying it out – or they would suffer the consequences of a court-martial. No allowances for extenuating circumstances were accepted. And that fact nearly got me into trouble.

'Close to midnight on the evening of the 9th, the officer from Kofl 4 knocked on my bedroom door and, when admitted to my humble place of rest, he personally read the order aloud before briefly commenting on the situation that made the move so necessary: following the Tommies' latest attack, one of our two-seat reconnaissance crews brought back information showing that British field artillery had already advanced so far that its guns could bring our current airfield under fire. I immediately alerted my pilots, while the ground crews prepared the aircraft for the earliest departure.

'In the morning, while a heavy layer of fog drifted across the 'field, we waited, shivering in our fur-lined jackets, for the dawn of the new day. At 7:00 a.m., normally a good time to take off, we could not even see Courtrai, two kilometres away, because the fog was so thick. Nearby factory chimneys, standing about 70 metres tall, were lost in clouds of rain and fog.

'The officer from Kofl 4 reminded me of the order he had brought. The time had come for Jasta 40 to depart.

'I replied: "I, alone, and not Kofl 4, bear responsibility for my pilots – and I will not order my Staffel to take off in this weather."

'He said nothing and walked away.

'After an hour of agonizing waiting, the ceiling had risen to about 300 to 400 metres. Experience with the changeable weather in Flanders now prompted me to begin moving out. Due to the scarcity of fuel, only six of my Fokkers could set out on the flight and even that had its hazards, as fatigue brought on by war weariness was beginning to take its toll of my pilots. They were not even able to maintain a good flight formation.

'My aeroplane, of course, was decorated with my white stag insignia, but it did not remain a beacon of direction for long. Soon after take-off, the other pilots lost sight of me and took different courses.

'Alone, I steered a northeast course to the new airfield that had been made for us at Wynghene. Then, quite suddenly, I realised that my engine was on fire. Quickly, I made a half-roll and turned the crate upside-down, hoping to snuff out the fire. It was risky, as my altitude was only slightly over 300 metres. That manoeuvre resolved the problem, however, and I was able to resume my flight. In a few minutes I caught sight of a row of poplars that marked an orientation point near our new field. After I landed, several mechanics came running toward my plane. I told them about the fire and they quickly took off the fuselage panels to have a look at the Mercedes engine. They pointed out to me that a part of one sparkplug had come loose and, while still glowing hot, had fallen into the carburettor and set fire to the fuel in it.

'Prior to our arrival at Wynghene the landing field was so rough that a gang of prisoners of war had been gathered to grade the area. It took several hundred men to turn up the soil and level it off, but they got the job done. Upon landing on the freshly graded airfield not a single machine nosed over. That was especially helpful, as spare propellers were not available by this time. Many of the depots that had supplied us with spare parts were already on their way back to Germany.

'I soon learned that I was the only one to make it to Wynghene. Ltn Adolf Auer and Unteroffizier Werner Hertel had gone on to Maria Aalter, and no report had come in yet from Leutnants Gilly, Jeschonnek and Rosenstein.'[3]

Adolf Auer recalled the worsening conditions that curtailed the Staffel's operations in mid-October, beginning with the flight from Menin to Wynghene. As he wrote in his diary:

'It was in a fierce storm such as I have never experienced in an aeroplane. At one point a British captive balloon that had got loose drifted close to me.

'First we landed at Wynghene, but, because we did not see the tents there, we flew a

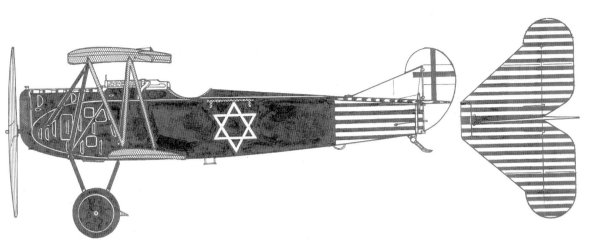

The Jasta 40 Fokker D.VII of Ltn.d.Res Adolf Auer when he scored his first and only aerial victory of the war on 23 October 1918. Auer's Fokker is the only known Jasta 40 aeroplane also to use striping on the white portion of the fuselage. *(Original artwork by Greg VanWyngarden)*

few kilometres further to Maria Aalter. I succeeded in landing there on the third try. My machine was pulled up by the winds of the storm, so I had to grasp the control column firmly to make the aeroplane land. At Maria Aalter, our machines were placed in an old bomber hangar. The other pilots had become lost, some flew to Ghent and others had landed anywhere they could.'

As bad as the weather conditions in Belgium were, however, they did not deter Allied ground forces from their determined push against German troops with every weapon they had. A key Allied objective was to force withdrawing German units to abandon their equipment – and, hence, the ability to wage war – and retreat as quickly as possible. For its part, the Royal Air Force sent up bombers that day and dropped 12.5 tons of ordnance[4] on German positions. And three S.E.5 pilots from one of Jasta 40's old adversaries, 85 Squadron, showed how courage and determination helped to reinforce their commanders' objectives:

'Capts Randall and Macdonald and Lieut Henson … attacked a line of [German] infantry who were holding up the advance of our cavalry. They dived again and again on the hostile troops, silencing their machine guns and causing them to retire behind a village. They repeated this operation at another place, causing the [German troops] to retire in confusion.'[5]

Further success by the advancing Allies followed their resumption of the Flanders offensive at 5:45 a.m. (British Time) on the following Monday, 14 October. The results of this action had the desired effect, as described by the RAF historian:

'The attack was delivered on the whole front from Dixmuide to Comines on the River Lys and was immediately successful. Roulers was surrounded on the same day, as was Thourout on the 15th, and … [four] days later the northern flank of the Allied armies rested on the Dutch frontier, and the Germans had no other concern than to extricate their troops as best they could from the Belgian pocket.'[6]

A Few More Victories
Among the units within that 'Belgian pocket' was Jasta 40. Degelow reported: 'As October wore on, fuel delivery was intermittent and sometimes I had only enough gasoline to take four other Fokkers with me on patrol. With the increasingly overwhelming number of enemy aircraft, this tactic soon took its toll and at times it was all we could do to bring all of our aeroplanes back intact.'

On the evening of 18 October, he led his five remaining Fokkers on a patrol southwest to Roulers, an area where former German airfields were then being used by the Allies. Despite the heavy cloud cover and fog over the Flanders Sector, French fighter units made five patrols that day,[7] looking to engage German aircraft.

One late-day patrol of Spad S.XIII fighters achieved its objective and encountered Jasta 40. As it turned out, the Spads were from Escadrille Spa 82, a unit that Jasta 40 had fought successfully just over two weeks earlier. On this occasion, Ltn.d.Res Hermann Gilly claimed two of the Spads for his seventh and eighth victories and Ltn Hans Jeschonnek shot down one, which was confirmed as his second victory. French records show only two Spa 82 losses[8] in that fight and no victories.

As Hans Jeschonnek did not score again, he did not attain the coveted status of Fliegeras [fighter ace], but he was remembered by Carl Degelow as 'a natural born soldier, if there ever was one. His low victory score of two confirmed victories while he flew with Jasta 40 belied the fact that he was often busy keeping aggressive Englishmen from getting to me and other members of our Staffel.'

Jasta 40 remained in the Belgian province of West Flanders until 22 October, when the unit relocated to East Flanders, closer to Germany and the border with The Netherlands, which maintained strict neutrality in the war. Degelow wrote: 'Despite the hard work of the prisoners, we did not use Wynghene airfield for very long. Events dictated another move, this one to the site of former Zeppelin sheds at Gontrode, southeast of Ghent. Soon, even our advance airfields were near Ghent.'

After days of foul weather, a slight improvement late on 21 October motivated Degelow to lead his now smaller Staffel into the air, even as the ground crew transferred equipment east to Gontrode.

Adolf Auer's diary recorded two eventful days:

'Tuesday, 22 October – Last night and this morning we made flights. There were no Tommies in the air; hence, many ground targets came under our fire. Many times I was down as low as fifty metres.

'Wednesday, 23 October – This morning we flew quite nicely along the frontlines; there was nothing at all going on. (Shortly after starting out, however, above us were quite a lot of enemy double- and single-seaters, dropping bombs in the area; of course, we could no longer surprise them.)

'As we had been flying for some time and had aroused the Tommy anti-aircraft

An example of the silver *Ehrenbecher für den Sieger in Luftkampf* [Honour Goblet for Victor in Air Combat] presented to Adolf Auer and German airmen following attainment of the first aerial victory.

Berlin, den *26.März*

An den *Leutnant d.Res.*

Herrn   A d o l f   A u e r

Jagdstaffel 40.

Vaterländische Freunde der Luftstreitkräfte haben mir eine Geldsumme zur Verfügung gestellt, die ich zur Schaffung eines

Ehrenbechers
für den Sieger im Luftkampfe

verwendet habe.

Es ist mir eine dankbare Freude, Ihnen als Anerkennung für die im siegreichen Gefecht bewiesene Tapferkeit den Becher überweisen zu können.

Der Inspekteur der Fliegertruppen

Major

The certificate that accompanied Auer's Ehrenbecher was dated 26 March 1919 but still signed by Major Willhelm Haehnelt, Air Force Inspector General of what was the decimated post-war German air arm.

Der kommandierende General
der Luftstreitkräfte

Nr. *137 389* Fl.A.

Gr. H.=Qu., den *12 Januar* 1919.

u. Jagdstaffel 40 durch Fdflng

Zu dort *2373/5* vom *25.10.* 1918.

Dem *Ltn. d. Rf. Auer, Adolf*
wird der Abschuß eines *Bristol-Figther*
am *23.10.18.* als *1.*
siegreicher Luftkampf anerkannt.

50 Sieg der Jagdstaffel *40.*

Fl.A.
J Lifte

Der Soldatenrat.

V. f. d. f. G. d. L.
M. Der Chef des Generalstabes.

The official confirmation document of Auer's victory, which was recorded as Jasta 40's fiftieth air combat success, was dated 12 January 1919 and signed by (then) Oberst [Colonel] Hermann von der Lieth-Thomsen, who remained Chief of Staff of Luftstreitkräfte until 11 January 1919. Note to the left of Thomsen's signature that the document was also approved by a functionary of the Soldatenrat (Soldiers' Council) which then exercised some authority in the German capital. When Thomsen joined the Luftwaffe on 1 November 1935, he was promoted to Generalmajor. He was promoted to Generalleutnant and then General der Flieger before he died on 5 August 1942 aged seventy-five.

batteries, puffs of smoke became evident to the north … [Then] very close to the Dutch border we surprised a British two-seater. Degelow fired first. As he let up and I was close enough, I aimed well and fired. After several shots right on the mark, the two-seater (Bristol Fighter?) began to smoke. Soon thereafter it went into a spin and crashed near Vosselaere. I circled the crash site several times. It was my first aerial victory.'[9]

Auer thought he shot down a Bristol F.2B, but while British records showed no F.2B losses in that area, they did note that an Airco D.H.9 was missing in the vicinity.[10] It was later learned that the pilot and observer had been killed.[11] In any event, Auer received full confirmation for the victory from Kofl 4, as well as an *Ehrenbecher*, the special commemorative goblet presented to every German airman on the occasion of his first confirmed aerial victory (see page 157). After the war, Auer told this author, 'there was still a sense of German orderliness and these small details received attention.'

Saturday morning, 26 October was a good day for flying and Degelow and his men went out to seek targets of opportunity. Soon, they spotted a lone Spad near Ghent, but were suspicious of such an 'easy' prey. However, there were not enough clouds in the sky at this time for a lone aeroplane to be used as 'bait' for a higher flying French formation eager to pounce on a flight of German fighters looking for a quick 'kill'. Several sweeps of the sky reassured the Jasta 40 pilots of their own security and then Degelow led them in a dive on the French fighter and sent it down in a slow spiral, trailing smoke. The Spad, seen to hit the ground, was recorded as Degelow's twenty-seventh victory. According to French records, one Spad was lost over Ghent that day and it was flown by Lt Maurice Quenioux, a pilot of a nearby Centre d'Aviation Militaire [Military Aviation Centre]. It can only be speculated that he may have been a new pilot, made overly confident by the Allies' steady advance toward Germany and not cautious enough for wartime conditions. Or Lt Quenioux could have been a ferry pilot delivering a new aeroplane to a frontline unit. Whatever the case, his lack of caution proved to be fatal.[12]

That afternoon, Jasta 40 joined with other German fighters to attack a large flight of Sopwith Camels from 65 and 70 Squadrons between Sotteghem and Alost, southeast of Ghent. Degelow shot down a Sopwith Camel, which one RAF source recorded as 'last seen going down in Flames near Esseghem at 1340 [hours]'.[13] It was confirmed as Degelow's twenty-eighth aerial victory.

The following day, 27 October, Ltn Willy Rosenstein shot down a Sopwith Camel for his ninth and final victory. By his tenacity and skill he proved once again to be the superior pilot and courageous fighter whom Degelow had recommended for the Knight's Cross of the Hohenzollern House Order.

Ltn Adolf Auer was not so lucky. After having flown more than 120 combat missions with Jasta 40 and attaining one aerial victory, Auer was forced down on 28 October. British balloons near Ooteghem were directing artillery fire onto German positions and Degelow was ordered to go up and shoot down as many of the gas bags as possible. Auer recalled the earlier lessons of Degelow's balloon attack, and he was lining up on one of the hydrogen-filled craft when a flight of S.E.5 fighters came down on him from out of the sun.

Capt Eric J. Stephens, an Australian member of 41 Squadron, RAF, later reported that he 'fired a short burst at one, which went into a spiral, then [I] saw Capt Soden get on its tail and follow it down'.[14]

As Canadian-born Capt Frank O. Soden's square-nosed S.E.5 closed in, Auer thought of his own fate in the worst possible terms. He later told this author that he clearly remembered his own aerial triumph over a Bristol F.2B five days earlier and did not think he would be as lucky as the F.2B crew that Degelow had 'captured' in the air. Auer twisted and turned, trying to shake off his pursuer. But the RAF pilot, who by then had shot down twenty-five German aeroplanes,[15] knew how to stay on Auer's tail.

According to Soden's combat report:

'At 1530 hours, whilst on [offensive patrol, we] attacked five Fokker Biplanes which were attacking our balloons [at] Ooteghem. I selected one E.A. and fired about 100

Spad S.XIII of the type engaged by Jasta 40 in October 1918.

rounds in four bursts, after which [the German pilot] seemed to want to land, so I ceased fire and followed him down. He landed OK and I landed near by to arrange for a guard; the pilot was wounded. Captain Stephens also fired a burst at this E.A.'[16]

Auer had made a good landing and provided his new hosts with a Fokker D.VII in reasonably good condition. One of Soden's bullets had ricocheted within the Fokker's metal framework and hit Auer in the right shin and foot. He had to be helped out of the aeroplane by two British infantrymen at the scene and was made comfortable by Capt Soden, who spoke to him in fluent German. Auer was well tended by his captors, but, as was so often the case, was not released and allowed to return home until 14 November 1919.[17]

The Kaiser's Last Troop Review

By now, US President Woodrow Wilson's government was busily exchanging telegrams with German officials in Berlin. Each succeeding message contained refinements for an armistice to put an end to the senseless fighting. One of the war's key planners, General Erich Ludendorff, Chief of the German General Staff, was forced to resign that post on 26 October.[18] With Ludendorff out of the way, Kaiser Wilhelm II was eager to leave Berlin, where increasing civil unrest made it less certain that he could be protected from his war-weary people. To get away, even for a short time, he used the excuse of wanting to visit some of his troops in Belgium.

The new General Staff Chief, General Wilhelm Groener, had another thought: '... that the Kaiser should go to the Front not to review troops or confer decorations, but to look for death ... If he were killed it would be the finest death possible. If he were wounded the feelings of the German people would completely change towards him.'[19]

Generalfeldmarschall Paul von Hindenburg, effectively Germany's military dictator at that point, favoured the Kaiser's abdication and was content to allow the monarch one last troop review in eastern Flanders, not far from the Supreme Headquarters in the field located in Spa, Belgium. Carl Degelow described the effect the imperial visit had on the German Luftstreitkräfte:

'When Kaiser Wilhelm made his last visit to the frontline troops, on 30 October 1918, German air units all along the Front were ordered to keep the airspace in the vicinity of the reviewing area free of enemy flyers. This was the last time that such a large number of German aircraft – numbering well into the hundreds – took to the air on combat patrols.

'A cold, but friendly autumn day and the expectation of being able to strike up a tune with the Tommy made our fighter pilots appear on the flight line earlier than usual. A grey morning mist lay over the meadows along the Schelde River, as our various Staffeln formed up into flights over our hastily improvised rear-area airfields. In our case, we flew to the vicinity of Ghent, near where the Kaiser was to review the troops.

'For a long time that day we criss-crossed the sector without seeing even one enemy airman. That pleased us little, as each of us would have been happy to break the silence with a little adventure. We were accustomed to having the Englishmen come over high above their bombers, ready to meet us.

'Then, puffs of anti-aircraft smoke showed us immediately that there was something within our airspace which, in the opinion of our anti-aircraft gunners, did not belong there. Almost in a single motion, all Jasta 40 aeroplanes changed direction to get at the enemy formation of seven bomb-carrying S.E.5s before they could bomb our troop concentrations. Each of us felt that with this aerial protection mission, we had taken on a very honourable and difficult assignment. Unlike some of our senior officers, we flyers felt we had to protect our Kaiser. Shortly before the attack, I glanced around at my Staffel and it seemed to me that all of our Fokkers were gripped by battle fever. Indeed, this would be their final war dance, for revolution was in the air and it was undermining the last vestiges of our military structure.

'This time the ratio of forces was fairly equal. There were seven British fighters to our seven Fokkers. The S.E.5s, encumbered by their bomb load, had difficulty in manoeuvring. Thus, when the battle began, they had no choice but to discard their bombs and pay attention to us.

'Even free of their bombs, however, the S.E.5s did not seem eager to engage us. Rather, they turned southwest and began heading for home. We chased them and, since I was at the head of our formation, I was the first to catch up with one of them. He went through the usual evasive tactics, moving from side to side, zig-zagging and going up

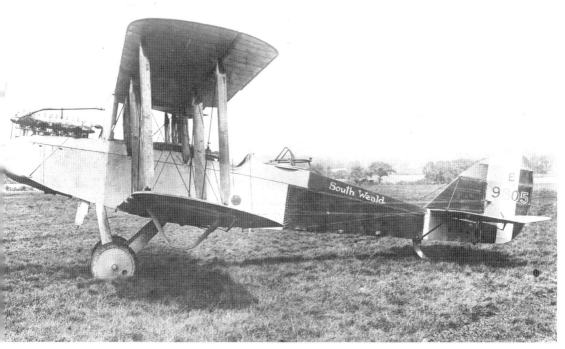

The Aircraft Manufacturing Company (Airco) at Hendon produced Geoffrey de Havilland's D.H.9 as the day-bombing successor to the D.H.4 two-seat bomber. The D.H.9 did not fare as well as its predecessor, but remained in service through most of the last year of the war. A D.H.9 of 104 Squadron, RAF became Carl Degelow's thirtieth and final aerial victory of World War I. The aircraft seen here was built under license by G. & J. Weir Ltd. of Glasgow.

and down. That made it easier for me, simply flying after him in a straight line, to close the distance. *Immer ran auf Meter, Meter!* Ever closer, metre by metre! With my first burst of machine-gun fire the S.E.5 suddenly bolted up and then dropped, falling like a leaf, in an erratic spiral, until he hit the ground near the forward lines.'

Jasta 40 very likely encountered one of two seven-aircraft flights of S.E.5s from 32 Squadron, RAF. One flight leader, Capt C.L. Veitsch, gave a slightly differing account, mainly to note that he and his men encountered more than the seven Fokkers of Jasta 40. According to his combat report:

'When leading his [Veitch's] flight on Escort Duty, pilot dived on two E.A. of large formation (of twenty-five Fokker Biplanes), firing about twenty-five rounds at each enemy machine, but without observing any results.
'On conclusion of dive, pilot pulled out in a steep climbing right-hand turn, on top of which he observed another E.A., 200 feet directly below, also climbing. Pilot half-rolled and dived vertically on E.A., firing 100 rounds with both guns at point-blank range. E.A. rolled over on its back, then went into an uncontrolled spin with large volume of smoke issuing from its engine, and continued its spin 'till observed to crash in bend between canal and railway at Ghislain.'[20]

The skies over Belgium and northern France were so full of aeroplanes that day that it is even more difficult than usual to determine the identity of Veitch's and Degelow's victim. The RAF historian called 'the 30th of October … the most intense day of air fighting which the war had provided.'[21] Ten S.E.5s were lost in that broad operational area that day,[22] and incomplete German records for the period do not offer a clue about Veitch's opponents; it is certain that Jasta 40 listed no casualties in the fight. In any event, Degelow's claim was credited as his twenty-ninth aerial victory and was most likely a member of 32 Squadron, who was not observed by Capt Veitch, but was noted by British sources.[23]

Degelow's Last Victory

As long as fuel and other supplies held out, German fighter aircraft took to the skies in final vain attempts to protect their troops, which were now in a full – and for the most part orderly – retreat. Degelow later recalled:

'A few days later, on 4 November, one week before the Armistice, we were flying north of Ghent, near the Dutch border, when we surprised a flight of De Havilland [Airco D.H.9] two-seat bombers. The De Havillands, which, due to their heavy, ponderous design, were no match in aerial combat for our single-seat fighters, were well aware of their vulnerability. When the battle began, the entire group was unified in its choice of tactics, which, in this case, was to withdraw to its own lines. For some unknown reason, this group had come over without fighter escorts, hence, it was left to provide its own defence.

'The British flight leader, knowing the best course of action, tried to lead his companions in a dive for home. That was the best solution for everyone but the swarm's port wingman. I came down and issued an unmistakable challenge with my guns. After two short bursts, the Englishman reacted to my invitation and we entered into a dogfight. I hung on behind and just below this fellow, keeping him within my sights, but keeping out of his line of fire. The pilot continued to descend, no doubt hoping to give his observer a chance to shoot at me. As he continued down in wide spirals, an awkward movement ended the fight and saved the crew from further bursts of my machine-gun fire. As the De Havilland came to within ten metres of the ground, it suddenly side-slipped in, thanks to some "dexterous" steering, and crashed in a meadow. I suspect that during our encounter the pilot had been wounded and that the less talented observer had thereupon decided to bring the crate down in one piece by using his back-seat emergency controls. From the manner of his flying, he looked like a pupil on his first solo at the controls.

'With the crash, the fuel tank must have sprung a leak, for suddenly the aeroplane, which until then had not been badly damaged, caught fire. Due to the poor landing, both crewmen were pinned in the craft and it took quite a while for them to free themselves from the burning machine. As a result, their flying suits caught fire and I saw them wildly beat themselves to escape the flickers of their misfortune. Meanwhile, some of our artillerymen had hurried to the spot from their nearby batteries and pulled the helpless pilot out of the wreckage. They extinguished his burning clothing with their own canteens of water and took care of the Englishmen as if they had been their own

The leading officers of Jagdgruppe 6, from left: Ltn Curt Rabe, JGru adjutant; Ltn.d.Res Karl Plauth, commanding Jasta 51; Ltn.d.Res Josef Carl Jacobs, Jasta 7; Hptm, Erhard Milch, JaGru 6 commander; Ltn.d.Res Carl Degelow, Jasta 40; and Oblt Waldemar Baron von Dazur, Jasta 20.

comrades. According to the inhumane traits attributed to us by our enemies, one should not have expected such help from the *"Boches"* and yet it seemed obvious to our men to do so.

'Unfortunately, I was able to learn nothing further of the immediate fate of the two captured British flyers,[24] as we lacked any means of communication. Even the so often praised and perhaps so often abused squadron staff car was no longer in running condition due to the shortage of tyres, so we would have been unable to fetch the Englishmen and invite them to our quarters for a bit of refreshment.

'In any event, our mission had been quite successful. We had kept the British bombers from harassing our already sorely pressed troops. Furthermore, through this encounter I was able to round off the number of my aerial victories to 30 officially confirmed. Both of the Englishmen who were shot down that day were decidedly lucky boys; for, in the first place, they came out of it with their hides intact (although, to be sure, slightly damaged) and secondly they were spared the dreariness of long imprisonment, as within the next few days their full freedom was restored to them with the coming of the Armistice and the revolution that was gaining momentum in Germany.'

The Orden Pour le Mérite, seen in its presentation case, with the black and white ribbon folded neatly above the badge. The Prussian colours are black and white; hence, the Iron Cross Second Class and the Knight's Cross of the Royal House Order of Hohenzollern with Swords are presented with similar-looking ribbons.

The blue enamel badge of the Orden Pour le Mérite.

Carl Degelow's sense of achievement was overstated. The last week of World War I was a time of great sacrifice on both sides. In that time the Royal Air Force 'claimed officially sixty-eight E.A. brought down and twenty-four driven down out of control ... sixty of our machines are missing ... [and] approximately 154 tons of bombs were dropped ...'[25]

The son of a poet and steeped in German culture, Degelow recalled the lines of Johann Gottfried Herder's poem about a Spanish hero's battles against the Moors: 'Rückwärts, rückwärts, Don Rodrigo! Deine Ehre ist verloren! ['Backwards, backwards, Don Rodrigo! Your honour is lost!']'[26]:

> 'Those words rang over and over in my ears like a thunderstorm ever since our Supreme Headquarters gave the order for the great withdrawal to positions along the Meuse. Our army was gradually being pushed back to Germany. It had long since become obvious that there would be no holding the line to regroup for an offensive in the spring of 1919. It had now become a matter of seeing how long it would take the politicians to recognise that the war was lost and that they must sue for peace.
>
> 'This period was especially hard for us flyers. Low on fuel and virtually devoid of badly needed spare parts, we undertook a nomadic existence of flying out of one airfield only to find we often had to land at another, as our former field was in danger of being overrun by the British.
>
> 'On 5 November, we made our last move, to a 'field just south of Antwerp, and there – as we ran out of fuel, ammunition and spirit – we had time to reflect on the past and try to sort out what the future held for us.'

The Last Pour le Mérite

The Imperial German government had been quick to 'fan the flames' of the Bolshevik Revolution in Russia in April 1917 by allowing V.I. Lenin and his supporters to pass from Zurich to Petrograd on the famed 'sealed train'. In November 1918 that same German government found itself 'fighting the fire' of similar social unrest which carried across Europe that spring, as Degelow recalled:

> 'Rumours of communist-inspired take-overs of other units had already infiltrated our ranks. Horror stories of "soldiers' councils" that took control of units and condemned their officers to death made the blood run cold.
>
> 'On the morning of 10 November 1918, Hauptmann Erhard Milch assembled the members of Jagdgruppe 6 – comprising Jastas 7, 20, 40 and 51 – for an announcement.
>
> '"Comrades," he said, "the war has gone badly for us and the outcome has been clearly decided. Nonetheless, we must keep up our courage. Sunshine follows rain. And now you will, I am sure, be happy to hear the report I have just received from Supreme Headquarters: 'His Majesty, our Kaiser Wilhelm II, has awarded to our valiant Leutnant Degelow the highest German decoration, the Orden Pour le Mérite.'"
>
> 'The following day, just hours before the armistice went into effect, I was summoned to the main field headquarters of General der Infanterie Sixt von Armin, commander of the 4th Army. There, I was formally presented with what I later learned was the last Pour le Merite[27] bestowed before the monarchy and all the pageantry of the once great German Empire passed into history.'

Unlike the Don Rodrigo of Herder's poem, Carl Degelow had not lost his honour. He had kept fast to his principles and had done his best to serve his country honourably. Perhaps the most fitting assessment of the laudable and worthy efforts of Degelow and his fellow members of the German Luftstreitkräfte came nearly twenty years after the end of World War I from a former adversary, RAF historian H.A. Jones:

'Finally, when the use, admittedly worthy, which the Germans were able to make of their air squadrons is generally reviewed, the question of equipment must be taken into full account. Except for one comparatively brief period the technical qualities of the best of the German aeroplanes were as good as or superior to those of the Allies …In the one period when German aeroplanes were technically inferior to the British, that is in 1916 … the German air service was ineffective. The morale of the service was shattered …'[28]

A similar situation occurred in the second half of 1918, when German technical superiority was still high but its results – aircraft and equipment – were starved by the lack of resources to support further fighting against the combined forces of the British Commonwealth, the French Empire and the United States of America.

Thus, Germany was outfought, outgunned and worn down, as Degelow noted:

'"Homeward, home and reunion." These words came to mind in varied and oft repeated sequence during the still hours of the night and as we stood at our posts facing our enemies during more than four years of war. They were the thoughts that to soldiers in the field bred a whole world full of hope and of yearning. We believed we had gone forth on behalf of our homeland and every one of us hoped that all of home's priceless virtues, which we had defended, would be there when we returned. We had, after all, kept the enemy from advancing into Germany itself.

'Therefore, a wit among us suggested that we flyers, considered to be élite troops, should go to Berlin and make a grand entrance through the Brandenburg Gate, or fly over the celebration in our battle-proven single-seaters. That was before our aeroplanes were confiscated and – as in the case of Jasta 40 – we were shipped home by rail or truck. The lucky few who did fly home almost always had "accidental" crashes at their final destinations to deny the use of our aeroplane to the victors.'

1   Franks, Bailey & Duiven, *The Jasta Pilots*, pp. 21, 62.

2   Bodenschatz, *Jagd in Flanderns Himmel*, pp. 41-42.

3   Auer letter to the author dated 19 April 1971.

4   Royal Air Force, *Communiqué No. 28*, 16 October 1918, p. 2.

5   RAF, ibid.

6   Jones, *The War in the Air*, Vol. VI, p. 539.

7   Grand Quartier Général, *Résumés des Opérations Aériennes*, No. 25.317, 19 October 1918.

8   Ibid., p. 1, Lt Henri Changine and Cpl Paul Trepp [Ref: Bailey & Cony, *The French Air Service War Chronology 1914-1918*, p. 318].

9   Auer, op.cit.

10 RAF, *Combat Casualty List*, 23 October 1918.

11 Capt Charles Graham Haynes, MC and 2/Lt G. Brown went down in Airco D.H.9 C.6314 of 108 Squadron, RAF [Ref: Hobson, *Airmen Died in the Great War 1914-1918*, pp. 149, 122].

12 Bailey & Cony, op.cit., p. 321.

13 RAF, *Combat Casualty List*, 26 October 1918; 2/Lt A.E. Moir, MM, age twenty-five, in Sopwith 1F.1 Camel H.7005 of 65 Squadron, RAF [Ref: Hobson, op.cit., p. 170].

14 41 Squadron, RAF, *Combat Report No. 269* by Capt Stephens, 28 October 1918.

15 Shores, Franks & Guest, *Above the Trenches*, p. 345.

16 41 Squadron, RAF, *Combat Report No. 270* by Capt Soden, 28 October 1918.

17 Auer, *Personal-Bogen*, 1919, p. 4.

18 Asprey, R. *The German High Command at War*, p. 484.

19 Ibid., pp. 485-486.

20 32 Squadron, RAF, *Combat Report* by Capt Veitch, 30 October 1918.

21 Jones, op.cit., p. 544.

22 RAF, *Combat Casualty List*, 30 October 1918;

23 2/Lt W. Amory in S.E.5a D.3440, wounded and taken prisoner [Ref: Henshaw, *The Sky Their Battlefield*, p. 448].

24 Lt J.G. Carey and 2/Lt D.C. MacDonald came down in Airco D.H.9 C.2224 of 103 Squadron, RAF; they were later reported to be 'safe in Louvain [Belgium]' [Ref: RAF, *Combat Casualty List*, 4 November 1918].

25 RAF, *Communiqué No. 32*, 14 November 1918, p. 1.

26 From the epic poem '*El Cid*' by Johann Gottfried Herder (1744-1803).

27 During the course of World War I the military Orden Pour le Merite was presented to 687 officers of the German armed forces and their allies. Of this number, 81 were awarded to aviation officers, of whom Leutnant der Reserve Carl Degelow was the last [Ref: Zuerl, *Pour-le- Mérite-Flieger*, p. 548].

28 Jones, op.cit., pp. 556-557.

CHAPTER TWELVE
A TURBULENT FUTURE

The Armistice and Beyond

In late 1918, many loyal military men, including Leutnant der Reserve Carl Degelow, were surprised by the Imperial German Navy mutiny that began on 4 November. Based on a widespread sentiment that a high seas fleet deployment planned for 30 October was, in fact, a suicide mission, many sailors refused to follow orders and their actions catalysed a movement that soon spread across Germany and culminated in revolutionary fever two days before the Armistice. In short order, the national frenzy led to organised groups of Bolshevik-type 'Soldiers' and Workers' Councils' whose aim was to create a new social order modelled after the success of the revolution in Russia.

Because World War I was concluded by an armistice – not a formal surrender – many German armed forces marched back to their homeland. Local regiments paraded with horses and equipment into their home cities and received heroes' welcomes. The general feeling created was that they had not been defeated in the field; rather, that they had been sold out by politicians. The *Dolchstoss* [stab in the back] sentiment was a balm to the national ego that was later used with great effect by such wartime veterans and Iron Cross recipients as Adolf Hitler.

There were no parades and festivities for Carl Degelow and his men when they crossed the border into Germany ingloriously crammed into the back of a lorry. By the time they arrived in Berlin for a formal demobilisation, the situation became worse, as Degelow remembered:

'A flyer should not philosophise about his future. What happened after the Armistice proved me unfortunately right; for the communist-inspired revolution and its attendant evils relieved us of an honour-saving homecoming.

'Shortly after the first wave of the political storm [of the naval mutiny] had passed over Germany, fate led me to the historical Brandenburg Gate in Berlin. I thought back to the days when we had joyfully envisioned this monument – this symbol of German character and strength – and when our only wish was to greet the sight of it with thankfulness and joy. But now, serious and grey, the structure had no air of festive feeling. My own unhappiness was intensified as I realized that my officer's epaulettes and Pour le Mérite were not looked upon with favour by people wearing red armbands. A thick briefcase and an official-looking bearing was the preferred style of appearance.

'The greeting I received was: "Do you not know about the revolution?" To which I replied with a smile – coarseness is often helpless when met with a smile – "You may be right I have not heard of the revolution. But have you not heard about the war?"

'It was inconceivable to me that such lack of concern should be the answer to the warm, spirited devotion with which we soldiers had marched to war in the first days of August 1914. At that time it was the common understanding for all who felt that home and family were threatened by the international threats and conspiracies of the alliance of the summer of 1914, to give their best – indeed, their all – for their Fatherland.

'We did not demand praise for this fulfilment of duty, nor thanks; all we expected was a little recognition as the defenders of the Fatherland. And those people whose homes we had kept safe from foreign invasion gave us soldiers no respect or gratitude for having fought and bled for them.

'Instead, on our return we met only with insult and abuse, bringing to mind the words of the 18th century dramatist Gotthold Ephraim Lessing: "The good that I intended is taken for the worst." During that sad post-war period in German history, I was tempted to feel, as did many other German soldiers, "If the call ever goes out again to fight for the Fatherland, I will gladly leave it to others."

'As the revolutionary mood persisted, however, one had to put personal feelings aside and show the world one was made of sterner stuff. The public disorder and mayhem they created soon got so far out of hand that the civilian police were virtually powerless to stop marauding gangs of Reds who roamed the streets, looking to take over by force what they could not win politically. During one such encounter near Hamburg, the conservative leader and wartime fighter ace of forty-four aerial victories Hauptmann Rudolf Berthold was captured by Reds. One of the scoundrels got behind Berthold and grabbed the strong, silver-threaded ribbon attached to his Pour le Mérite medal and strangled him to death with it.

'"Fight fire with fire" became the watchword. I returned to Hamburg after I was discharged from the army, and I joined with several other former soldiers to establish a private, semi-military organisation to deal effectively with the Reds. Together we formed the *Hamburger Zeitfreiwilliger-Korps* [Hamburg Volunteer Corps] and, in league with like-minded groups, helped chase the rascals out of the city.'[1]

But, before conservative forces were successful, another casualty among German airmen during the volatile post-war period was the first commanding officer of Jagdstaffel 40. Oberleutnant Eilers, who remained in aviation after the war and became Kommandeur der Flieger for the northern Freikorps area in Germany's former Baltic territories, was killed during a street battle with a communist unit in Hamburg-Fuhlsbüttel on 29 April 1919.

Honours and Awards

When Carl Degelow was finally released from military service on 7 July 1921, he was accorded the brevet rank of *Oberleutnant der Reserve ausser Dienst* [Reserve First Lieutenant, Retired]. At the age of thirty, he was retired from active service rolls, but did not qualify for a pension. Indeed, aside from that rank title and his Pour le Mérite, Degelow had few honours to show for his service. He earned the Second and First Class awards of the Iron Cross, which became vastly diluted in importance as the war continued – with some 5,210,000 of the former and about 218,000 of the latter[2] awarded for bravery in combat.

Degelow is a case in point to demonstrate the haphazard nature of the German awards system. As a non-Hessian native who enlisted in the Grand Duchy of Hesse's military arm and served in combat in three Hessian infantry units, Degelow would have qualified for Hesse's *Allgemeines Ehrenzeichen für Tapferkeit* [General Honour Decoration for Bravery],[3] as did his Jasta 40 comrade Adolf Auer,[4] but he was simply overlooked. A Hamburg resident, Degelow attained such stature that he could have been awarded the *Hamburgisches Hanseatenkreuz* [Hanseatic Cross of Hamburg], of which some 50,000 were presented,[5] but he missed that one, too. Degelow also earned the *Verwundeten-Abzeichen für das Heer* [Wound Badge for the Army], which was authorised by Kaiser Wilhelm II on 3 March 1918,[6] but, despite his having been wounded in 1915, Degelow never applied for it. He received the Kaiser's *Abzeichen für Militär-Flugzeugführer* [Military Pilot's Badge],[7] mainly because it was conferred upon him. As noted previously, he was awarded the distinguished Knight's Cross of the Royal House Order of Hohenzollern with Swords, and the Pour le Mérite – the latter almost certainly the result of military political manoeuvring by JaGru 6 commander Erhard Milch, who had friends in high places. Other fighter pilots whose victory scores were higher than Degelow's did not receive the Pour le Mérite, however, as the Kaiser was not able to sign their award documents before he went into exile on 9 November 1918.[8]

When the body of Germany's leading World War I fighter ace Manfred von Richthofen was returned to Berlin in November 1925, it was escorted by an honour guard from the Knighthood of the Order Pour le Mérite. Then Oberleutnant der Reserve a.D. Carl Degelow was the second to the last member of the outside left column. Directly behind him was then Major Alfred Keller. Behind the honour guard, in the centre of the first row of mourners, was Kunigunde Freifrau von Richthofen, by then the widowed mother of the Red Baron. German President Paul von Hindenburg walked behind her, accompanied by her sole surviving son, Bolko Freiherr von Richthofen.

Degelow returned to work in the cement industry in 1919 and kept up his former military aviation connections with membership in the *Ring der Flieger* [Flyers' Ring] organisation, as well as the *Stahlhelm* [Steel Helmet] veterans' association. He also attended events of the more exclusive *Ritterschaft des Ordens Pour le Mérite* [Knighthood of the Order Pour le Mérite].

His association with the Pour le Mérite veterans provided Degelow with a one-time and final connection to Germany's famed Red Baron. Rittmeister Manfred Freiherr von Richthofen was also a Pour le Mérite recipient and, after he was killed in combat in April 1918, his body was buried in Bertangles, France, not far from where he fell. Subsequently moved to a German military cemetery in Fricourt, France, Richthofen's remains were returned to Germany in November 1925. Carl Degelow was among the national heroes selected to participate in funeral and reburial ceremonies in the national cemetery in Berlin. His role was described in a contemporary media account of events from the tomb of Prussia's renowned warrior king, Frederick the Great, at the Garnison-Kirche in Potsdam to the Invalidenfriedhof in Berlin:

'Veteran fighter pilots in field uniforms, all Knights of the Order Pour le Mérite, escorted [the coffin]. Under the solemn tolling of bells they [served as a] company of honorary pall bearers and brought out the coffin. They placed the coffin on a gun-carriage. An immense funeral procession followed the coffin through the gates of the Invalidenfriedhof [to the gravesite]. Aeroplanes circled above in the grey November air.'[9]

Changing Times
The decade that followed was a time of great turmoil as Degelow testified:

'Freedom returned to Germany, followed by bad economic times and then what appeared to be salvation by the National Socialists. My mistake was in not being more fully aware of politics. Dressed up and at a street parade in 1934, I was naïve enough to think that, because I was not a member of the Nazi party, I did not have to give the stiff arm *"Hitler-Gruss"* [salute] when the swastika banners passed by. Abruptly, some *Gestapo* [secret state police] men – in method not unlike that of the Reds we had chased from Hamburg – seized me and hauled me off to jail.

'It was not until some hours later that a sympathetic guard spotted the Pour le Mérite at my neck and asked me to identify myself. He then disappeared and in short order, a local party official stood before my opened cell and apologized for "the inconvenience", telling me that it was not the party's intention to embarrass national heroes. I paid scant attention to what he said. But I should have been more attentive, as he went on and on, telling me about the grandeur that would some day prevail in Germany. Little did I know that, in a way, his words were the opening tunes of Germany's *Götterdämmerung* [twilight of the gods], the country's ruination.'

After sixteen years of mostly covert development, the German Luftwaffe [literally air weapon] was publicly unveiled on 1 March 1935.[10] Germany was still in difficult financial straits and, as the cement industry was not a high priority in the coming preparations for

When Carl Degelow was promoted to Major der Reserve, he posed for this portrait wearing his Pour le Mérite.

war, Degelow agreed to be re-activated in the new air arm to earn a decent wage. On 15 August 1936, he was back in uniform – with the rank of Hauptmann der Reserve. His date of rank was recorded as 1 January 1931 to give him sufficient seniority befitting a German national hero.

Although he had not piloted an aeroplane since the war, Degelow was posted to the *1. Teil Eignungsübung bei III./Lehrgeschwader* [1st Section of Flight Aptitude Testing for the 3rd Training Wing] at Greifswald in Pomerania. A few weeks later he was assigned to the Wing's 2nd Section. But the shift was of little consequence, as the unit's first Geschwaderkommodore [Wing Commander] was a man Degelow knew from their time together in Jagdstaffel 40, Major Hans Jeschonnek.

Hans Jeschonnek

Unlike Degelow, Jeschonnek remained in uniform after the Armistice. As was typical of officers who served with the post-war Reichswehr, Jeschonnek endured slow career development. He was given permanent rank as a Leutnant in 1922 and promoted to Oberleutnant three years later. It was another seven years before he was promoted to Hauptmann on 1 June 1932, but, with the ascension of Hitler's National Socialists in 1933, Jeschonnek's promotions came much quicker: Major in 1935, Oberstleutnant [Lieutenant-Colonel] two years later and, nineteen months after that, Oberst [Colonel] on 1 November 1938.[11]

Suffice to say, in the autumn of 1936, Hans Jeschonnek was at the beginning of a meteoric career rise. Whether by accident or design the thirty-nine-year-old major was surely glad to be reunited with his former Jasta-Führer [fighter squadron leader] and mentor. Indeed, this stroke of good fortune was but one of many 'lucky breaks' that Carl Degelow received over the next nine years.

Being assigned to the *2. Teil Eignungsübung bei III./LGG* [2nd Section of Jeschonnek's Gruppe] in March 1937, would have utilised Degelow's flight expertise – such as it was – with the newly forming training wing. On 1 November 1938, *Lehrgeschwader Greifswald* became *Lehrgeschwader 1* and Degelow remained with the unit until just before the outbreak of World War II.

Indeed, on 1 August 1939, he was promoted to Major der Reserve, the highest rank he attained in the Luftwaffe. When asked why Degelow was not promoted further, his World War I comrade Adolf Auer, whose career also peaked at that rank, explained: 'Officers from the Great War who later achieved high rank were generally those who were on active duty or returned to active duty on their own in 1933.'

Degelow's Further Assignments

By his own admission, Carl Degelow was at least naïve and at worst a bumbler when it came to political matters. Degelow told this author that he felt he could rely on his association with his former Jagdgruppe Kommandeur [fighter group commander] Erhard Milch, who left active duty as a Hauptmann in 1920 and, after helping successfully to launch the Lufthansa airline, was reactivated at the rank of Oberst in 1933.[12]

Degelow met Hermann Göring at several gatherings of the Knighthood of the Order Pour le Mérite and took him at his word when Göring offered to be of any assistance in life. Degelow soon outwore his welcome with the future Reichsmarschall [Supreme Marshal] after the Nazis consolidated their political power.

On two occasions, Degelow called Göring's office to seek help for Jewish friends who feared the worst during the virulently anti-Semitic Third Reich and felt they needed to leave Germany. The first request was fulfilled with little fuss. After the second request was granted and a possible trend sensed, however, Degelow was informed that any further communications with (by then) Generaloberst [Colonel-General] Göring were to be forwarded through the Luftwaffe's chain of command.

By that time, Degelow's one-time boss Erhard Milch was also a Luftwaffe Generaloberst and, upon learning of Degelow's falling out of favour, he intervened to keep his old friend away from Göring. Thus, in conjunction with Degelow's final Luftwaffe promotion, he was assigned briefly to *Luftwaffenführungsstab, Abteilung 5 (Fremde Staaten)* [Luftwaffe High Command Staff, Section 5 (Foreign Nations)]. The office assessed aviation strengths and capabilities of potential German enemies of the Luftwaffe such as the British Commonwealth, the Soviet Union, Poland and France. Just as he had had no recent flying experience when assigned to Jeschonnek's training command, Degelow had no intelligence or military analytical training when posted to an office responsible for information collection within the Luftwaffe's senior command.

Five weeks after the German invasion of Poland on 1 September 1939, Degelow was assigned to be *Kommandant des Stabsquartier des Stabes Luftgau-Kommando II* [Headquarters Commander for the staff of Air Defence District II]. That command was based in Posen, the major city in the largest subdivision of occupied Poland to be annexed by Germany. The area had been the former Kingdom of Prussia's Wartheland before it was restored to the post-World War I Polish Republic. Back under German control following the conquest of Poland, the area showed no signs of hostile air operations. Hence, Degelow's job was essentially that of a paper shuffler.

From 19 May to 13 July 1940, Degelow was assigned to the staff of the *Generalluftzeugmeister* [general in charge of aviation equipment], then General der Flieger [Lieutenant-General] Ernst Udet, who, as a World War I fighter pilot, had attained sixty-two confirmed aerial victories[13] and was Germany's highest ranking living fighter ace. With this move, Degelow now worked for a fellow Pour le Mérite recipient and fighter pilot whom he knew for many years. Given Udet's reputed lack of commitment to his job and propensity for partying, it is likely that Degelow found this assignment to be very enjoyable, albeit not productive.

At the time, Udet was having problems with his superior, Generaloberst Milch, who had to explain away various situations to his boss, Generalfeldmarschall Hermann Göring. Looking out for Degelow once again, Milch had him transferred to a less visible role. When asked about his role as Degelow's 'protector', Milch wrote to this author that Degelow was 'an especially first-rate human being and soldier who I have always valued.'[14] In any event, Degelow was out of that office when Udet, accused by Milch and Göring of causing Luftwaffe equipment failures during the Battle of Britain, committed suicide in Berlin on 17 November 1941.[15] The German public was told that Udet died in a flying accident, testing a new fighter aeroplane, and he was given a formal state funeral. He was buried in Berlin's Invalidenfriedhof, near his World War I mentor, Manfred von Richthofen.

Germany's last knights of battle gathered for a reunion in 1968. Aviation members of the Knighthood of the Order Pour le Mérite were: fighter pilot Josef Jacobs (front row, third from right), aviation observer Jürgen von Grone (second row, far left), fighter pilot Carl Degelow (second row, far right), naval fighter pilot Theodor Osterkamp (third row, far right), and bomber squadron commander Alfred Keller (top row, far right). Coincidentally, fighter pilots Degelow, Jacobs and Osterkamp were congratulated together a half century earlier in a 4th Army report dated 8 October 1918.

In any event, those political storm clouds were more than a year away, when, on 14 July 1940, Degelow was appointed *Verbindungsoffizier des Reichsmarschalls für den Binnenschiffarht im bestezengebieten–Belgien* [Reichsmarschall's Liaison for Inland Navigation for Occupied Territories (based in) Brussels]. Göring was initially responsible for the European inland canal system, as part of his *Vierjahresplan* [Four Year Plan] to help develop production capabilities of raw materials for German industry's wartime production. His nominal oversight of moving primary raw materials from occupied countries to Germany entitled Göring to have a representative on the committee that oversaw this aspect of supplying factories. Degelow's management background in the cement industry made him qualified to handle this job and the invisible hand of Erhard Milch arranged the assignment. But it turned out to be a do-nothing post that was not needed when the entire supply function came under German Arms Minister Albert Speer, a member of Hitler's inner circle. Speer added it to his portfolio after Göring was humiliated by the Luftwaffe's failure to prevail in the Battle of Britain.

In August 1941, Degelow was detached from his military duties – and with not a single medal or honour this time. He was still nominally responsible to Four Year Plan State Secretary Paul Körner, but he no longer had a real function. With the cement industry then at the height of its production, supplying materials for bunkers and various fortifications,

Degelow returned to his old job at the cement industrial complex in Pomerania. In the heady days before the German Army was defeated at Stalingrad, it was easier to release a non-conforming, under-performer like Carl Degelow than to expend time and energy finding a place for such an 'old-timer' in the military. Hence, he spent the remainder of the war on the island of Wollin, off the Baltic coast of what is now Poland. At the end of World War II, Degelow and his family had to flee Wollin, as its Soviet occupiers expelled the German population and replaced them with eastern Polish expellees from territories ceded to the USSR. Degelow and his wife Maria and their son Manfred made their way to Lübeck, a western German city on the Baltic Sea. Eventually, they followed other refugees to Hamburg, where they were able to re-establish residency based on Degelow's having once lived there.

Life After World War II

Carl Degelow celebrated his fifty-fifth birthday on 5 January 1946 in Hamburg. While his long-time friend and benefactor Erhard Milch went on to spend nine years in prison for war crimes, Degelow emerged from the post-World War II denazification process with a clean sheet. His lack of success in the Luftwaffe and antipathy toward the Nazis, which no doubt occasioned his release from active duty in 1941, were favourable factors. And he was greatly helped by post-war letters of support and testaments to his character by two Jewish former Jagdstaffel 40 subordinates: Anton Raab, who had moved to Italy, and Willy Rosenstein, who then resided in South Africa.

As West Germany's post-war 'economic miracle' took hold and the country's social service network grew, Carl Degelow enjoyed a modicum of comfort. Between his Luftwaffe and national pensions, he lived well enough to be able to visit old friends and attend Aero Club of Germany meetings. Most of all, he enjoyed getting together with his contemporaries at the Knighthood of the Order Pour le Mérite; as he told this author, he relished his role as the 'junior member' of the exclusive group.

Carl Degelow was in declining health in his final year, and when he died on 9 November 1970 – less than two months short of his eightieth birthday – he was among a small group of surviving German fighter pilots of The Great War. At Degelow's funeral, one of his favourite lines from scripture was read and it summed up his life, the value of personal honour and his refusal to accept rewards from the hands of an evil dictator:

'Peoples' hearts plan the way, but the Lord alone directs the steps.' (Proverbs 16:9)

1   Deutscher Offizier-Bund, *Ehren-Rangliste des ehemaligen deutschen Heeres*, p. 741.

2   O'Connor, *Aviation Awards of Imperial Germany and the Men Who Earned Them*, Vol. II, p. 11.

3   O'Connor, op.cit., Vol. VII, pp. 172-191.

4   Auer, *Personal-Bogen*, 1918, p. 4.

5   O'Connor, op.cit., Vol. VII, p. 402.

6   Neubecker, *Für Tapferkeit und Verdienst*, p. 28.

7   Ibid.

8   Zuerl, *Pour-le-Mérite-Flieger*, p. 488.

9   Ring der Flieger, *Flieger-Ring Nachrichtenblatt Nr. 33*, 1 December 1925, p. 5.

10 Ries, K. *Luftwaffe: Die Maulwürfe – Geheimer Aufbau 1919-1935*, p. 117.

11 Hildebrand, *Die Generale der deutschen Luftwaffe 1935-1945*, Vol. I, pp. 138-139.

12 Ibid., Vol. II, p. 394.

13 Franks, Bailey, & Guest, *Above the Lines*, p. 220.

14 Milch letter to the author dated 16 December 1970.

15 Franks, Bailey & Guest, op.cit.

APPENDIX I

CARL DEGELOW AND JAGDSTAFFEL 40 VICTORY LIST

Author's note: The following list of aerial victories and resulting casualties was compiled from the official *Nachrichtenblatt der deutschen Luftstreitkräfte* weekly intelligence summary, various *Kommandeur der Flieger* bi-monthly, weekly and other reports, and research material provided by the late Dr. Gustav Bock. Other information was provided by the late Erich Tornuss. Comparable British and French reports provided potentially corresponding casualty and other information. Dates are stated in the German numerical style (day, month) and times are expressed in military time, with chronological sub-headings to clarify whether the local time was an hour ahead of British/French time, or matched it. Airfields used by Jadstaffeln 7 and 40 are also noted, to indicate the victors' proximity to the air combat sites noted. For two-seater casualties, pilots are listed first, observers second. Fates of the airmen are indicated by the abbreviations: DoW = Died of Wounds; KiA = Killed in Action; PoW = Prisoner of War; WiA = Wounded in Action. When no abbreviation is given, it is assumed the man was uninjured and returned to his own lines. Aerial victories claimed, but not confirmed are indicated by n/c, and aircraft Forced to Land (which may have been credited as victories) are identified by FtL.

Date	Time	Location	Aircraft	Victor & No.		Crew and Disposition
1917						
17.4		German time one hour ahead of British time				
22.5		southwest of Braye	Caudron G.4	Ltn Degelow, FAA 216 shared with Ltn Kürten	$^1/_2$	
25.5		southwest of Bailly-Braye	Caudron G.4	Ltn Degelow, FAA 216 shared with Ltn Kürten	$^1/_2$	Lt Graff, Esc C.43 (WiA)
5.6			Caudron G.4	Ltns Degelow & Kürten	n/c	
		Wynghene airfield (Jasta 7: 22.8 – 14.9.17)				
3.9	0825	west of Dixmuide	Sopwith Camel	Ltn Degelow, Ja 7	n/c	
		Mars-la-Tour airfield (Jasta 40 : 14.9.17 – 15.3.18)				
30.10		Savonières	Nieuport 27 B.3627	Ltn King, Ja 40	2	2/Lt E.D. Scott, 1 Sqn, RFC (KiA)
		Aertrycke airfield (Jasta 7: 15.9.17 – 1.3.18)				
8.12	1400	southwest of Passchendaele	Sopwith 2-seater	Ltn Degelow, Ja 7	n/c	
12.12	P.M.		Sopwith Camel	Ltn Degelow, Ja 7	n/c	

Date	Time	Location	Aircraft	Victor & No.		Crew and Disposition
1918						
23.1	1600	Dixmuide	Sopwith 1F.1 Camel B.7184	Ltn Degelow, Ja 7	n/c	F/S/L J.E.Youens, 3 Sqn, RNAS (PoW)
25.1	1350	Courtemarck	Bristol F.2B B.883	Ltn Degelow, Ja 7	2	Sgt H.O. Smith & 2/Lt H.S. Clemons, 20 Sqn, RFC (WiA, PoW)
11.2		Pont à Mousson	Spad S.XIII	Ltn King, Ja 40	3	
10.3		German time synchronized with British time				
16.4		German time one hour ahead of British time				
		Rumbeke airfield (1.3 – 14.3.18)				
21.4	1110	east of Armentières	Sopwith 1F.1 Camel B.9315	Ltn Degelow, Ja 7	3	Lt R.J. Marion 54 Sqn, RAF (KiA)
		Roubaix airfield (6.4 – 5.5.18)				
25.4	1500	Dickebusch – Reninghelst	Airco D.H.9	Ltn King, Ja 40	4	Lt C.J. Gillan & C.6079 Lt W. Duce, 98 Sqn, RAF (PoW)
		St. Marguerite airfield (Jasta 7: 29.3 – 1.10.18)				
16.5	1230	Vlamertinghe	R.E.8	Ltn Degelow, Ja 7	4	2/Lt R.C. Mais 7 Sqn, RAF (WiA)
		Mouscron airfield (Jasta 40: 5.5. – 6.6.18)				
24.5			enemy aircraft	Ltn Gilly, Ja 40	n/c	
5.6	2050	Poperinghe	captive balloon	Ltn Dilthey, Ja 40	7	2nd Balloon Wing 5th Co., 2nd Section, RAF
5.6	2055	Poperinghe	captive balloon	Ltn Gilly, Ja 40	1	2nd Balloon Wing 5th Co., 25th Section, RAF
		Lomme airfield (6.6. – 24.8.18)				
11.6	1550	Vlamertinghe	R.E.8 C.2203	Ltn Jeschonnek, Ja 40	1	2/Lt W.W. Saunders (WiA), PBr E.L. Gouder, 7 Sqn, RAF
18.6	0930	Vieux Berquin	S.E.5a C.8870	Ltn Degelow, Ja 40	5	Lt R.G. Pierce 29 Sqn, RAF
25.6	2025	Zandvoorde	Sopwith 1F.1 Camel C.8238	Ltn Degelow	6	Lt O.J.F. Jones-Lloyd, 54 Sqn, RAF (PoW)
27.6	0945	Armentières	Sopwith 5.F1 Dolphin	Ltn Gilly	2	Capt W.A. Forsyth or T/Lt F.S. Ganter 79 Sqn, RAF
27.6	0935	Bailleul	Sopwith 5F.1 Dolphin	Vzfw Rausch	2	79 Sqn, RAF
27.6	0940	Le Leuthe southeast of Bailleul	S.E.5a C.9573	Ltn Degelow	7	Lt F.R. Brand, 29 Sqn, RAF (KiA)
2.7	0740	Kruistraat	S.E.5a B.8524	Ltn Degelow	8	Lt W.E. Durant, 29 Sqn, RAF (KiA)
13.7	0940	Erquinhem	S.E.5a C.1818	Ltn Degelow	9	Lt W.S. Robertson, 85 Sqn, RAF (KiA)

181

Date	Time	Location	Aircraft	Victor & No.		Crew and Disposition
14.7	0930	southeast of Vieux Berquin	S.E.5a C.6490	Ltn Degelow	10	2/Lt N.H. Marshall, 85 Sqn, RAF (PoW)
14.7	0935	southeast of Vieux Berquin	S.E.5a C.6447	Ltn Rosenstein	4	2/Lt B.N. Garrett, 64 Sqn, RAF (PoW)
14.7	0940	west of Merville	S.E.5a D.405	Ltn Degelow	11	Lt H.A. Whittaker 29 Sqn, RAF (WiA)
14.7	0940	near Vieux Berquin	S.E.5a	Ltn Gilly	3	29 Sqn, RAF
22.7	0930	Lestrem	Bristol F.2B F.5810	Ltn Degelow	12	Lt W.E. Coulson & 2/Lt W.H.E. Labbett, 62 Sqn, RAF (PoW)
25.7	0930	Wytschaete	Sopwith 1F.1 Camel D.1889	Ltn Degelow	13	Lt W.A. Carveth, 208 Sqn, RAF (PoW)
10.8	1010	Swartenbrouck	S.E.5a	Vzfw Groll	2	
17.8	0925	Lomme airfield	Sopwith 1F.1 Camel D.1961	ground gunner		Lt E.P.E McCleery, 4 Sqn, AFC (KiA)
		Halluin-Lille airfield (24.8. – 9.9.18)				
		Reckem airfield (9.9 – 28.9.18)				
18.9	1615	Poperinghe	captive balloon	Ltn Degelow	14	2nd Balloon Wing 17th Co., 36th Section, RAF
20.9	1055	north of Annappes	Bristol F.2B D.2260	Ltn Degelow	15	Lt M.F.R. Mahony & 2/Lt J.N. Kier, 48 Sqn, RAF (PoW)
21.9	0945	north of Ypres	R.E.8 F.5976	Ltn Degelow	16	Lt W.G. Allanson & 2/Lt W.I. Anderson, 7 Sqn, RAF (KiA)
24.9	1900	near Zillebeke Lake	S.E.5a E.4074	Ltn Degelow	17	Capt C. Crawford, 41 Sqn, RAF (PoW)
27.9	1530	Valenciennes	Bristol F.2B E.2153	Ltn Degelow	18	Lt C. Foster & Sgt T. Proctor, 88 Sqn. RAF (KiA)
		Bisseghem airfield (28.9 – 8.10.18)				
28.9	1250	Passchendaele	Sopwith 1F.1 Camel	Ltn Degelow	19	70 Sqn, RAF
29.9			F.2B (or D.H.9)	Ltn Rosenstein	5	211 Sqn, RAF
1.10	1430	Menin	S.E.5a F.54674	Ltn Degelow	20	Lt A.M. Sanderson, 74 Sqn, RAF (KiA)
2.10		Roulers	Sopwith 1F.1 Camel F.3121	Ltn Degelow	21	Capt M.L. Cooper, 213 Sqn, RAF (KiA)
3.10		Roulers	Spad S.VII	Ltn Degelow	22	Esc. Spa 82
3.10		Roulers	Spad S.VII	Ltn Rosenstein	6	Esc. Spa 82
3.10		Roulers	Spad S.VII	Ltn Gilly	4	Esc. Spa 82
3.10		Roulers	Spad S.VII	Vzfw Groll	3	Esc. Spa 82
4.10	1850	Landelede	Sopwith 1F.1 Camel	Ltn Degelow	23	65 Sqn, RAF
4.10	1850	Landelede	Sopwith 1F.1 Camel	Ltn Rosenstein	7	65 Sqn, RAF
5.10	1100	Roulers	Airco D.H.9 E.8872	Ltn Degelow	24	2/Lt V.G.H. Phillips & 2/Lt A.F. Taylor, 211 Sqn, RAF (both WiA)

Date	Time	Location	Aircraft	Victor & No.		Crew and Disposition
7.10	1130	Ghent	Sopwith 1F.1 Camel	Ltn Degelow	25	65 or 70 Sqn
7.10	1130	Ghent	Sopwith 1F.1 Camel	Ltn Gilly	5	65 or 70 Sqn
7.10	1130	Ghent	Sopwith 1F.1 Camel	Vzfw Groll	4	65 or 70 Sqn
7.10	1130	Ghent	Sopwith 1F.1 Camel	Ltn Rosenstein	8	65 or 70 Sqn
		Menin airfield (8.10 – 10.10.18)				
8.10		over frontlines	Sopwith 1F.1 Camel D.3382	Ltn Degelow	26	2/Lt R.W. Hopper, 210 Sqn, RAF (POW)
		Wynghene airfield (10.10 – 22.10.18)				
18.10	1930	Roulers	Spad S.XIII	Ltn Jeschonnek	2	Esc. Spa 82
18.10	1930	Roulers	Spad S.XIII	Ltn Gilly	6	Esc. Spa 82
18.10	1930	Roulers	Spad S.XIII	Ltn Gilly	7	Esc. Spa 82
		Gontrode airfield (22.10 – 5.11.18)				
23.10	1230	Vosseleare	Airco D.H.9 C.6314	Ltn Auer	1	Capt G.C. Haynes & 2/Lt G. Brown, 108 Sqn, RAF (KiA)
26.10		over Ghent	Spad S.XIII N° 18816	Ltn. Degelow	27	Lt. M. Quenioux, C.A.M (KiA)
26.10	1440	Esseghem	Sopwith 1F.1 Camel H.7005	Ltn. Degelow	28	2/Lt A.E. Moir, 65 Sqn, RAF (KiA)
27.10			Sopwith 1F.1 Camel	Ltn. Rosenstein	9	
30.10		Ghislain	S.E.5a	Ltn. Degelow	29	32 Sqn, RAF
4.11		near Dutch border	Airco D.H.9 C.2224	Ltn. Degelow	30	Lt J.G. Carey & 2/Lt D.C. MacDonald 103 Sqn, RAF (PoW)

Antwerp airfield (5.11 – 11.11.18)

APPENDIX II

GLOSSARY

Military ranks / offices / terms

Abteilung(en)	Two seater squadron(s)
Abteilungsführer	Two-seater squadron leader
Aeroplanbau	Aircraft construction factory
Armee-Oberkommando	Army Group Command
Fahnenjunker	Officer Cadet
Fähnrich	Army Ensign
Feldwebel (Fwbl)	Sergeant
Fliegeras	Fighter ace
Flugzeugwerk	Aircraft factory
Gefreiter (Gefr)	Lance Corporal
Generalfeldmarschall	Field Marshal
General der Infanterie	General of the Infantry
Generalleutnant	Lieutenant-General
Generalmajor	Major-General
Generaloberst	Colonel-General
Hauptmann (Hptm)	Captain
Jagdflieger	Fighter pilot
Jagdfliegerei	Fighter aviation
Kaiser	Emperor
Kommandierende General der Luftstreitkräfte (Kogenluft)	Commanding General of the Air Force
Kommandeur der Flieger (Kofl)	Army Corps officer in charge of aviation
Landser	Private (lowest rank)
Leutnant (Ltn)	Second Lieutenant
Leutnant der Reserve (Ltn.d.Res)	Second Lieutenant, Reserves
Oberflugmeister (Oberflgmstr)	Chief Petty Officer [Imperial Navy]
Oberleutnant (Oblt)	First Lieutenant
Oberleutnant zur See	Naval Lieutenant, junior grade
Oberst	Colonel
Oberstleutnant	Lieutenant-Colonel
Offizierstellvertreter	Warrant Officer
Offizier zur besonderen Verwendung	Officer seconded for special assignment
Rittmeister (Rittm)	Cavalry Captain
Staffel-Führer	Fighter squadron leader
Stellvertretender Staffel-Führer	Deputy squadron leader
Unteroffizier (Uffz)	Corporal
Vizefeldwebel (Vzfw)	Sergeant-Major

Military units

Centre d'Aviation Militaire	French Military Aviation Centre
Escadrille	French word for squadron
Feld-Fliegerabteilung	Field Aviation Section (Squadron)
Flieger-Abteilung	Aviation Section (Squadron)
Flieger-Ersatz-Abteilung (FEA)	Aviation Replacement Section (Squadron)
Fliegertruppe	Flying Force
Infanterie-Regiment (Inf-Reg)	Infantry Regiment
Inspektion der Fliegertruppen	Inspectorate of *(Idflieg)* Military Aviation
Jagdeschwader (JG)	Fighter Wing
Jagdgruppe (JaGru)	Fighter Group
Jagdstaffel (Jasta)	Fighter Squadron
Jagdstaffelschule (Jastaschule)	Fighter Pilots School
Kette	Flight
Landsturm	Local Militia
Luftstreitkräfte	Air Force
Marine-Jagdstaffel	Naval fighter squadron
Schlachtstaffel (Schlasta)	Attack Section
Staffel (n)	Squadron(s)

184

Appendix III
Belgian Place Names

Author's note: Belgian place names in this book are spelled as they appeared on British and German maps in World War I. To avoid any confusion, names from that time and current Flemish spellings are listed below.

Aelbeeke	Aalbeke	Harlebeke	Harelbeke	Sotteghem	Zottegem
Aertrycke	Aartrijke	Iseghem	Izegem	Thouroube	Torhout
Alost	Aalst	Keyem	Keiem	Thourout	Torhout
Bisseghem	Bissegem	Kruistraat	Kruisstraat	Vlamertinghe	Vlamertinge
Brugges	Brugge	Kuerne	Kuurne	Vosselaere	Vosselare
Comines	Komen	Langemarck	Langemark	Warneton	Waasten
Courtemarck	Kortemark	Menin	Menen	Wervicq	Wervik
Courtrai	Kortrijk	Messines	Mesen	Wynendael	Wijnendale
Dadizeele	Dadizele	Nieuport	Nieuwpoort	Wynghene	Wingene
Dickebusch	Dikkebus	Ooteghem	Otegem	Wytschaete	Wijtschate
Dixmude	Diksmuide	Ostende	Oostende	Ypres	Ieper
Esseghem	Essegem	Passchendaele	Passendale		
Gheluwe	Geluwe	Pervyse	Pervijze		
Ghent	Gent	Poperinghe	Poperinge		
Ghislain	St. Ghislain	Reckem	Rekkem		
Ghistelles	Gistel	Reninghelst	Reningelst		
		Roulers	Roeselare		

BIBLIOGRAPHY AND SOURCES

Books:

Asprey, R. *The German High Command at War*, New York, 1991

Bailey, F. & Cony, C. *The French Air Service War Chronology 1914-1918*, London, 2001

Bodenschatz, K. *Jagd in Flanderns Himmel*, Munich, 1935

Bowyer, C. *For Valour – The Air VCs*, London, 1978

Bruce, J. *British Aeroplanes 1914-1918*, London, 1969

Buckler, J. *Malaula! Kampfruf meiner Staffel*, Berlin, 1939

Clark, C. *Iron Kingdom – The Rise and Downfall of Prussia*, Cambridge (Massachusetts), 2006

Cutlack, F. *The Australian Flying Corps in the War of 1914-1918*, Sydney, 1933

Degelow, C. *Mit dem weissen Hirsch durch dick und dünn*, Altona-Ottensen, 1920

Deutscher Offizier-Bund. *Ehren-Rangliste des ehemaligen Deutschen Heere*s, Berlin, 1926

Dhanens, P. & Dedecker, C. *Een eeuw luchtvaart boven Gent*, Erembodegem, 2008

Eberhardt, W. von (ed.). *Unsere Luftstreitkräfte 1914-1918*, Berlin, 1930

Esposito, V. *A Concise History of World War I*, New York, 1965

Franks, N. *Albatros Aces of World War I*, Oxford, 2000

Franks, N., Bailey, F. & Guest, R. *Above the Lines*, London, 1993

Franks, N., Bailey, F. & Duiven, R. *The Jasta Pilots*, London, 1996

––. *Casualties of the German Air Service 1914-1918*, London, 1999

Haehnelt, W. *Ehrentafel der im Flugdienst während des Weltkrieges gefallenen Offiziere der Deutschen Fliegerverbände*, Berlin, 1920

Henshaw, T. *The Sky Their Battlefield*, London, 1995

Hildebrand, K. *Die Generale der deutschen Luftwaffe 1935-1945*, Vol. I, Osnabrück, 1990

––. *Die Generale der deutschen Luftwaffe 1935-1945*, Vol. II, Osnabrück, 1990

Hindenburg, P. (Translated by F. Holt) *Out of My Life*, London, 1920

Hobson, C. *Airmen Died in the Great War 1914-1918*, London, 1995

Hoeppner, W. von. *Deutschlands Krieg in der Luft*, Leipzig, 1921

Imperial War Museum. *Handbook of the German Army in War* [reprint], London, 1996

Jones, H. *The War in the Air*, Vol. II, Oxford, 1928

––. *The War in the Air*, Vol. III, Oxford, 1931

––. *The War in the Air*, Vol. IV, Oxford, 1934

––. *The War in the Air*, Vol. VI, Oxford, 1937

Kilduff, P. *Germany's Last Knight of the Air*, London, 1979

−−. *Over the Battlefronts*, London, 1996

Kollegium. *Kaiser-Karl-Schule Itzehoe 1866-1991*, Itzehoe, 1991

Liddell Hart, B. *The Real War 1914-1918*, Boston, 1964

Langsdorff, W. von (ed.). *Flieger am Feind*, Gütersloh, 1934

Loewenstern , E. von & Bertkau, M. *Mobilmachung, Aufmarsch und erster Einsatz der deutschen Luftstreitkräfte im August 1914*, Berlin, 1939

Moncure, J. *Forging the King's Sword*, New York, 1993

Neubecker, Dr. O. *Für Tapferkeit und Verdienst*, Munich, 1956

Neumann, G. *Die deutschen Luftstreitkräfte im Weltkriege*, Berlin, 1920

O'Connor, M. & Davis, M. *Nieuports in RNAS, RFC and RAF Service*, London, 2007

O'Connor, N. *Aviation Awards of Imperial Germany and the Men Who Earned Them*, Vol. II, Princeton, 1990

−−. *Aviation Awards of Imperial Germany and the Men Who Earned Them*, Vol. IV, Princeton, 1995

−−. *Aviation Awards of Imperial Germany and the Men Who Earned Them*, Vol. VII, Princeton, 2002

Perthes, J. *Ehrentafel der Kriegsopfer des reichsdeutschen Adels 1914-1918*, Gotha, 1921

Raleigh, W. *The War in the Air*, Vol. I, London, 1922

Revell, A. *High in the Empty Blue*, Mountain View (California), 1995

Richthofen, M. von. *Der rote Kampfflieger*, Berlin, 1917

Robertson, B. *British Military Serials 1911-1971*, London, 1971

Schmidt, O. *2. Nassauisches Infanterie-Regiment Nr. 88*, Oldenburg/Berlin, 1922

Shores, C., Franks, N. & Guest, R. *Above the Trenches*, London, 1990

Supf, P. *Das Buch der deutschen Fluggeschichte*, Vol. I, Stuttgart, 1956

−−. *Das Buch der deutschen Fluggeschichte*, Vol. II, Stuttgart, 1956

Täger, H., Heerde, D., Franke, H. & Ruscher, M. *Flugplatz Grossenhain – Historischer Abriss*, Meissen, 2007

Uebe, F. *Ehrenmal des preussischen Offizier-Korps*, Berlin, 1939

Wenzl, R. *Richthofen-Flieger*, Freiburg im Breisgau, ca. 1930

Werner, J. *Boelcke der Mensch, der Flieger, der Führer der deutschen Jagdfliegerei*, Leipzig, 1932

Wise, S. *Canadian Airmen and the First World War*, Toronto, 1980

Woodman, H. *Early Aircraft Armament – The Aeroplane and the Gun Up to 1918*, London, 1989

Zuerl, W. *Pour-le-Mérite-Flieger*, Munich, 1938

Documents:

Grand Quartier Général des Armées Nord et du Nord-Est, *Résumés des Opérations Aériennes*, in the field, 1918

Kommandierende General der Luftstreitkräfte (Kogenluft). *Nachrichtenblatt der Luftstreitkräfte*, Vol. I, in the field, 1917

−−. *Nachrichtenblatt der Luftstreitkräfte*, Vol. II, in the field, 1918

−−. *Richthofen-Bericht*, Nr 42360. Fl. II, Idflieg Nr 1166/18. Z. III, Charlottenburg, 26 April 1918

Kommandeur der Flieger der 4. Armee (Kofl 4).*Tagesbefehle*, in the field, 1917

−−. [Weekly] *Meldungen*, in the field, 1917

−−. *Wochenberichte*, in the field, 1918

Kommandeur der Flieger der 6. Armee (Kofl 6). *Flieger-Wochenbericht*, 1918

Kriegsministerium (organisational manual), *Teil 10 Abschnitt B, Flieger-Formationen*, Berlin, 1918

National Archives (U.K.). 20 Squadron, RFC, *Combat Reports*, in the field, 1918 (PRO File Air 1/1223/204/5/2634/20 Sqdn)

−−. 29 Squadron, RAF, *Squadron Record Book*, in the field, 1918 (PRO File Air 1/173/15/162/1)

--. 32 Squadron, RAF, *Combat Reports*, in the field, 1918 (PRO File Air 1/1222/204/5/2634/32 Sqdn)

--. 41 Squadron, RAF, *Combat Reports*, in the field, 1918 (PRO File Air 1/1222/204/5/2634/41 Sqdn)

--. 48 Squadron, RFC, *Combat Reports*, in the field, 1917 (PRO File Air 1/1223/204/5/2634/48 Sqdn)

--. 65 Squadron, RAF, *Squadron Record Book*, in the field, 1918 (PRO File Air 1/175/15/183/3)

--. 74 Squadron, RAF, *Squadron Record Book*, in the field, 1918 (PRO File Air 1/176/15/186/1)

--. 79 Squadron, RAF, *Combat Reports*, in the field, 1918 (PRO File Air 1/1226/204/5/2634/79 Sqdn)

--. 85 Squadron, RAF, *Combat Reports*, in the field, 1918 (PRO File Air 1/1227/204/5/2634/85 Sqdn)

--. 211 Squadron, RAF, *Combat Reports*, in the field, 1918 (PRO File Air 1/1228/204/5/2634/211 Sqdn)

--. 213 Squadron, RAF, *Squadron Record Book*, in the field, 1918 (PRO File Air 1/2027/204/324/13)

--. 3 Squadron, RNAS, *Combat Reports*, in the field, 1917 (PRO File Air 1/1216/204/5/2634)

Royal Flying Corps / Royal Air Force. *Combat Casualty List*, in the field, 1917, 1918 (PRO File Air 1/967/204/5/1097 – 969/204/5/1102)

--. *Communiqués*, in the field, 1918 (PRO File Air 1/2097/207/13/1)

--. 5 Group, *Dover Patrol Fortnightly Summaries*, in the field, 1918 (PRO File Air 1/109/15/9/397)

--. *Summary of Air Intelligence*, in the field, 1918 (PRO File Air 1/1572/204/80/64)

--. *War Diary*, in the field, 1918 (PRO File Air 1/1185 – 1188/204/5/2595)

Royal Flying Corps / Royal Air Force. *Communiqués*, in the field, 1917, 1918 (PRO File Air 1/2097/207/14/1)

--. *War Diary*, 1917, 1918 (PRO File Air 1/1185 – 1188/204/5/2595)

Royal Naval Air Service. *Communiqués*, in the field, 1917 (PRO File Air 1/55 15/9/474345)

Reichsarchiv. *Kriegstagebuch der königlich preussischen Jagdstaffel 24*, Potsdam, n.d.

--. *Kriegstagebuch der kgl. preuss. Jagdstaffel 36* (summary), Potsdam, n.d.

Articles, Monographs, Periodicals and Papers:

Bailey, F. Bock, G., Browne, P. & Chamberlain, C. 'German Balloon Claims During 1918' in *Cross & Cockade* Journal, Vol. XXIV, Whittier (California), 1983

Bock, G. *Jagdstaffel 7 Kriegstagebuch* abstract, n.d.

--. *Jagdstaffel 28w Kriegstagebuch* abstract, n.d.

--. *Jagdstaffel 40s Kriegstagebuch* abstract, n.d.

Cron, H. (Translated by P. Grosz) 'Organization of the German Luftstreitkräfte' in *Cross & Cockade* Journal, Vol. VII, Whittier (California), 1966

Degelow, C. (Translated by P. Kilduff) 'Reminiscences of Jagdstaffel 40' in *Cross & Cockade* Journal, Vol. XII, Whittier (California), 1971

Gill, R. 'The Albums of Willy Rosenstein' in *Cross & Cockade* Journal, Vol. XXV, Whittier (California), 1984

Grosz, P. *Fokker D.VII Windsock Datafile 9*, Berkhamsted, 1989

--. *Albatros D.III – A Windsock Datafile Special*, Berkhamsted, 2003

--. *DFW C.V Windsock Datafile 53*, Berkhamsted, 1995

--. *Pfalz D.III Windsock Datafile 107*, Berkhamsted, 2004

Kilduff, P. 'Combat Fliers of Baden' in *Over the Front*, Vol. IV, Dallas (Texas), 1989

Miller, M.G. 'Of Lice and Men: Trench Fever and Trench Life in the AIF', http://www.vlib.us/medical/liceand.htm, based on a paper given to the Second Anzac Medical Society Meeting, France, 1993

Puglisi, W. 'Jacobs of Jasta 7 – Highest Ranking Living German Ace of World War I' in *Cross & Cockade* Journal, Vol. VI, Whittier (California), 1965

--. 'German Aircraft Down in British Lines' in *Cross & Cockade* Journal, Vol. X, Whittier (California), 1969

Ries, K. Luftwaffe: *Die Maulwürfe – Geheimer Aufbau 1919-1935*, Mainz, 1969

Ring der Flieger. *Flieger-Ring Nachrichten-Blatt Nr. 33*, Berlin, 1925

Zickerick, W. 'Verlustliste der deutschen Luftstreitkräfte im Weltkriege' in *Unsere Luftstreitkräfte 1914-1918*, Berlin, 1930

Other Sources:

Auer, A. *Personal-Bogen*, 1918; diary entries, 1918; correspondence with the author, 1971-1986

Carveth, W. Personal summary, n.d.

Degelow, C. *Flugbordbuch*, 1917

––. Correspondence with the author, 1967-1970

Gilly, H. *Personal-Bogen*, 1918

King, A. *Personal-Bogen*, 1920

Kreuzer, E. *Personal-Bogen*, 1917

Milch, E. Correspondence with the author, 1969-1971

Nami, P. Correspondence with the author, 1970-1987

Raab, A. Miscellaneous correspondence with A. Auer, 1961

––. Correspondence with the author, 1969

Rosenstein, W. *Personal-Bogen*, 1918; miscellaneous correspondence with A. Auer, 1946-1949

INDEX

Further Information

Readers interested in obtaining additional information about military aviation of the First World War may wish to contact websites of research-oriented, non-profit organizations, including:

The Aerodrome
URL: http://www.theaerodrome.com/

Australian Society of World War I Aero Historians
URL: http://asww1ah.0catch.com

Cross & Cockade International (UK)
URL: http://www.crossandcockade.com

League of World War I Aviation Historians (USA)
URL: http://www.overthefront.com

Das Propellerblatt (Germany)
URL: www.Propellerblatt.de

World War One Aeroplanes (USA)
URL: http://www.avation-history.com/ww1aero.htm